The Material Culture of Basketry

D1572778

The Material Culture of Basketry

Practice, skill and embodied knowledge

EDITED BY STEPHANIE BUNN AND VICTORIA MITCHELL

BLOOMSBURY VISUAL ARTS
LONDON · NEW YORK · OXFORD · NEW DELHI · SYDNEY

BLOOMSBURY VISUAL ARTS
Bloomsbury Publishing Plc
50 Bedford Square, London, WC1B 3DP, UK
1385 Broadway, New York, NY 10018, USA
29 Earlsfort Terrace, Dublin 2, Ireland

BLOOMSBURY, BLOOMSBURY VISUAL ARTS and the Diana logo are trademarks of Bloomsbury Publishing Plc

First published in Great Britain 2021
Paperback edition published 2023

© Editorial content and introductions, Stephanie Bunn and Victoria Mitchell, 2023
© Individual chapters, their authors, 2023

Stephanie Bunn and Victoria Mitchell have asserted their right under the Copyright,
Designs and Patents Act, 1988, to be identified as Editors of this work.

For legal purposes the Acknowledgements on p. xxiii constitute an extension
of this copyright page.

Cover design by Louise Dugdale
Cover image: Lois Walpole, 2015, one of the table mats, in progress, for *There Were
15 to Feed at Midbrake*, an installation for the touring exhibition *Weaving Ghosts*,
of fifteen mats made from found rope. Photograph: Lois Walpole.

All rights reserved. No part of this publication may be reproduced or transmitted
in any form or by any means, electronic or mechanical, including photocopying, recording,
or any information storage or retrieval system, without prior permission
in writing from the publishers.

Bloomsbury Publishing Plc does not have any control over, or responsibility for,
any third-party websites referred to or in this book. All internet addresses given in
this book were correct at the time of going to press. The author and publisher
regret any inconvenience caused if addresses have changed or sites have ceased to exist,
but can accept no responsibility for any such changes.

A catalogue record for this book is available from the British Library.

Library of Congress Cataloging-in-Publication Data
Names: Bunn, Stephanie, editor. | Mitchell, Victoria, editor.
Title: The material culture of basketry: practice, skill and embodied knowledge /
edited by Stephanie Bunn and Victoria Mitchell.
Description: London ; New York : Bloomsbury Visual Arts, 2020. | Includes bibliographical references and index. |
Identifiers: LCCN 2020011225 (print) | LCCN 2020011226 (ebook) | ISBN 9781350094031 (hardback) |
ISBN 9781350094048 (epub) | ISBN 9781350094055 (pdf)
Subjects: LCSH: Basketwork. | Material culture. | Basketwork–Social aspects. | Nature (Aesthetics) |
Art and technology. | Art and science. | Basketwork–Therapeutic use.
Classification: LCC NK3649 .M38 2020 (print) | LCC NK3649 (ebook) | DDC 746.41/2—dc23
LC record available at https://lccn.loc.gov/2020011225
LC ebook record available at https://lccn.loc.gov/2020011226

ISBN: PB: 978-1-3503-5990-1
         HB: 978-1-3500-9403-1
         ePDF: 978-1-3500-9405-5
         eBook: 978-1-3500-9404-8

Typeset by Refine Catch Limited, Bungay, Suffolk
Printed and bound in Great Britain

To find out more about our authors and books visit www.bloomsbury.com
and sign up for our newsletters.

Contents

List of Illustrations

Contributors

Paulina Adamska

Since 2008 Paulina Adamska has been devoted to promoting and developing basketmaking through the Serfenta Association. She is both an author of research projects and a handicraft instructor. A graduate of anthropological studies at the Silesian University in Cieszyn and the Folk University of Arts and Crafts, she has travelled in Poland and abroad to meet and learn from traditional basketmakers what she goes on to describe in the exhibitions and books of Serfenta. In 2016, she was awarded a grant from the Polish Ministry of Culture and National Heritage to explore techniques and materials connected with weaving.

Dr Lissant Bolton

Lissant Bolton is Keeper (Head) of the Department of Africa, Oceania and the Americas at the British Museum. Her research focuses on Melanesia – especially Vanuatu where she has worked with the Vanuatu Cultural Centre for many years – and more recently in relation to Indigenous Australia. Her publications include *Unfolding the Moon: Enacting Women's Kastom in Vanuatu* (2003), co-authored works including *Art in Oceania: A New History* (2012), and edited collections such as *Melanesia: Art and Encounter* (2013). She has curated a number of exhibitions for the British Museum, including an exhibition published as the catalogue *Baskets and Belonging: Australian Indigenous Histories* (2011), and most recently *Reimagining Captain Cook: Making Histories in the Pacific* (catalogue 2019).

Paula Brown (BSc Hons)

Paula Brown has been Project Coordinator for An Lanntair's Arora/Cianalas project since 2015. This project won Best Dementia Friendly Community Project in the Scottish Dementia Awards, 2016. Originally from Portsmouth, with a background in Cell Pathology, Care and Nursery Management, including community art festival and publishing experience, Paula's sense of adventure and curiosity brought her to the Western Isles and she spent her time there watching and learning traditional hand-skills from Hebridean women. A natural facilitator, Paula has supported the community to create physical and digital cultural resources and has widely shared arts, cultural and heritage opportunities intergenerationally.

Dr Stephanie Bunn

Stephanie Bunn is Leverhulme Emeritus Research Fellow at the University of St Andrews. She has conducted research through practice into Central Asian felt textiles and basketry worldwide. She collected and curated the first ever British Museum exhibition of Kyrgyz felt textiles, is author of *Nomadic*

Felt (British Museum Press) and editor of *Anthropology and Beauty* (Routledge). She has curated numerous exhibitions and recently coordinated Woven Communities, www.wovencommunities.org exploring Scottish social history through its baskets, working with Scottish basket-makers and museums. She is currently working on the *Forces in Translation* project, collaborating with mathematicians and basket-makers to study how skilled handwork enhances cognition.

Hilary Burns

Hilary Burns is a British basketmaker, researcher and writer. She is interested in the complexity of basketry techniques, constructing three-dimensional forms and the processes involved in preparing materials. Making is physical, practice is essential; passing on skills to keep the craft alive and collaboration with other makers is what she likes to do. Her work is linked to place and the seasons through materials she uses such as homegrown varieties of willow, small diameter wood, bark, bast and fibre-giving plants. Research, understanding basket history, our connection to this most close-to-nature of crafts still feeds our imaginations today. Hilary is co-founder with Geraldine Jones of not-for-profit company *Basketry and Beyond*, a yeoman of The Worshipful Company of Basketmakers and a member of the Devon Guild. Author of *Cane, Rush and Willow*, weaving with natural materials, she has written articles about textiles and craft and curated basketry exhibitions. She co-managed (2016–18) the First World War research-based project, *Basketry Then and Now*, (Everyday Lives in War, University of Hertfordshire). hilaryburns.com basketryandbeyond.org.uk

Mary Butcher MBE

Mary Butcher was originally a zoologist, studying the Arachnid populations on a small fenland at the University of Wisconsin, USA. She became a willow specialist, learning traditional skills from Alwyne Hawkins in Kent and from apprenticed makers. She has researched basket history and recorded traditional makers at work, both technical details and their changing practices in response to consumer demand. This gives a good record of changing economies and industries and the nature of basketmaking today. Her techniques and materials now vary from the traditional to the contemporary, using natural stems, leaves, bark, wire, plastics, vellum, paper and lots of colour. Mary is committed to the transmission of basket knowledge, technical, historical and contemporary. She teaches a range of skills based on those traditional techniques she learned first, then building on these with a diverse collection of methods. She has written a number of technical books and catalogues for several major exhibitions she has created, as well as having a lifelong involvement with the Basketmakers' Association and being Trade Advisor to The Worshipful Company of Basketmakers for many years.

Florence Cannavacciuolo

Florence Cannavacciuolo divides her time between occupational therapy, teaching and creation in the art of weaving plants. She offers her patients basketry in her role of Occupational Therapist. In 2012, she received an award from the *Fondation de France* to combine crafts and occupational therapy. From there, she has developed the Wood Basketry Workshop, a place of transmission through practical workshops. Florence Cannavacciuolo is engaged in many artistic projects that reveal the universe of plant fibres and their links, and in weaving, through the realization of volumes and spaces in a logic of landscape revelation or the creation of social links and collective work.

Professor Hugh Cheape

Hugh Cheape set up a postgraduate programme in material culture for *Sabhal Mòr Ostaig*, University of the Highlands and Islands, in 2005 and moved to Skye in 2007 to teach the new course. Graduating with a degree in Scottish Historical Studies, he worked as curator for both ethnology and the applied and decorative arts in the National Museums of Scotland for 33 years and has brought this knowledge and experience into the academic sphere. He has published widely in the subject-fields of agricultural history and ethnology as well as musicology, with a PhD thesis and two books on the bagpipe and piping in a European context.

Mary Crabb (BEd.Hons)

Mary Crabb is an artist, tutor and mathematics teacher. With an initial career in primary teaching then museum education, Mary later developed her creative practice, beginning with the learning of traditional willow basketry skills. This evolved into an experimental style of working with a mix of traditional and contemporary materials using adapted basketry and textile techniques. Mary is interested is in the connections made between mathematical thinking, making and creativity. Alongside sharing her creative work through workshops, talks and exhibiting, has been the teaching of maths in a variety of settings, for a wide range of ages and abilities.

Caroline Dear

Caroline Dear studied botany, then qualified as an architect and now works as an artist who explores the intertwined, interdependent relationships between plants and people. Interested in structures, ancient traditional skills of basketry and working with natural fibres, her work seeks to engage and question our involvement with the plant life which surrounds us. She has exhibited worldwide, recently in Finland and Canada, as well as Scotland and the UK. She has received many awards, including from Creative Scotland, and commissions, including from ATLAS Arts to curate and deliver a series of walks on Skye. At present she is doing an MA in Art and Social Practice through the Centre for Rural Creativity in Shetland, part of UHI. www.carolinedear.co.uk

Dr Ian Ewart

Ian Ewart is a Lecturer in Digital Technologies at the University of Reading. He worked as a mechanical design engineer for many years before turning to anthropology as a way of studying the place of technology in the world around us. He has conducted research into rural houses and bridge-building in Borneo and among steam railway enthusiasts at Didcot Railway Centre. He was awarded an ESRC Future Research Leader fellowship (2013–17) for a research project combining ethnography with digital modelling and 3D virtual reality, investigating the links between house design and concepts of health. His current research investigates the perception and application of technologies in the context of the built environment, the practices this influences, and how these inform the real, social experience of the world.

Professor Cathrine Hasse

Cathrine Hasse is full professor in learning and technology and research program leader of the *Future Technologies, Culture and Learning* program at the Danish School of Education, (DPU), Aarhus University and an honorary professor in techno-anthropology at Aalborg University. She specializes in cultural anthropology and learning theory – especially in cultural psychology, postphenomenological philosophy of technology, as well as new materialist feminist science studies. She has a long expertise in studying the learning, technology and culture of organizations. Apart from being a research program leader, since 2002, she has been coordinating a variety of projects, including two Horizon2020 projects and a major project financed by the Danish Research Council. All her projects are interdisciplinary and she hosts a number of researchers from different disciplines, including psychology, neurobiology and engineering, in her present research program. She is the author of *An Anthropology of Learning*, (Springer) and *Posthumanist Learning*, (Routledge), along with many international peer reviewed articles and anthologies on learning, technology, concept formation and robots in real-life settings.

Dr Lucie Hazelgrove-Planel

Lucie Hazelgrove-Planel has a PhD in Social Anthropology from the University of St Andrews (2019) and a BSc in Pure Mathematics (2010). She received a University of St Andrews 600th Anniversary scholarship for her doctoral research, which considered how ni-Vanuatu basket-makers explore and express complex ideas in their everyday practices of making. Lucie is fascinated by ways of working and motivated to support communities in achieving their goals. She researched the potential role of Pacific Island museums in sustainable development for *Heritage Matters: Culture and Development in the Pacific*, collaborating with the national museums of Kiribati and Solomon Islands. She currently supports farmer research networks conducting agro-ecological research with IDEMS International.

Professor Susan D. Healy

Susan D. Healy is a New Zealander who is Professor of Biology and Director for the Centre of Biological Diversity at the University of St Andrews, Scotland. She is also the European Executive Editor of *Animal Behaviour*. Her research integrates cognitive ecology, neurobiology and psychology in both wild and laboratory animals with a focus on birds. The common thread to her research is her interest in the role that natural selection has played on shaping cognitive abilities. For the past 10 years she has been especially interested in why birds build the nests they do.

Joe Hogan

Joe Hogan has worked as a basketmaker since 1978, being attracted to the idea of growing willow and being involved in the whole process from harvesting willow through to making a basket. He came to basketmaking as the living tradition of rural Irish basketmaking, with its many unique designs, was declining, and spent many years researching and making the various indigenous Irish baskets. For the past fifteen years he has devoted much of his time to making artistic or sculptural baskets prompted by a desire to develop a deeper connection to the natural world. Publications include *Basketmaking in Ireland* (2001) which focuses on the indigenous baskets of Ireland, *Bare Branches Blue Black Sky* (2011) and *Learning From the Earth* (2018). His website is www.joehoganbaskets.com

Professor Sabine Hyland

Sabine Hyland is an American anthropologist at the University of St Andrews. She is best known for her work studying *khipus* and hybrid *khipu*-alphabetic texts in the Central Andes and is credited with the first partial phonetic decipherment of Andean *khipus*. She has written extensively about the interaction between Spanish missionaries and the Inka in colonial Peru, focusing on language, religion and missionary culture, as well as the history of the Chanka people. Hyland's research has appeared in media outlets around the world, such as the BBC World Service, *The Times* (UK), *National Geographic* and *Scientific American*. Her awards include fellowships from the National Endowment for the Humanities and the John Simon Guggenheim Foundation.

Dr William P. Hyland

William P. Hyland is an American historian and Lecturer in Church History at the University of St Andrews. He has published extensively on medieval monastic culture and spirituality, and is a co-founder of the British Cusanus Society. He shares a deep interest in the development of Christianity in colonial Peru, and in the spread of scribal and textual traditions in the Andes. He has conducted fieldwork on ethnographic *khipus* in the Peruvian Andes, and was a co-investigator with Sabine Hyland on a grant, *Hidden Texts of the Andes*, funded by the National Geographic Society Global Exploration Fund.

Professor Tim Ingold

Tim Ingold is Professor Emeritus of Social Anthropology at the University of Aberdeen. He has carried out fieldwork among Saami and Finnish people in Lapland, and has written on environment, technology and social organization in the circumpolar North, on animals in human society, and on human ecology and evolutionary theory. His more recent work explores environmental perception and skilled practice. Ingold's current interests lie on the interface between anthropology, archaeology, art and architecture. His recent books include *The Perception of the Environment* (2000), *Lines* (2007), *Being Alive* (2011), *Making* (2013), *The Life of Lines* (2015), *Anthropology and/ as Education* (2018) and *Anthropology: Why it Matters* (2018).

Felicity Irons

Felicity Irons is a rush weaver, founder of Rush Matters, one of the last remaining rush weaving companies in Britain. Felicity started her practice in 1992, teaching herself the techniques and processes of rush weaving. Working from Grange Farm, Felicity Irons harvests her own bulrushes from the Great Ouse river. The rush is harvested in the summer months, totalling over 2 tons a day and left to dry naturally before being plaited by Felicity and her team into bags, baskets and homewares. http://www.rushmatters.co.uk

Tim Johnson

Over the past 25 years artist and basketmaker Tim Johnson has explored the relationships of material, place, nature and culture. Exhibiting internationally Tim's diverse creative practice encompasses basketmaking, sculpture, costume, performance, photography and painting. He combines a deep respect for traditional basketmaking with his own innovations and enjoys using a wide variety of materials and techniques gleaned from his travels, research and his own creative practice. Originally from Newcastle Upon Tyne, England, Tim has lived in various parts of England and Ireland and is currently based in Catalonia. Tim is an experienced tutor and has been awarded the prestigious Marsh Award for Excellence in Gallery Education and several awards for his baskets in Spain and Poland. www.timjohnsonartist.com

Geraldine Jones

Geraldine Jones has been a professional basketmaker since 1985, after learning how to make a gypsy basket from blackberry stems from an elderly Travelling man, Tom Aldridge. She was then taught the tricks of the trade from retired basketmaker, Richard Moon. Over the years she has been fascinated to discover how many natural formations and life forms can be replicated using a variety of basket-weaving techniques and materials from all over the world. Work in progress can develop into surprising and mathematically precise pieces of work. Geraldine co-founded the organisation *Basketry and Beyond* with Hilary Burns, in 2000, to promote the craft of basketry through entertaining and educational events. Since 1990 her workplace has been at Salt Cellar Workshops in Porthleven, overlooking the sea and harbour. She co-manages this business as a collective of artisan studios with Claire Francis, hat-maker. basketryandbeyond.org.uk

Joanne B. Kaar

Joanne B. Kaar (BA Hons, MA) is a research-based artist inspired by journeys over land, sea and through time and lives in Dunnet, on Dunnet Head, Caithness, Scotland, only 2 miles from Brough, where she grew up. Joanne has been self-employed since graduating in December 1992, starting as artist in residence for the Isle of Skye a few weeks later. Her artwork is varied, taking inspiration from our heritage and is as much at home in museums as art galleries. As both participant and instigator of arts and heritage projects and collaborations she has worked in Taiwan, South Korea, Iceland, USA, Canada, Estonia, Catalonia and exhibited in Japan, Germany, Australia, Sweden and Finland.

Professor Susanne Küchler

Susanne Küchler is Professor of Anthropology and Material Culture at University College London. She has conducted ethnographic fieldwork in island Papua New Guinea and Eastern Polynesia over the past 25 years, studying the modular, composite image in its relation to political economies of knowledge from a comparative perspective. Her work on the history of the take-up, in the Pacific, of cloth and clothing as 'new material' and 'new technology' has focused on social memory and material translation, and on the epistemic nature of pattern. The question of the return to the object and its theoretical and methodological imperative is the central theme of her forthcoming work which follows publications on *Malanggan: Art, Memory and Sacrifice* (2002); *Pacific Pattern* (2005) and *Tivaivai: The Social Fabric of the Cook Islands* (2009).

Joyce Laing OBE

Joyce Laing has a BA in Fine Art from the University of Aberdeen and an MA in Art and Psychotherapy. Her books include *Angus McPhee, Weaver of Grass* (Taigh Chearsabhaig 2000) and *Art from the Barlinnie Special Unit* (CCA). She has curated numerous exhibitions on Art Extraordinary and Outsider Art.

Professor John Mack

John Mack is an anthropologist who specializes in the arts and material culture of sub-Saharan Africa, particularly the Congo Basin, eastern Africa and the islands of the western Indian Ocean.

Since 2004 he has been Professor of World Art Studies in the Sainsbury Research Unit at the University of East Anglia. Prior to that he was Keeper of the Museum of Mankind and Senior Keeper of the British Museum. His many publications explore themes in artistic production across cultures as well as monographs on specific African societies and regions. His latest book is *The Artfulness of Death in Africa* (2019).

Jon Macleod

Jon Macleod is a multidisciplinary artist and project curator for An Lanntair. *Cianalas* is the latest incarnation of a series of funded projects initiated by Macleod in 2012, designed to examine the nature of memory and memory loss within the context of the Outer Hebrides and the role of creativity and an oral tradition as tools for expression and rehabilitation. He also works a croft on the westside of the Isle of Lewis.

Victoria Mitchell

Victoria Mitchell works with the theory, practice and history of textiles and basketry, with a particular interest in relationships between materials, making, metaphor and meaning. She was a co-investigator on the Arts and Humanities Research Council project *Beyond the Basket: Construction and Understanding*, 2009–2011. She is a Research Fellow at Norwich University of the Arts, UK, formerly Senior Lecturer in Contextual Studies and Course Leader for MA Textile Culture, and is on the advisory board for *Textile: Cloth and Culture* and *Craft Research*.

Professor Ricardo Nemirovsky

Ricardo Nemirovsky is professor at the Manchester Metropolitan University in Manchester, UK. He has directed educational projects in Argentina, Mexico, USA, and currently in Europe. He is conducting research and theory development on the interplay between embodied cognition, affects, and mathematics learning. Part of his work focuses on the synergy between art, crafts and mathematics. He has been working with several science and art museums in mathematics-oriented projects that combine research, development and museum staff professional development. Additionally, he has designed numerous mechanical devices and software to enrich the learning of mathematics, including several maths-oriented exhibits for science and technology museums.

Dr Tim Palmer

Tim Palmer has been making baskets and teaching basketmaking for almost 30 years, fitting them around his post as Consultant Pathologist in Inverness. An interest in historical baskets, particularly relating to the fishing industry, led to involvement in the *Woven Communities* and *Everyday Lives in War* projects, researching the use of basketmaking in rehabilitation of injured servicemen and making copies and replicas of old baskets, including seats for replica First World War aircraft. Retirement from full-time medicine left time to start working with patients with brain injury at Raigmore. The combining of his medical background and basketmaking experience followed a *Woven Communities* project symposium and is proving both a benefit to the patients and a most rewarding and stimulating activity.

Dr Catherine Paterson MBE, MEd, FRCOT

Catherine F. Paterson is a retired occupational therapist, trained in Edinburgh in the 1960s. At that time, basketry, one of the many crafts learned, was still used therapeutically. Her clinical career spanned psychiatry, spinal injuries and care of the elderly and she used basketry in each setting. In 1972, as a Churchill Fellow she visited Australia. She trained as a teacher of occupational therapy and then, as a King's Fund Fellow, researched the training needs of the remedial professions. She set up the course in occupational therapy in Aberdeen in 1976, where she worked until retirement in 2002. Dr Paterson published many papers on clinical, educational and historical aspects of occupational therapy, including a book *Opportunities not Prescriptions: the Development of Occupational Therapy in Scotland 1900–1960*, 2010 (Langstane Press).

Des Pawson MBE

Des Pawson MBE is a professional ropeworker with over 50 years' experience. He is one of the world's leading authorities on knots, rope and sailors' ropework. A researcher and historian on the subject, he is the author of many books and papers. In 1982 he was co-founder of the International Guild of Knot Tyers. He feels passionately about the preservation and celebration of all aspects of sailors' ropework and, with his wife Liz, opened the first Museum of Knots and Sailors' Ropework in 1996, in Ipswich, Suffolk (UK). With Liz, Des has run a successful business, Footrope Knots, for more than 40 years. He was awarded an MBE for services to the world of knots and rope in 2007.

Dr Ian Tait

Dr Ian Tait is a native of Shetland, and has worked at the Shetland Museum for the whole of his career. His specialism is ethnology, although the general nature of the museum's collections and clientele means he has broad interests in local heritage as a whole, especially where it concerns working practices, tools and traditions. He is particularly concerned with the artefacts and buildings from the Early Modern period and the folklife that derived from subsistence economics. Dr Tait has published articles on a diversity of aspects and has created many exhibitions on local topics, all of which have examined indigenous traditions and the forces that eroded them. Beyond ethnology, the all-round nature of the work has encouraged him to create exhibitions and articles on such things as emigration, shipping, warfare, trade and, most recently, birds. Dr Tait has made several traditional Shetland baskets, and learned thatching over thirty years ago.

Dr Maria Cristina Tello-Ramos

Maria Cristina Tello-Ramos is a Mexican biologist working at the University of St Andrews. She has studied the behaviour of wild free-living birds in Mexico, Canada, the United States of America and South Africa. Her research has focused in the cognitive abilities of wild birds including work on the foraging behaviour of hummingbirds and the variation in spatial abilities of mountain chickadees living at different elevations. She is now working on the role of social learning and cultural transmission in shaping the morphology of structures built by white-browed weavers.

Dr Pat Treusch

Pat Treusch is a postdoc of the Berlin-wide Program 'DiGiTal', situated at the Centre for Interdisciplinary Women's and Gender Studies and the Department of General and Historical

Educational Science, Technical University Berlin. She is a feminist Science and Technology Scholar, specializing in qualitative research on human-machine relations with a focus on interactive AI technologies. Lately, she explored the possibilities of knitting collaboratively with a robot arm. Details of the work of the interdisciplinary project 'Do robots dream of knitting?' are documented here: https://blogs.tu-berlin.de/zifg_stricken-mit-robotern/

Dr Lois Walpole

Lois Walpole was born in London of Anglo-Scottish heritage. She graduated from Central Saint Martins School of Art, London with a BA(Hons.) in Sculpture in 1975 and obtained City and Guilds qualifications in Creative Basketry, from the London College of Furniture in 1982. In 2003 she completed a Doctorate in the Design department at the Royal College of Art in London. Since 1982 she has worked full time as an artist/basketmaker taking part in and curating national and international exhibitions, working to commission, designing for production, teaching and writing. From 1972 to 2005 she lived in London. Now she divides her time between the Shetland Islands and the Charente, in south-west France, where her studio is based.

Professor Willeke Wendrich

Willeke Wendrich is an archaeologist who has published on the social context of ancient Egyptian basketmakers (PhD Leiden University, the Netherlands, 1999). She is the Director of the Cotsen Institute of Archaeology at the University of California, Los Angeles, holds the Joan Silsbee Chair in African Cultural Archaeology and is professor of Egyptian Archaeology and Digital Humanities in the Department of Near Eastern Languages and Cultures at UCLA. Some of her publications on archaeological basketry include *Who is afraid of basketry? a guide to recording basketry and cordage for archaeologists and ethnographers* (1991) and *The World According to Basketry; an Ethnoarchaeological Interpretation of Basketry Production in Egypt* (1999), both available in open access. Her latest books are *Egyptian Archaeology* (Wiley-Blackwell, 2010); *Archaeology and Apprenticeship, Body Knowledge, Identity, and Communities of Practice* (University of Arizona Press, 2012) and *The Desert Fayum Reinvestigated* (CIoA Press, 2017).

Acknowledgements

This book begins from a perspective that scholarly understanding of craft skills such as basketry proceeds from practice. The initial research for this book was championed by three practitioners, members of the Scottish Basketmakers' Circle, Liz Balfour, Julie Gurr and Dawn Susan. Many of the strands, themes and even the structure of this book reflect the research we began together in the *Woven Communities* project and we thank them wholeheartedly. We would also like to thank all our contributors, many of whom responded to the requests of this project to take part in our symposia and others who responded to requests to provide an international perspective to our research.

Our research has taken a collaborative and emergent approach. Thanks go to An Lanntair on the Island of Lewis, with whom we developed our work with people living with dementia. Also thanks to the Scottish Fisheries Museum in Anstruther, the Highland Folk Museum, Shetland Museum and the National Museums of Scotland, all of whom helped us develop our approach to heritage. The organisation *Basketry and Beyond* encouraged us to explore links between basketry, injury and occupational therapy. We thank them, along with the University of Hertfordshire, who supported this work. Our work with mathematics and basketry was inspired by working with children from schools in Uist and Shetland, our thanks to all classes, teachers, individuals and institutions who made this possible. *Basketry and Beyond* also encouraged this interest, and thanks again to them. We would also like to thank Raigmore Hospital, Inverness, who enabled development of the stroke recovery work research on which one of our chapters is based, especially Dr Ashish MacAden of the Stroke Recovery Unit, Dr Tim Palmer, and basketmaker Monique Bervoets who helped develop this work.

The exceptional *Knowing from the Inside Project* at the University of Aberdeen, led by Professor Tim Ingold, confirmed the practical approach we wanted to take and supported us throughout. Thanks to all members of this wide group. The group not only provided a helpful 'intellectual soup' in which this research could develop, it also provided much needed research time and financial support. We extend especial thanks to Tim for also reading through all the contributions and writing a stimulating 'afterword' in response. We have also received very welcome funding from the Arts and Humanities Research Council, who supported each stage of the research underpinning this book, the Royal Society of Edinburgh, who enabled colour publication, and the University of St Andrews Knowledge Exchange and Impact Fund, which enabled us to explore new and emergent themes.

We are very grateful for the patience, skill and generous support provided by our editors, Rebecca Barden, Claire Collins, Olivia Davies and Amy Jordan, and to the design and production teams at Bloomsbury. Thanks also to the longstanding support of Jon Warnes who has provided continued advice and other help through the duration of this project.

Finally, it might seem ironic to thank each other as co-editors, but the many stimulating conversations, determination to keep going when one or the other of us was out of action and rigorous attention to different kinds of detail, have enabled us to bring the multiple perspectives of this book together.

Introduction

Stephanie Bunn

1. Take 2 or 3 strands of moss
2. Match up with someone else – each of you make a small circle using the moss
3. Join your circles together with another strand of moss
4. Link up with another pair and join your circles up
5. Continue until all the circles are joined up

CAROLINE DEAR, 2012

Moss, and making circles out of moss, led a group of scholars and basketmakers to begin talking to each other at a symposium on basketry and anthropology.[1] People twined their circles and, in touching and intertwining hair moss, they aligned and intertwined their conversations, their intellectual concerns, their inspiration and their communities. This book was born out of these intertwined conversations. It draws on the experience and knowledge of practitioners, experts and scholars across many disciplinary boundaries.

On the one hand, the goal in this meeting was to explore basketry as fabric of society, to use a familiar artefact – the basket – as a lens through which to explore social patterns and cultural history. On the other hand, the aim was to begin with practice, taking basketry's interwoven nature, and to explore what its making, interweaving and interconnections could engender. This took us to a world of analogies and interconnections in both discussion and theory. A world that expanded to show us we had to begin with materials – plants, their gathering and sorting, and the ways humans (and other animals) twiddle, twine, weave and knot. It led to the things we make and do with basketwork, from simple artefacts of containment and transportation, to the condensations of meanings and metaphors that the artefacts inspire and provoke, from kinship, to human origins, to ritual. Thus, the book aims to explore how baskets-in-the-making help tell of our past, build our present and assist us to grow and develop.

In this anthropological, yet interdisciplinary, *Material Culture of Basketry,* we explore basketwork through people and their relationships with the environment, focusing on process, the body in action. We move from materials to learning and skill – to pattern, space, time and rhythm. Alongside considering history, we explore memory, meaning and mind. Our concern with embodiment and learning has also led us to look at that aspect of basketry associated with recovery, healing and rehabilitation, with cognition and human development; and the slow design of the work of the human hand (Bunn 2015; Mitchell, this volume).

Basketry practices also raise questions of labour, of hard work and changing global economics. The same globalized, mass-production imperative which now characterizes consumption has made the basket largely obsolete, replaced by plastic bags and metal shopping trolleys on a huge scale. The associated privatization of land also impacts on necessary materials. So, the basket is an artefact indicative of social change on many levels. These subjects are addressed but are not the only focus of the book. When hand-skills such as basketry are driven solely by an economic imperative, they tell a different story, as the image by Andreas Gursky reveals (Fig 0.1). Here, our concern has been to explore the value of such bodily practices for what makes us human. We consider their relevance for a future where they are recognised as significant human actions, formative of our human intelligence and enquiry, worthy of frequent renewal, an element of how new learners come to know the world.

Who can tell about basketry?

Just as interdisciplinary research has helped us understand the processes encompassed by basketwork, so interdisciplinary writing can tell the bigger picture of their making. Authors contributing to this volume include basketmakers, artists, knot-workers, curators, art historians, anthropologists, archaeologists, mathematicians, occupational and art therapists, community workers, engineers, biologists, pathologists, educationalists and roboticists.

Presentation of their material spans academic writing and visual essays, drawings, diagrams and tables. This rich description, from multiple perspectives, aims to break open any one linear, long-held approach, while providing analogies and resonances, interweaving multiple stories and patterns of how basketry works, as the basket itself is woven. While the approach of the artist and the anthropologist reveals certain parallels in the emergent, social and qualitive nature of their studies, that of the medical scientist and occupational therapist gives it a grounded, visceral physicality, and these perspectives bind together body, mind, society and environment, revealing they are aspects of one process.

Materials, techniques, definitions

Our definition of basketry begins with materials and techniques. Most basketry materials originate from plants – from soft materials such as rush, sedge or pandanus, to hard materials such as willow, rattan or bamboo. In general, the relationship between maker and basketry material is not one of imposing form onto substance or making it do what one wants, but rather of knowing the life-cycle, habitat and potential of the material and listening to the wisdom that it may impart. To be a basketmaker, as Peri and Paterson showed for Pomo basketmakers, is to be familiar with plant materials and local ecology. 'The basket is in the roots,' they say (Peri and Paterson 1976).

FIGURE 0.1 *Rattan furniture factory. Andreas Gursky, 2004, Nha Trang. © Andreas Gursky. Courtesy Sprüth Magers Berlin London/ DACS 2018.*

FIGURE 0.2 *Gathering sedge for Pomo baskets. Photo Courtesy Creative Commons.*

This way of practicing basketry may parallel the anthropological 'plant turn' (Myers 2015; Tsing 2015), it is an 'interspecies interaction' – an interaction which basketmakers have long known. Basketmakers and their plant materials certainly interact with, sense and respect each other, as Kimmerer describes (2013), this is a world of mutual sense-making.

Yet alongside listening and responding to the material as it grows into a basket, 'becoming with and alongside plants and their material form' (Myers 2015), basketmaking also tells makers about themselves and their humanity. Basketry techniques are bodily techniques. Basketmakers know the pleasures of skill, of marrying and parrying their bodily rhythms with the force in materials through the strokes, movements, patterns and effort of making baskets. They know the challenge of resistance as they transform material into artefact through bodily engagement. They enjoy the dexterity of working hands and materials in rhythmic engagement to create structural patterns which at the same time hold the basket form together and produce a result.

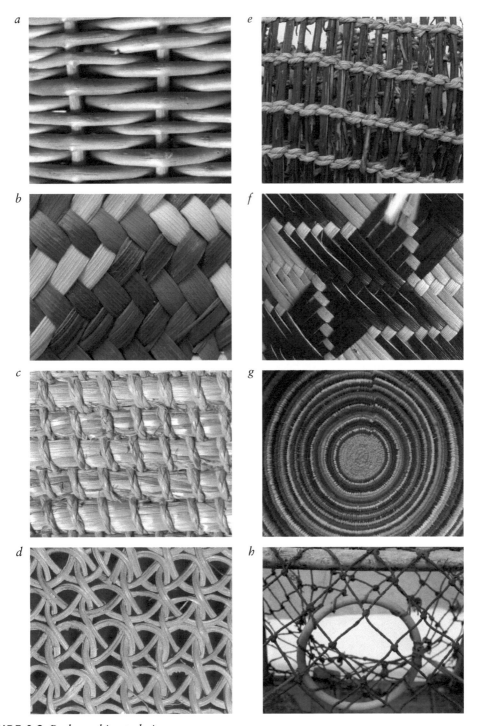

FIGURE 0.3 *Basketmaking techniques.*

a) Woven willow; b) Plaited palm; c) Coiled straw and sisal; d) Looped rattan; e) Twined dock and wild rush; f) Plaited and twilled pandanus; g) Coiled grass and wool; h) knotted string and wooden frame.

These techniques include:

- weaving – using stakes as warp and strands as weft, creating form through tension;

- twining or waling – using two or more weavers crossing at each stake in turn;

- plaiting – where three strands or more are interlaced in different directions;

- coiling – a continuous core (twisted, plaited or twined) is stitched to itself as the form unfolds, beginning from the centre, working outwards and upwards;

- looping – where just one strand is pulled through loops in sequence;

- knotting, and even netting . . .

Many baskets incorporate several of these techniques. The tension and strength they incorporate into materials produce two- or three-dimensional forms, from string to plaited sails, mats to boat fenders. As with all bodily techniques, from walking, to sitting, to digging, they also reflect cultural specificity in terms of details of skilled practice and meaning.

These basketry techniques also appear to reflect a kind of 'vital' knowing. Their vitality is such that they are one of the few handcrafted artefacts which could not be made by machine, as Otis Mason claimed in his late nineteenth century *Origins of Invention*, and this is still largely true (1895). A 3D printer can make a basket-like artefact, but it will not be held together by the same forces and techniques as a handmade basket. This is because the basket's three-dimensional form develops in the making, acting as both the technology – the loom or frame on which the basket is made – and, at the same time, forming the structure of the basket itself. While on the one hand this is liberating (see Albers 1961; 1965), on the other it can be restrictive, and any commercial requirement for high quantity means highly labour-intensive work and, frequently, uncontrolled harvesting from the natural environment.

This emergent, three-dimensional making process is further complicated by plant materials' organic nature. Being variable, uneven and often short, they frequently need adjustment during weaving, requiring the maker to problem-solve and make creative decisions from stroke to stroke and from one newly introduced stake or strand to the next. We have here 'a continuous variation of variables', 'simultaneous equations in multiple unknowns' (Deleuze and Guattari 2004, 510; Powers 2018). You have to think like a tree or a tangled creeper to solve them.

While basketry's plant-based, perishable qualities have meant that there are few ancient basket remains, creating structures held together by tension or friction produced by the hands in engagement with materials provokes discussion of just how closely interwoven basketwork is with the origins of being human. Basket-like containers are not just dependent on the supple actions of human hands, however, since other creatures weave – from the majority of birds to the Osmia Bee, albeit using their beaks or mouths. The latter carries stems of grass in its mouth, cutting and weaving them into a thatched cover over the snail shell it inhabits, while all the time flying and hovering in the air, using its entire body. And as Susan D. Healy shows, Weaver Birds do not simply weave and knot their nests through instinct, but they appear to learn aspects of this skill through observation and imitation (part 1). Thus, the creation of form by weaving materials in-tension reveals an 'intention' that is manifest in both humans and other animals. Indeed, the etymological link between 'intention' and 'in-tension' could arguably reflect the quality and forceful nature of these two processes, where the outcome is an artefact where movement is immanent but held in check, arguably a feature of growth and learning in diverse species (Herrera).

The rhythms and movements of basketry

Movements held in check by textile production describe forms, arcs, curves in space, as a person's arms and body stretch, bend, fold or pull the materials under constraint. These movements, whether sweeping, or neat and precise, mark proportions and relationships, and their repeated action over time creates patterns which emerge as the basket, mat or sculptural form take shape. Such movements express a bodily understanding of geometric relationships and dynamic forces, a non-verbal expression of a mathematician's or an engineer's understanding of balance, space and stresses, the process often being one of 'forces in translation' (from numbers to patterns, from twisting to strength etc).

Such gestural moves can reveal a spatial and geometric comprehension that a person is not necessarily able to articulate verbally (Goldin-Meadow 2013; Nemirovsky 2012). This is not a classical formal mathematics, nor is there any frozen system hidden behind these skilled movements (see Marchand 2018). While basketwork does reveal fundamental relationships such as proportion and strength, not to mention also counting and pattern, it also reveals 'the possibility of entirely different forms of mathematics that may not in any way resemble academic mathematics,' as Marchand eloquently argues (*ibid* 303). Other thinkers have shown how weaving on a loom can

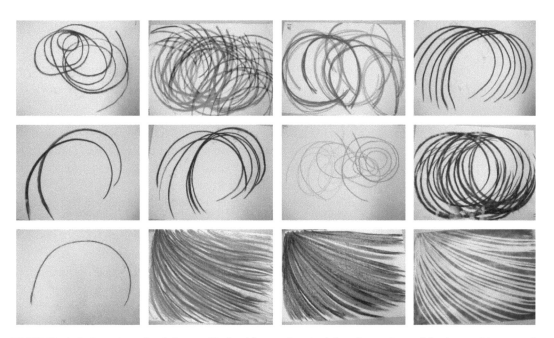

FIGURE 0.4 *Drawings by Johanne Verbockhaven inspired by the action of basketry. Photograph: Stephanie Bunn.*

provide a basis for both mechanization and computer modelling (Albers 1965; Harzelius-Klück), yet basketwork, in its challenge to mechanization, reveals a more embodied side to problem-solving and mathematical thinking, a maths which is not the pure or abstract process that scholars such as Bertrand Russell have described (de Freitas 2017).

This should not detract from basketry's mathematical potential, since it has the capacity to explore processes involving diverse elements all working at the same time – not just binaries, but 3s, 5s, 9s, 35s . . ., often in different directions, on different planes, at diverse angles, and each one, as discussed above, offering slight variation. But this does reveal how mathematics is nevertheless a form of 'material labour', a kind of work where actions such as drawing, sketching, diagramming and forms of making such as basketry, are conducted alongside, and sometimes articulate, more mental computations (see Figure 0.4; de Freitas 2017; Nemirovsky 2012). Thus, you cannot have design or engineering without the effort of the hand, cannot have planning and drawing without gesture and inscription, cannot have the model without the making.

Furthermore, this mathematical bodily engagement is both personal *and* social, subjective *and* intersubjective, evoking on the one hand a feeling of meditative calm once the skill is mastered and comes 'ready to hand' (Heidegger 1927), and on the other, a sense of connectedness and even well-being, when done on the company of others. The process of *learning* basketry may not always be so positive – learning the rhythms of strokes and the nuances of materials can be frustrating, even annoying when trying to do this and create form for the first time. Yet patience, as Sennett describes, is also part of the process, allowing the maker to adopt a particular way of being with the materials and the skill to be mastered (2008). And working together in company, materials in hand, allows for analogies, resonances and, new combinations of ideas to emerge.

The knowledge in the basket: care, memories, meaning

The knowledge gathered in learning and making baskets provides illustration of Ryle's classic notion of the 'intelligent act', where bodily skills and actions such as weaving or other hand-skills are not distinct from operations of the mind, they are the same as them (1949). Basketry knowledge is, however, more all-encompassing than Ryle's simple distinction between 'knowing how' (such as knowing how to weave) and 'knowing that' (propositional or factual knowledge) (*ibid*). In the concerns of our contributors, 'knowing how' extends beyond 'skill' to 'care for skill', while 'knowing that' encompasses 'knowing when' and 'knowing about' – memories contained and triggered by seeing and interaction[2] handling, touching and making, both materials and artefacts. There is also a 'knowing through' how belief and world view can be both articulated through and even generated by basketry moves, patterns, forms and by basketry potential such as containment.

Care in basketry skill extends from ecological knowledge (collecting, growing, harvesting, sorting, processing materials), to the dexterous (twisting, plaiting, binding forms of bodily movement). Making also generates motivation and care: to improve skills, to learn new forms, to actively seek out new systems and techniques. Basketmakers also want to learn about the materials, about historic practices, often doing their own autodidactic research. For many there is real concern that such skills should continue, not be forgotten, that these skills are important. Joe

Hogan's chapter on his journey into learning Irish basketry illustrates this well (part 3), as does Des Pawson's chapter on knots (part 5). This is not nostalgia, nor 'salvage ethnography', but clear enjoyment of the skill and an acknowledgement of the significance of these skills for our human development. It is also a kind of elicitation or provocation to the human from the artefact, from the creativity and skill of past makers embodied in the artefact and from the material.[3]

The roles that baskets fulfil also provoke cultural meanings linked to bodily resonances. Marcel Griaule's *Conversations with Ogotommêli* describes Dogon baskets as an aspect of the universe's unfolding, from cosmos to granary to human to basket, all reflecting the one process of Dogon creation (1965). Similarly David Guss, describes Yekuana basketwork in Venezuela, from gathering and preparing materials to weaving and using baskets, as conforming to a singular poetics of creation, that is, conforming 'to the same structure of meaning that determines all its other aspects, and therefore possess[ing] the same power to reveal it' (1990, 126).

Within this approach to knowledge, Küchler (part 2) shows how practices such as weaving or knotting cords in the Pacific do not so much *represent* political practices, such as Hawaiian kingship ritual, through resemblance, as make associative and contiguous links. – 'It is not what the cord looks like that is important . . . It is the processes of binding and opening to which the cord is subjected which constitutes the mystical subject of kingship.' Knots are, she says, a 'mode of being', and according to the emphasis that different Pacific societies place on specific forms of binding, the emphasis on their political and social practices may vary, or vice versa. Reflecting this diversity, indigenous Australian basketry conversely evokes, not temporal events, notions of memory, nor linear history, since for these indigenous makers the sacred is beyond time (see Bolton, part 3). Rather, their baskets evoke a notion of country, land, place and belonging. 'The land,' they say, 'inspires us to make things'.

Basketry as regrowth, recovery, renewal

We should not ignore how these actions work on the body, or body-mind. This is not to say that basketry experiences can be reduced to the physical, but that a neuro-science perspective may provide further insight as to why basketwork can assist recovery and why feelings like well-being arise through hand-skills such as basketry.[4] In this book, skilled hand-work is shown to help overcome psychological trauma, assist in memory recollection for people with Dementia, and help recovery from the effects of brain injury and stroke, not just physically, but also with skills such as problem-solving, concentration and self-confidence.

Our summary view is that this is due, in part anyway, to the combined effects of the effort of learning the skills and the new neural pathways that this learning of basketwork creates; the special kind of integrated left-right attention that basketry requires; rhythmic, repeated action; producing an end result; and the fact that this work is often done in the company of others. Authors in part 4 of this volume develop these themes in-depth (see also Bolte Taylor 2009).

Neuro-phenomenologists Varela and Evan Thompson give further insight to the sense of well-being which arises during basketwork (Varela, Thompson and Rosch 1993; Thompson, 2006). In their views, if cognition is 'the exercise of skillful know-how in situated action', then experience and practice become central to any understanding of mind. Thompson's insights come through studying Buddhist meditation and contemplation. Turning the mind inwards in meditation, Thompson suggests, is a way of observing how the mind works. Meditation trains the attention, acting as a means of gathering focus and stilling the mind.

While meditation turns the attention inwards, craft practices such as basketry, we suggest, turn the attention outwards, through the hands and materials to the wider environment, while also commanding the kind of distributed focus that skillfulness requires. This expanding of attention as a piece of work unfolds, its rhythm, the smell of the materials, the emerging form and pattern as the artefact grows while the maker exercises judgement, strength, balance and dexterity, is another externally directed form of focusing. Basketwork could thus also be seen as a form of contemplation, an expanding of the self into the wider environment, again stilling the mind, and revealing a person's decentred connectedness with the wider world (including other people) which some makers describe as producing well-being, even joy.

Renewing through hand work

Our enquiry begins and ends with one practice, basketwork. It travels through a stream of apparently unrelated themes – materials, maths, memory, recovery, renewal, all of which can be grounded in this practice, the hand work of basketmaking. In some ways, little has changed in basketry over the past centuries, given basketwork's continued need of the hand. But economically, everything has changed to the extent that basketwork is generally now perceived as obsolete and such hand work as irrelevant. Yet our authors argue that basketwork still has relevance. Our understanding of the value of basketwork is enlivened by the anthropological 'plant-turn', but that is not the whole story, because there is also a 'crafty and skilful turn' that comes with the hand work required to make baskets, and our contributors show that both considerations are of continued significance and importance today. So much human learning and understanding of the world is generated by skillful practical engagement, that, like our final author, Tim Ingold, we propose that such practices should be recognised as important human actions, alongside skills such as handwriting, reading, and digital activities. Practised in conjunction with each other, these skills are formative of our human intelligence and enquiry. They are worthy of frequent renewal – not obsolete, so that 'basket-ing' is part and parcel of how humans come to know the world and develop themselves within it.

Notes

1 *Woven Communities 1* (2012), followed by *Woven Communities 2: Making, Memory and Mind* (2017).

2 See also K. Barad on intra-action. *Meeting the Universe Halfway*, Durham, NC: Duke University Press, 2007.

3 For Tomasello (2009), this capacity to build on past skills and take them forward to the future illustrates another uniquely human endeavour. In Tomasello, M. 2009.

4 See, for example, the work of Betsan Corkhill on knitting as therapy; Kate Davis on knitting following a left-brain stroke; Clare Hunter's work on embroidery in her *Threads of Life*; and Jögge Sundqist on *Slöjd*.

Bibliography

Albers, A. [1943] 1961 *On Designing*. Middletown, CT: Wesleyan University Press.
Albers, A. 1965 *On Weaving*. New York: Dover.
Bolte Taylor, J. 2009 *My Stroke of Insight*. London: Hodder and Stoughton.
Bunn, S.J. 2015 'Who designs Scottish vernacular baskets?' *Journal of Design History*, 29 (1): 24–42.
Bunn, S.J. 2015 'Weaving solutions to woven problems'. In T. Marchand (ed.), *Craftwork, Problem Solving*. Farnham: Ashgate Publishing.
Dear, C. 2012 Introductory worksheet for 1st *Woven Communities* Symposium.
De Freitas, E. 2017 In S. Bunn (ed) *Anthropology and Beauty*. London: Routledge.
Deleuze, G. and Guattari, F. 2004 *A Thousand Plateaus*, trans B. Massumi. London: Continuum.
Goldin-Meadow, S. 2013 *Hearing Gesture: How our hands help us think*. Cambridge, MA: Belknap Press.
Griuale, M. 1965 *Conversations with Ogotommeli*. Oxford: Oxford University Press.
Guss, D. 1990 *To Weave and Sing: Art, Symbol and Narrative in the South American Rainforest*. Berkeley, CA: University of California Press.
Harzelius-Klück, E. https://penelope.hypotheses.org
Heidegger, M. 1927 *Being and Time*. 2008 reprint, New York: Harper.
Herrera, C. E. G. n.d. 'Winding bodies: intentionality, harmony and memory in rope-making'.
Hurcombe, L. 2014 *Perishable Material Culture in Prehistory*. Routledge: London.
Kimmerer, R. W. 2013 *Braiding Sweetgrass: Indigenous wisdom, scientific knowledge, and the teachings of plants*. Minneapolis: Milkweed Editions.
Marchand, T. H. J. 2018 'Towards an anthropology of mathematizing'. *Interdisciplinary Science Reviews* 43 (3–4): 295–316
Mason, O. T. 1895 *The Origins of Invention*. London: Walter Scott Ltd.
Mauss, M. 1934/1935 'Techniques of the body', *Journal de psychologie normal and pathologiques* XXXII: 271–293.
Myers, N. 2015 'Conversations on plant sensing: notes from the field', *Nature Culture* 3: 35–6.
Nemirovsky, R. 2012 'Modalities of bodily engagement in mathematics activity and learning', *Journal of the Learning Sciences* (21) 2: 207–215.
Peri, D. and Paterson, S. 1976 'The basket is in the roots, that's where it begins. *Journal of California Anthropology* (2): 17–32.
Powers, R. 2018 *The Overstory*. New York: Norton.
Ryle, G. 1949 *The Concept of Mind*. Chicago, IL: University of Chicago Press.
Sennett, R. 2008 *The Craftsman*. London: Penguin.
Thompson, E. 2006 'Neurophenomenology and contemplative experience'. In P. Clayton (ed.), *The Oxford Handbook of Religion and Science*. Oxford: Oxford University Press, 226–235
Tomasello, M. 2009 *Why We Cooperate*. Cambridge, MA: MIT Press.
Tsing, A. 2015 *The Mushroom at the End of the World: On the possibilities of life in capitalist ruins*. Princeton, NJ: Princeton University Press.
Varela, F. J., Thompson, E., and Rosch, E. *The Embodied Mind: Cognitive Science and Human Experience*. Cambridge, MA: MIT Press.
Venkatesan, S. 2010 'Learning to weave, weaving to learn. What?' *JRAI Special Issue on Knowledge*, pp 158–175.

PART ONE

Materials and processes: From plant to basket and beyond

Introduction
Victoria Mitchell

Basketry exemplifies and articulates ways in which humans have adapted and continue to adapt to the environment through the selection and manipulation of plants and other pliable materials. In 'Materials and processes: from plant to basket and beyond', materials take centre stage – as if each contributor is engaged in conversation with, or transformation of, materials, and learning through them how knowledge itself is formed and formative across a range of practices. It is as if materials and their characteristics themselves become embodied, adapting to the technicity that nurtures them. They have their own agri-cultural history, being tended and processed over time to enable the complex needs and desires of makers and users to be fulfilled. However, materials once regarded as 'natural' have been so commodified they are no longer always ecologically sustainable and in some current-era practices this has led to a search for new, often recycled, materials, which in turn leads to timely inventiveness.

Humans do not tell the whole 'basketry' story. The evolution of materials and making might also emerge through morphology, as in living matter which pertains to basketry-like formations such as the glass sponge known as the Venus flower basket (*Euplectella aspergillum*). Although not typically regarded within a basketry typology, exoskeletons, traps and animal 'architecture' are not dissimilar in kind. Through scientific observation Susan D. Healy and Maria Tello-Ramos consider ways in which the basket-like nests of certain birds are formed through selection and artful manipulation of choice materials and adaptation to the needs of habitat. They coin the notion of 'manufacturing convergence' to indicate mutual characteristics of basketmaking and nest building, though why baskets are 'made' and nests are 'built' reveals a significant divergence, hopefully one which their inclusion within Materials and Processes can begin to heal.

Basketry culture predates history, but because traditional basketry materials are so easily perishable in most environments, there are many, and huge, gaps in the material evidence, geographically and across time. However, as archaeology increasingly identifies not-quite-perished traces, much can be gleaned especially when, as in the work of archaeologist Willeke Wendrich, the research draws on traces unearthed from ancient Egyptian sites *and* on observation of contemporary basketmakers in Egyptian villages. Past and present also inform each other in the practice of artist Caroline Dear, who indicates connections between the two through the lens of a length of handmade rope. While her transformation of materials is poetic and visually stimulating, it also manifests a detailed engagement with the skills and plant husbandry of those for whom basketry was once part of everyday life. Similarly, the artist and basketmaker Tim Johnson makes use of basketry artefacts to 'to converse with the material in hand'. In a process he likens to the playing of music, the intertwining, looping and interlacing of materials are recreated in pencil on paper and in three-dimensions through string, in preparation for reconstruction and invention.

Ingenuity has long served to sustain what might otherwise be lost. Wendrich's example of the *sabat tilifun*, a basket to carry mobile phones from room to room, is a case in point. Mary Butcher's concerns for current threats to willow production in the United Kingdom and to the loss of skills and techniques which were once commonplace may point to an uncertain future, but seen alongside Lois Walpole's scouring of Scotland's beaches for the flotsam and jetsam detritus of 'ghost gear' and the use of traditional techniques to transform this into basketry forms, it is clear that basketry is, for the time being, not lost so much as having the potential to be reinvented and renewed. Material resources and techniques are adapted to meet new uses but also new 'audiences', as in the art-gallery context within which much contemporary practice is displayed.

1

Bird nest building

Susan D. Healy and Maria C. Tello-Ramos

Animals of all kinds build different purpose structures by manipulating and transforming materials into something new. These structures can be used as a sexual display, a shelter or as a nest into which eggs are laid and offspring are raised. Some of the structures that animals make are remarkably similar to objects that humans manufacture e.g. baskets, in the object/structure's shape, its purpose and even the process by which it is made. From gathering the right material at different stages of construction, bending it and weaving it to form an object/structure, nests built by birds and the baskets humans have been making for millennia are an example of 'manufacturing convergence'. Whether similar decisions are being made by birds and humans when building is not known, but there are increasing data that shed light on at least some of the decisions made by nest-building birds.

Famously, bower birds in Australia and Papua New Guinea build stick and grass bowers, which they then decorate with berries, shells and other objects in order to attract females to mate with them. Males from different species differ in the colours of objects they prefer for their decorations (e.g. satin bowerbirds prefer blue objects, even if man made). For the great bowerbird *Ptilonorhynchus nuchalis*, at least, it's not just the right objects (bleached snail shells, white and grey stones) that are important to the male's attractiveness but also the way in which he presents them to the female on his bower: he arranges them such that the smaller objects are at the immediate end of the avenue and larger objects are further away. When a female stands the middle of the avenue of a male's bower looking out at the decorations she is, then, provided with a forced perspective of the decorations (Kelley & Endler 2012).

The entirely-for-display constructions of bower birds are, however, an uncommon example of the constructions most typically built by birds and for which they are best known. Bird nests are built to contain and protect their eggs and the resulting offspring (from the heat, cold or rain and from predators). Across species, nests vary in the materials from which they are made (e.g. grass, reeds, feathers, animal hair, sticks, manmade materials such as string, wire, plastic), where they are built (e.g. on cliffs, in trees and bushes, on the ground, in holes) and the shape they take (e.g. a platform, a cup, a cup with a dome). Although this variation has generally been considered to be the result of some kind of 'genetic blueprint', there is now increasing evidence that this is not the whole story and that birds learn from others, they learn from their own building experience and that where, when and how they build their nest depends on the environment in which they build.

FIGURE 1.1(a-f) *Top left: the first blade of grass woven on to a branch by a nest-building Southern Masked Weaver* Ploceus cucullatus; *top right: male weaving the first few blades of grass; middle left: the male has formed ring; middle right: a female sits in the forming nest, which now has the beginnings of a roof while the male hangs beneath; bottom left: male building inside the nearly completed nest; bottom right: the female in possession of the completed nest. Note: Not all the photos are of the same male or nest. Photographs: S. Healy*

There has been sporadic interest in bird nest building over the past century and a half, including by well-known evolutionary biologist Arthur Russell Wallace, but perhaps the first substantial body of research began in in the late 1950s by Elsie and Nicholas Collias on a colony of captive Village weaverbirds *Ploceus* (previously *Textor*) *cucullatus* (Collias & Collias 196). Nest building by weaverbirds has long been fascinating because of the ways in which they manipulate material into forming the nest and the resultant structures bear more than a passing resemblance to the baskets made by people. The Collias' described multiple stages of a weaver's nest building: the initial attachment on a branch, weaving grass into a ring, building the roof, then the egg chamber, followed by the antechamber, the entrance and then the entrance tube. Rather like Village weavers, the Southern Masked Weaver *Ploceus velatus* prepares the site first by removing any leaves around the attachment site. He then attaches first one long blade of grass, holding one end under one foot and moving his bill along the length of grass bit by bit until weaving the free end of the grass over and under the branch and through itself (Fig. 1).

Once he has several pieces of grass woven to form the attachment, he weaves together the loose ends to form a ring. It appears that at least in the Southern Masked weavers, the males may build at a rate that is associated with the presence of a female: the more she visits or the longer her visits, the faster the male builds. In that species, at least, building doesn't begin until the male has enticed a female to become his mate. In other species, however, such as the Cape weaver *P. capensis*, males build multiple nests before a female chooses whether to lay her eggs and raise their offspring in one or other nest. Nests then, may also be used by the male to signal his quality.

Material colour

The Collias' described the kinds of materials used by weavers: long strips of fresh, green, flexible elephant grass or palms, with shorter leaves once the outer shell was built and then females often add feathers and soft grassheads. They also had the opportunity to describe the knots the birds used, some nine of them, including the bowline.

To examine whether birds had particular preferences for certain material attributes, the Collias' presented their captive weavers with toothpicks of different colours, of which the birds preferred yellow or green toothpicks over toothpicks that were blue, red, black or white. Because birds that had been hand-reared without experience of normal nest materials also preferred green toothpicks, it may be thought that these birds have an innate preference for materials of 'natural' colours (Collias & Collias 1984).

Subsequent investigation into preferences for nest material colour in other species has, however, resulted in variation that is not easy to explain: for example, domestic canaries prefer red to white string, zebra finches sometimes prefer brown material to green and red, sometimes green rather than brown, or when offered, blue over yellow. These colour preferences do appear to be specific to nest materials because while the colour preferences of zebra finches for nest materials can be strong they do not prefer one colour of food over another (Muth et al. 2013).

One might expect that birds would pay some attention to the colour of materials if the colour has some function, such as enabling the bird to camouflage its nest against the background in order to reduce the threat of predation. And yet, the evidence that birds do this is surprisingly sparse or even contrary to this expectation. Diamond Firetails *Stagonopleura guttata*, for example, decorate their nests with very colourful flowers that make their nests extremely conspicuous but do not experience more predation as a result (McGuire & Kleindorfer 2007). It is also possible that birds do not choose material in order to camouflage their nests but choose material based on the availability of materials in the habitat around them, a choice that leads to nests matching their background. Bailey et al. (2015b) showed experimentally, however, that zebra finches, at least, will choose nest materials that match the background: birds provided with a cage with coloured wall paper and nest box covered with the same paper, chose paper strips of the same colour with which to build their nest.

At least sometimes, then, birds may choose materials of a colour that is functionally appropriate. They will also learn to associate the colour of a material with their own reproductive success: zebra finches that build with material of a colour they do not prefer but produce offspring from that nest, for their next breeding attempt will preferentially choose material of that colour (Muth & Healy 2011). This suggests that whatever initial colour preferences birds might have as naïve builders, those preferences are not fixed but depend on the bird's own experiences.

Material rigidity

Although the Collias' weavers did prefer some coloured toothpicks to others, when given the opportunity these birds preferred flexible over more rigid materials, a choice also seen in the nest building of Southern masked weavers (Fig.1). Weavers also choose materials based on their strength: Cape weaver *P. capensis* chose sedges that were long and strong for the attachment and outer shell of their nests but increasingly chose shorter, weaker materials as their nest progressed (Bailey et al. 2016). It has also been suggested that weavers will choose stronger materials when they are building in windy habitats but this has not been tested (Crook 1963).

Zebra finches do not weave materials to form their nests, but they will do quite a lot of tucking of materials (typically grasses in the wild, but all sorts of material in the laboratory, including string) to form a nest that is a cup covered by a dome. Perhaps because they tend to build a dome (probably to protect their eggs and chicks from the sun of the Australian deserts) they prefer material that is not too flexible. Indeed, with increasing experience of flexible materials, they will increasingly prefer more rigid material. This appears to be due to the number of pieces of flexible material required to form the appropriate nest, which can be twice as many (>800) as required when building with more rigid material (around 400) (Bailey et al. 2014). These data suggest that the birds can learn the mechanical properties of the materials with which they build. They also suggest that preferred or appropriate material properties depend on the kind of nest a bird builds.

Building to a template?

The increasing evidence that birds learn at least something about what materials with which to build suggests that any innate component of nest building would be a template that is moulded by experience. Examination of the variation in the morphology of Village and Southern Masked weavers also suggests that although the nests built by these species are often identifiable as to which species was the builder, the degree of variation among males in the nests they build is greater than that expected from a genetic contribution alone (Walsh et al. 2010). Both are useful species in which to examine variation in nest morphology because males build multiple nests in a season, providing the opportunity to determine whether each male builds the same nest over and over. In both species, nest length, height and weight diminish over the season, independently of the total number of nests built and of a male's body size. And, although there is evidence for repeatability in a male's nest measurements, this is rather low, suggesting that a weaver male's nest morphology may be a response to the current weather conditions (e.g. wind, rain, sun), available materials, perhaps even the number of eggs his mate may lay. Morphology may, however, be a rather gross measure of individual variation as it is possible to attribute weaver nests to the individual that built them (albeit somewhat short of 100% classification): in essence, it appears that male weavers each produce something that might be described as a signature weave pattern (Bailey et al. 2015a).

Builders may also become more competent at building the more nests they build: detailed analysis of the movements performed by male Southern masked weavers as they built their nests showed that males became more dexterous the more they built and much less likely to drop grass (Walsh et al. 2011). This detailed analysis also showed that the direction in which and how the birds inserted a blade of grass as they wove varied across males. For example, some males were more likely to insert blades of grass into the left side of the nest as they built than to the right, some more likely to have a right-side bias and others had no bias at all. The greater the side bias a male had, the faster he was to complete the ring stage of the nest, but more lateralized males did not finish a nest more quickly or build more nests across the season. The variability in how males carried grass and where they inserted it into the nest seemed most likely to be a result of the particulars of each blade of grass, rather than the result of a series of fixed action patterns.

A fixed action pattern also did not seem to explain the behaviour of Southern masked males once they had more than one nest. Indeed, these birds do not seem to finish completely a nest if they manage to attract another female for whom to build the next nest. They then begin work on the new nest while continuing to bring material to the nearly-complete nest. As they add nests, males revisit all their nests continuously, sometimes bringing new material, and at other times appearing to 'tidy up' a nest, tucking in or biting off pieces of material that stick out from the nest. The lack of pattern to the order in which they visit older nests is not consistent with an obvious stereotyped rule of building or of repair. This apparent 'tidiness' is also apparent in the complete removal of a nest should a breeding attempt fail. Taken together it appears that a male knows the status of his nests and keeps this information updated as the breeding season proceeds (he does not feed the young or his mate).

One might speculate on whether the descriptions of females bringing materials such as soft grasses and feathers to a nest that has been largely built by her mate is not because she is the one who does the 'decorating' but rather because her male stops building as soon as she is prepared to move into the nest and begin egg laying, it then falls to her to finish the nest to the standard necessary to produce fledglings. When a female is the builder (e.g. in blue tits, blackbirds), she does all of the building and not just the last touches.

Learning from others?

If birds can learn how and what materials with which to build, it seems possible that they may learn something of the trade from others, especially those social and/or long-lived species that have the opportunity to see others building. The data are still very sparse, but it does appear that zebra finches (a social species) will copy at least some building decisions from others: first-time male builders switch their preference for one colour of material to another after watching an experienced bird building with the material of colour they do not like. But this occurred only when the demonstrator was familiar to the observer. When the demonstrator was unfamiliar the observer's material preference was unchanged by the demonstration (Guillette et al. 2016). At least some aspects of building expertise, then, can be transmitted socially. And, indeed, it appears that zebra finches also pay attention to nests themselves: to date, this manipulation has been confined to the colour of the material but nonetheless, naïve builders that observed just a nest of a colour they did not like, when offered materials of two different colours lost their initial preference for a particular colour and instead chose the material of the same colour as that of the nest they had observed (Breen et al. 2019). A nest artefact, then, can also shape a builder's decisions albeit perhaps not to quite the same extent as when there is an individual attracting attention, especially if that individual is in the cage next door. Observers that watch a video of demonstrator building also change their preferences for material colour to match that used by the video demonstrator but not to the same degree as those that watch a live neighbour (Guillette & Healy 2019). These findings strongly suggest that, at least in zebra finches, nest-building behaviour is socially influenced.

Conclusion

Our understanding of the role that learning plays in the choice, the manipulation and the design of nests by birds is still in its infancy. But there is increasing evidence that learning, both individual and social, plays a role in the materials a builder chooses, and in the nest that he or she builds.

Bibliography

Bailey, I. E., Backes, A., Walsh, P. T., Morgan, K. V., Meddle, S. L., & Healy, S. D., 2015a 'Image analysis of weaverbird nests reveals signature weave textures', *Royal Society Open Science* 2. doi: 10.1098/rsos.150074.

Bailey, I. E., Morgan, K. V., Bertin, M., Meddle, S. L., & Healy, S. D., 2014 'Physical cognition: birds learn the structural efficacy of nest material', in *Proceedings of the Royal Society B* 281, 20133225. doi: 10.1098/rspb.2013.3225.

Bailey, I. E., Morgan, K. V., Oschadleus, H. D., DeRuiter, S. L., Meddle, S. L., & Healy, S. D., 2016 'Nest-building males trade off material collection costs with territory value', *Emu* 116: 1–8. doi: 10.1071/mu15022.

Bailey, I. E., Muth, F., Morgan, K., Meddle, S. L., & Healy, S. D., 2015b 'Birds build camouflaged nests', *Auk* 132: 11–15. doi: 10.1642/auk-14-77.1.

Breen, A., Bonneaud, C., Healy, S. D. & Guillette, L. M., 2019 'Social learning about construction behaviour via an artifact', *Animal Cognition* 22: 305–315.

Collias, E. C. & Collias, N. E., 1964 'The development of nest-building behavior in a weaverbird', *Auk* 81: 42–52.

Collias, N. E. & Collias, E. C., 1984 *Nest Building and Bird Behavior*. Princeton, NJ: Princeton University Press.

Crook, J. H., 1963 'A comparative analysis of nest structure in the weaver birds (*Ploceinae*)', *Ibis* 105: 238–262.

Guillette, L. M., & Healy, S. D., 2019 'Social learning in nest-building birds watching live streaming video demonstrators', *Integrative Zoology* 14: 204–213.

Guillette, L. M., Scott, A. C. Y., & Healy, S. D., 2016 'Social learning in nest-building birds: a role for familiarity', *Proceedings of the Royal Society B* 283. doi: 10.1098/rspb.2015.2685.

Kelley, L. A. & Endler, J. A. 2012 'Illusions promote mating success in great bowerbirds', *Science* 335: 335–338. doi: 10.1126/science.1212443.

McGuire, A. & Kleindorfer, S. 2007 'Nesting success and apparent nest-adornment in Diamond Firetails (*Stagonopleura guttata*)', *Emu* 107: 44–51. doi: 10.1071/mu06031.

Muth, F. & Healy, S. D., 2011 'The role of adult experience in nest building in the zebra finch, *Taeniopygia guttata*', *Animal Behaviour* 82: 185–189. doi: 10.1016/j.anbehav.2011.04.021.

Muth, F., Steele, M., & Healy, S. D., 2013 'Colour preferences in nest-building zebra finches', *Behavioural Processes* 99: 106–111. doi: 10.1016/j.beproc.2013.07.002.

Walsh, P. T., Hansell, M., Borello, W. D., & Healy, S. D. 2010 'Repeatability of nest morphology in African weaver birds', *Biology Letters*: 149–151. doi: 10.1098/rsbl.2009.0664.

Walsh, P. T., Hansell, M., Borello, W. D., & Healy, S. D., 2011 'Individuality in nest building: Do Southern Masked Weaver (*Ploceus velatus*) males vary in their nest-building behaviour?' *Behavioural Processes* 88: 1–6. doi: 10.1016/j.beproc.2011.06.011.

·

2

Binding place

Caroline Dear

In front of me sits a small piece of heather rope (Fig. 2.1). I gathered it many years ago from inside a derelict house on North Uist and I treasure it. It is something that I am inherently interested in as an artist.

This handmade rope once ran continuously across the roof space from gable to gable over the rafters, instead of the timber traditionally used for this purpose. It supported turf slabs, into which rush thatch was fixed. Embedded within the rope is knowledge of how, when and where to gather the correct heather, who made the rope, when and how it was made and even suggestion of the season and number of people who helped place it within the roofing of the house. Its fragile DNA can be extracted, pieced together, understood and learned from. I believe this knowledge and these subtle hand-skills are vitally important and relevant for us now and in the future.

One of the first skills I learned, over thirty years ago, was that of making heather rope by hand, in the traditional Highland way. I was taught this on Skye, where it was called *sìoman* (Dwelly, 1994), from a man who had learned it from an older Orcadian, this skill having already died out on Skye. I am still learning about heather and its rich and varied characteristics, including toughness and longevity. It was traditionally used for thatching, mooring ropes, creels, *cassies*, brushes and

FIGURE 2.1 *Caroline Dear, 2018, section of heather rope, pen and ink drawing.*

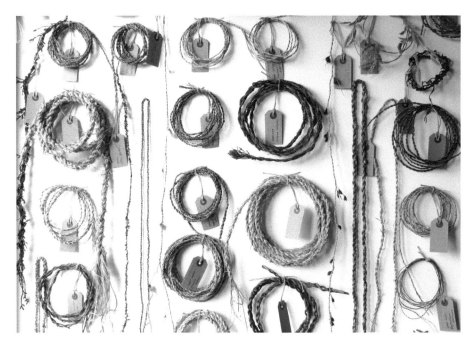

FIGURE 2.2 *2012,* Entwined/suainte *(fifty local Skye plants). One hundred ropes, one hundred days, each labelled in Latin and English. Photograph: C. Dear.*

FIGURE 2.3 *2013,* Cupar Coat of Good Luck *(bog myrtle). Wreaths of bog myrtle appear on Cupar's coat of arms. Photograph: C. Dear.*

Figure 2.4 *2013,* Encircled by gold *(dandelion, bog cotton, soft rush, birch). Life-size mantles referencing 'Brigid', an Iron Age woman excavated on Skye. Photograph: C. Dear.*

Figure 2.5 *2016,* Soundings IV *(common reed). Part of Vassen Susar,* The Whispering Reeds, *an exhibition exploring the common reed (*Phragmites australis*) in response to its invasive nature in Finland. Photograph: C. Dear.*

as the base layer for roads across boggy areas. There is an eighteenth-century house near me where, it is said, heather was used as nails to hold slates in place.

The landscape we live in reflects how we use, think about and relate to it. Plants needed for making are husbanded, but as needs change and certain plants are no longer needed, so too the landscape changes. An example of this is soft rush, *Juncus effusus*, once used for thatching, bedding, lamp wicks and bags, amongst other things. A *seic*, for example, was a bag for holding grain made wholly of *sìoman luachair*, a rope made of rushes (Dwelly, 1994). Near where I live is a small enclosed area beside the burn where, neighbours tell me, rush was grown for communal use. This area was carefully managed and controlled, harvested regularly and the produce used. Nowadays, left to itself, the rush has spread, turning good grazing areas into boggy ground due to its dense root system. Pesticide is now sprayed in order to control it.

In understanding our place within a local landscape and our relationship with the plants around us we are able to understand our place in the wider world. This is fundamental to me in my work as an artist (fig 2.2–2.5). Preserving local skills and knowledge and adapting these for use now and in the future is an important role of the artist. Connecting people with plants, binding the thread of knowledge which links past, present and future, leads to a deeper understanding of the place we are in now.

Bibliography

Dwelly, E. 1994 *The Illustrated Gaelic–English Dictionary*, Glasgow: Gairm Publications.

3

Archaeological basketry and cultural identity in Ancient Egypt

Willeke Wendrich

Introduction

Basketry has received little attention from archaeologists, partly because it rarely survives. In most environments organic materials decay into non-existence. Baskets and mats, made mostly of dried plant material are, furthermore, often reused and at the end of their object life-cycle used as fuel, leaving no physical trace behind. Basketry remains survive best in anaerobic circumstances, closed off from microbial activity, for instance in permafrost, waterlogged or, most frequently, in extremely arid circumstances. These environments determine what type of basketry survives: in Northern Europe most basketry finds are fish traps, left behind in waterways and ditches. Deserts, caves and rock-cut tombs provide often extremely dry circumstances in which organic materials are preserved well. Even if we find a wealth of basketry, the question should always be what these objects represent, especially when dealing with grave goods: are these the baskets and mats that the deceased used throughout his or her life? Were they especially produced for the tomb? Which types of objects were *never* included, and thus have not survived?

The circumstances of preservation not only determine *what* survives, but also *how* basketry remains are found, and this directly influences our interpretation of the society that produced and used this material. In addition, the important role of basketry is reflected in other cultural expressions, such as art and architecture. After a comparison of very early evidence for basketry in two Neolithic cultures of Anatolia and Egypt, we will explore information on basketry and matting gleaned from impressions, imitations, depictions and present day basketry production and use. In order to gain some understanding of the social function of basketry we can in addition use a simple exercise: consider your own surroundings and replace all plastic articles with objects made from natural materials. It inevitably leads to reflection on the wide range of properties, the specificity of function and the many levels of meaning that basketry and matting would have had in ancient society.

Neolithic basketry

That basketry was a very early human invention, and well developed during prehistoric times, is clearly demonstrated at two Neolithic sites: Çatalhöyük in Turkey (approximately 7500–5500 BC), and the Fayum in Egypt (approximately 5000–4200 BC). These two Neolithic sites provide very different narratives on the production, use, reuse, discard and preservation of basketry.

Excavations in Çatalhöyük by a large interdisciplinary team under direction of Ian Hodder have yielded matting impressions of large tabby plaited mats with phytolith remains in clay floors, as well as impressions with traces of phytoliths (siliceous plant remains, literally 'plant stones'), of small coiled mats and large coiled baskets (Fig. 3.1).

The latter were used in burials of children and adults inside the houses (Wendrich 2006). The dwellings at this site were built of mudbrick and were entered through hatches in the roof. The floor space was divided into different sectors raised at various levels, thus forming low platforms underneath which the dead were laid to rest (Hodder 2010). Some of the floors, possibly limited to those in rooms that had ceremonial significance, (the previous excavator called them shrines, cf. Mellaart 1967), were covered with large plaited mats made of broad, even strips of plant material in a simple over-one, under-one pattern. Although there was evidence of use wear on the burial baskets, no basketry containers were found in the house outside the platform. Remains of coiled mats the size of dinner plates were found on the surface of some of the platforms, specifically in the northern area of the excavation (Tringham and Stevanovic 2012).

The context of the Egyptian Neolithic basketry is very different. The settlement areas in the Fayum, a basin west of the Nile Valley and fed by a branch of the Nile, have yielded no traces of dwellings and consist of several layers of hearths, interspersed with 'clean' and 'dirty' areas. No

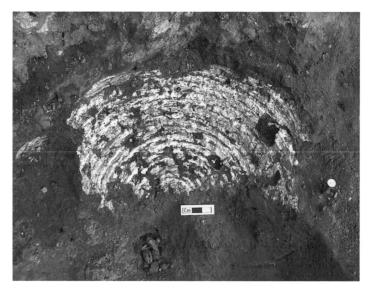

FIGURE 3.1 *Phytolith Neolithic basketry remains at Çatalhöyük: coiled lid covering a skeleton. Copyright: Catalhoyuk Research Project. Photograph: Peter Boyer.*

clear posthole pattern is discernible, nor traces of sturdy matting or other indications of shelters. This is probably due to adverse circumstances of preservation, because on a high ridge overlooking the habitation area more than a hundred grain storage pits were found, many of which retain coarsely coiled basketry lining (Wendrich and Cappers 2005). The coiling of these round baskets with a diameter of approximately 1 m. and a height of 0.75 m. was done with wheat straw (Fig. 3.2).

The widely spaced stitches were not made with a separate winder, but rather with a small section of the bundle material. In the same area a fragment of very finely coiled basketry was found in 2005, decorated with a dark rim. It is similar to a complete basket found in one of the storage pits in 1924 (Caton-Thompson and Gardner 1934), now in the British Museum (Fig. 3.3).

This basket was equally regular and finely made, but in addition to the rim, coloured winders were employed in the base and sides to create patterns.

FIGURE 3.2 *Basketry lining of grain storage pits in the Fayum (Egypt). Copyright UCLA/RUG/UoA Fayum Project. Photograph: Willeke Wendrich.*

FIGURE 3.3 *Neolithic basket found inside one of the grain storage pits in the Fayum (Egypt), now in the British Museum. Copyright: © Trustees of the British Museum.*

The interpretation of the function and meaning of the material from Fayum and Çatalhöyük, the social context of its producers and users, can easily be slanted because of accidents of preservation. If we do have basketry surviving, what is the information we can glean from it if we take into account what might be missing? The two types of Fayum basketry are both found in an elevated ridge away from possible high stands of the lake that borders the settlement site. Apart from the storage pits, the area is devoid of evidence of human occupation. The baskets found as pit lining are utilitarian and specifically made for their purpose in this particular place. The fine decorated coiled basketry, however, may have been used as scoops, to take out grain from the pits, and this could potentially be a secondary use. If we consider the grain storage pits as a kind of 'industrial area', two kilometres away from the settlement, then the finely decorated basket may have been left there, reused as grain scoop after more glorious days as food presentation basket. On the other hand, if we see the pits as a storage area for a community's most prized possessions, such as the agricultural reserves, or seed capital, then a decorated basket found within a storage pit should perhaps be considered a treasure or heirloom. The only way to decide between such different interpretations is to weigh all other available evidence. Even such a holistic approach to the archaeological record will often provide conflicting trends. In any case, the gorgeously produced basketry found within the pits provides a radically different view of Fayum Neolithic society from the dilapidated remains of the settlement near the lake shore.

The narratives that the Neolithic basketry from Çatalhöyük potentially presents us with are quite different. The lack of large baskets in the area of the living, in contrast to their presence in the realm of the dead, underneath the platforms, can be explained in different ways. We may suppose that the finely coiled basketry was prepared specifically for use in burials. There are indications, however, that the burial baskets were previously used; the presence of dense patches of white phytoliths seem to represent bundle fibres, exposed at the surface. This would indicate that Çatalhöyük burial baskets were not new baskets, but ones that showed damages from use: some of the winders had worn off and the coils were bared. What this indicates about the care of the living for the dead is still a matter of debate. Were the buried bodies considered unimportant, not worthy of a specially made container? Considering that the dead were kept close to the world of the living, literally underfoot within the house, makes this an unlikely assumption. Were baskets perhaps very expensive? Were they heirlooms, that served a person during life and in death? Was the age and appearance of the container unimportant, as long as the deceased was physically separated from the surrounding soil? Was it difficult to find raw materials at some times of the year, the choice of used baskets indicating a burial in winter? Many of these questions are unanswerable, but they nevertheless form the foundation of the archaeological work, because without these we would have no direction in studying and recording the material culture remains within their archaeological context. They form the building blocks of our reconstruction of ancient society.

Impressions

In some cases we find traces of basketry even if the actual baskets or mats no longer exist. Pots which were put to dry on a mat may have the structure of the weave impressed in the still wet clay of their bases (Crowfoot 1938). Matting weave or plait patterns have likewise been preserved as impressions in the mud of floors or roof covering layers. Sometimes these impressions still have some remains of the original fibres, in the form of phytoliths. Because phytoliths are specific to the plant species producing them, they can be used to identify the plant families used in producing basketry, the provenance of the raw materials used to make the baskets or mats, and in some cases even the ecological systems and circumstances.

Representations

Although impressions might give information on decorative weaving, plaiting or coiling patterns, they do not provide evidence for the use of colour, while we know from extant examples that intricate coloured patterning has been attested in coiled basketry from very early on. By looking at additional evidence, for instance skeuomorphs, imitations of basketry in ceramics, stone or metal or representations of basketry in reliefs and wall paintings, we can gain insight in decoration methods and styles. Such research should always be approached in conjunction with the study of archaeological material, however, because geometric decorative patterns do not necessarily represent basketry, or may not represent a basketry technique in ways that seem logical to modern observers. In addition, it is important to consider the period and the region to which the evidence belongs and to take into account the general developments in the material culture and the art styles.

Several examples may serve to illustrate this point. In early Egyptian Old Kingdom tomb paintings (ca. 2575 BC), offering bearers, who symbolize the different estates or domains contributing to the wealth of the king or the tomb owner, are depicted carrying a plethora of baskets (Khaled 2008). Most of these are straight sided with a narrow bottom and a wider top. No extant basketry has been found dated to the Old Kingdom, but the tomb paintings seem to represent a type of coiled basketry, which has been attested in later, New Kingdom contexts (ca. 1350 BC). There are also modern equivalents of such round baskets with straight sides, a shape which can be easily produced by coiling. This technique is depicted most frequently as simple horizontal lines, which denote the coiled rows (Wendrich 2000). In slightly later Old Kingdom tombs (ca. 2500 BC) blocked patterns occur on the same shape of baskets, interspersed with the ones with simple horizontal lines, which can perhaps be interpreted as a different basket type, or more likely a different type of decoration, because apart from an increase in basketry shapes over time, there is also an increase in quantity and variety of offered grave goods. The checked pattern in the baskets does not seem to denote a different technique, but shows a schematic view of the individual stitches of the winder. In some cases, these blocked patterns are not just alternating tan and black squares, but vividly coloured with green and red, possibly indicating not only the use of coloured winders, but also larger decorative chevron patterns over the entire side of the basket. Clear and unequivocal depictions of highly patterned coiled basketry with intricate motifs, including animal and human figures, occur a millennium later in paintings on the walls of the tomb of Rekhmire, the vizier of Pharaoh Thutmoses III (ca. 1500 BC), as part of 'tribute' from Kush (Southern Nubia) (Fig. 3.4).

Similar blocked patterns occur also on the thrones of the gods, mostly attested on New Kingdom temple walls, for instance in the Temple of Ramesses III in Medinet Habu (ca. 1250 BC).

FIGURE 3.4 *Wall relief from the tomb of Rekhmire depicting decorated baskets as tribute from Kush (Southern Nubia). Drawn by the author after Davies 1973.*

Ethnoarchaeology

Ethnoarchaeology is a method to study present day society using archaeological research questions. These can vary from very practical concerns, such as the wear marks that particular activities cause, to complicated questions of cultural identity. Ethnoarchaeological research is a search for tangible and intangible archaeological correlates. By observing or partaking in certain human activities in the present, an ethnoarchaeologist develops a sensitivity to develop possible alternative explanations of the material traces from the past. The method has some enormous pitfalls, however. A scholar who believes that relations between past and present are fixed, determined, immobile, or linked to a cultural continuity will block the development of alternative explanations and limit interpretation to an obstructed view of the past. In Nubian basketry, for instance, the use of colourful patterned decoration was important in the past as it is at present. The materials and techniques, however, differ much from those of a millennium ago (Wendrich 1999).

The combination of archaeological, philological, iconographic and ethnoarchaeological research can focus on a wide range of topics. In order to understand the production process, the selection and provenance of the raw materials, the techniques used, the order in which parts of the production process take place, the time investment and the technological solutions, it is important to find the archaeological correlates of each phase of the production. The concept of *chaîne opératoire* (Leroi-Gourhan 1964) understands an object as the result of a process, with points of decision (and thus potential variation) at each step of the process. Observing or working with present day basketmakers allows insight in the production process and all its demands, including the amount of effort and time the different phases require.

One of the aspects which we can record during a modern production process, especially with the help of video recordings, is the working rhythm of basketmakers. Most technological processes have long periods of repetitive actions and the best way of sustaining these is by maintaining a steady work rhythm. This is the basis for work songs, heaving cries, and the almost mesmerizing percussion sounds of carpentry, masonry and certain types of basketmaking. Even if the material is soft, and the process itself almost noiseless, the regular swishing, articulated by sudden stops, marks the working rhythm of the producer. The archaeological correlate of these sounds is a certain regularity in the work. Ethnoarchaeological work has demonstrated that skilled basketmakers maintain a steady working rhythm, while unskilled basketmakers falter and halt irregularly. In the resulting work this can be recognized as a very regular size or distance of stitches in coiling, or a well divided tension in weaving (Wendrich 1999).

Objects are made in a particular way following a preconceived notion of the producer, which is often closely linked to the expectations and demands of the users, be this the basketmaker him or herself, or a broad client base. A good example is the basketry from present day Egyptian Nubia. After the building of the Aswan High Dam in the 1960s, the Nubians were forced to resettle in the region north of Aswan, because their villages were flooded by Lake Nasser. They have developed a unified lobby aimed at the Egyptian government and present themselves effectively as one group. On a different level, however, they identify themselves as two distinct groups: Kensi and Fadidja speak a different language and live in separate villages. The difference between Kensi and Fadija is clearly born out in the material culture, most obviously in clothing, but the basketry shows marked differences as well. On the one hand Nubian basketry is distinct from Egyptian basketry through appearance and function: Egyptian coiled basketry is made by women, mostly for their own use inside the house. Two shapes are most common: simple round trays, with a diameter of approximately 0.75 m., used to stack the unleavened bread that is baked in the villages of Middle Egypt, and round baskets with straight sides used for multiple purposes. Apart from these there are small lidded coiled baskets used to keep trinkets, decorative baskets with open worked zig-zag sides, and special purpose baskets, such as the *sabat tilifun*: a tray with handle on which to carry the telephone from room to room (clearly a classic in the present time of ubiquitous mobile telephones). These baskets are made of date palm leaf, with bundles of the hard fibres of the shredded stem on which the dates grow. They are mostly plain, although sparse decoration with coloured ribbons does occur.

In contrast the Nubian coiled baskets are mostly used as covers for cups, plates or large trays on which food is laid out. These food covers are lavishly decorated with coloured winder patterns, or with inlaid patterns of dyed straw (imbrication). The Nubian basketry made after the resettlement shows clear differences between Fadidja and Kensi producers. The doam palm, the primary raw material for coiled basketry in ancient times, was common in Pharaonic Egypt, but gradually retreated to the South. In the early twentieth century it was a familiar palm species in the Nubian landscape, but by the 1960s when the Nubians were resettled, it had become quite rare in Upper Egypt. More than the choice of patterns, it is the selection of raw materials which at present differentiates Fadidja and Kensi basketmakers. The Fadidja women make brightly-coloured baskets from dyed doam palm leaf. They do everything in their power to obtain the materials they used for basketmaking before the resettlement, although they use chemical dies to colour the strands. Kensi women are much more innovative and produce baskets of whatever coloured material they come across: dyed date palm leaf, but more often brightly-coloured wool or cotton yarn over a bundle of the same date palm fibre as is used in Middle Egypt. In addition, I have come across food covers made of plastic washing line, and even candy wrappers (Wendrich 1999) (Fig. 3.5).

In interviews the Fadidja women say that doam palm leaf simply is superior material, and that is why they prefer to use it. They are not weary of innovation; they actually boast that they are better basketmakers than their mothers, because they use more colours (which is difficult) and invent new decorative patterns. The decorative patterns show greater variety than those of the previous generation. It is unclear if this is in any way related to the physical and geographical changes to the settlements. The villages are located much closer together, at a few minutes distance by car along the asphalt roads of New Nubia, rather than a day or more on foot or by boat in Old Nubia. One man told me that in the old days each village had its own recognizable patterns, but this was not confirmed by any of the women.

In spite of the differences between Kensi and Fadidja baskets, the Nubian coiled baskets corpus is characterized by its function as food covers. With the exception of meal times, when they are in use, the baskets normally hang on the wall. In Fadidja households the tops of the coiled food covers are oriented away from the wall, showing off their brightly-coloured decorative palm leaf sides. In addition, the wall is sometimes decorated with painted circular shapes patterned in a way that is strongly reminiscent of the basketry designs (Fig. 3.6).

In many of the Kensi households the food covers also hang on the walls but are wrapped in textiles – often quite old and not particularly attractive – to protect them against dust. The Kensi way is not less traditional but seems to be characterized by a very practical adaptive approach, a similar integration of tradition as the imaginative choice of raw materials: the goal is to create colourful baskets, the means are to use whatever is available.

Understanding the Kensi and Fadidja expression of cultural identity requires a broader approach than the study of their basketry only. A comparison of food ways, for instance, shows that the 'traditional' palm leaf Fadidja and the 'innovative' cotton Kensi baskets cover the same food trays with the same type of dishes. Criticism of ethnoarchaeology by anthropologists has centred on the selective recording archaeologists are often involved in. Pierre Lemonnier, for instance, maintains that many of the studies that emphasize social aspects or meaning of material culture focus on too few aspects. They are concerned with what humans communicate through material culture, by studying the shape ('type') or decoration of an object. Such studies 'do not deal with the prime and obvious reason why technology deserves a sociological approach, which is: because techniques are first and foremost social productions.' (Lemonnier 1993: 3). Each artefact belongs to an integrated technological, economic, functional and communication system, which cannot be reduced to a simplified 'message' carried by a certain material, shape or decorative pattern. Artefacts are highly significant in social communication, but their meaning is rarely distinct or unambiguous, and is greatly dependent on the circumstances of use.

FIGURE 3.5 *Two Kensi baskets employing non-traditional materials to produce traditional coiled food covers. To the left: coiling with coloured washing line, to the right: coiling with cotton yarn. Photograph: Willeke Wendrich.*

FIGURE 3.6 *Fadidja room decoration with baskets and painted designs imitating basketry. Photograph: Willeke Wendrich.*

Conclusion

How then are archaeologists supposed to understand the meaning of objects within a culture, and especially in expressing cultural identity? Archaeology is characterized by many specializations, which tend to concentrate on a certain class of objects such as basketry, paying specific attention to a limited number of recordable attributes. Often it is difficult to record even the shape or material fabric of archaeological specimens, and the effort to place one's analysis in the context of all the other specialized studies is a major, but necessary task. Ethnoarchaeology should serve as a constant reminder that objects, materials and technology are actively negotiated. We do need the in-depth study of objects, however. If we try to study all aspects of society, we will not be able to analyze the subtle idiosyncrasies and variations, the technological details which are not obvious or readily discernible, either in the end product or the production process. It is these details which allow us to define micro-variables, in what appear to be similar techniques. Such variations are related to learned behaviour, indicative of the transfer of knowledge in a community of practice, and therefore form the roots of a tradition and cultural identity (Wendrich 2012).

For basketry these are, for instance, the different methods for fastening off strands, the inlay of new strands, the finishing of the rim, and the start of the basket. In order to record these micro-variables ideally the basketry objects should be well-preserved, but damaged enough that the usually well-hidden details are discernible. The worse the preservation, the more difficult it will be to find and define these micro-variables, through which we can begin to understand enculturation, tradition and innovation among those who make baskets, and trace what the preferences are of those who use baskets. This information lies at the basis of understanding the constantly negotiated cultural identity within the social context of technology.

Bibliography

Bongioanni, A., and Croce, M.S. 2003 *The Treasures of Ancient Egypt from the Egyptian Museum in Cairo*. New York: Rizzoli.

Crowfoot, G. M., 1938 'Mat Impressions on Pot Bases', *Annals of Archaeology and Anthropology*, 25: 3–11.

Davies, N. de G. 1973 *The Tomb of Rekh-Mi-Reē' at Thebes*, Publications of the Metropolitan Museum of Art, Egyptian Expedition v. 11. New York: Arno Press.

Khaled, M. 2008 'Old Kingdom funerary domains: a question of dating', in H. Vymazalová and M. Bárta (eds), *Chronology and Archaeology in Ancient Egypt (the Third Millennium B.C.)*. Prague: Czech Institute of Egyptology, Faculty of Arts, Charles University in Prague, 194–213.

Kitchen, K. A., 2003 *Ramesside Inscriptions: Merenptah & the late Nineteenth Dynasty*. Oxford: Wiley-Blackwell.

Lemonnier, P. 1993 *Technological Choices: Transformation in material cultures since the Neolithic*. Abingdon: Routledge.

Leroi-Gourhan, A. 1964. *Le geste et la parole I*. Paris: Albin Michel.

Smith, W. S. and Simpson, W. K. 1998 *The Art and Architecture of Ancient Egypt*. New Haven, CT, and London: Yale University Press.

Tringham, R. and Stevanovic, M. 2012 *Last House on the Hill: BACH Area Reports from Çatalhöyük, Turkey*. Los Angeles, CA: Cotsen Institute of Archaeology Press.

Wendrich, W. 1999 *The World According to Basketry: An Ethno-Archaeological Interpretation of Basketry Production in Egypt*. CNWS publications no. 83. University of Leiden: Research School of Asian, African and Amerindian Studies.

Wendrich, W. 2000 'Basketry'. In P.T. Nicholson and I. Shaw (eds). *Ancient Egyptian Materials and Technology*. Cambridge: Cambridge University Press, 254–267.

Wendrich, W. (ed.) 2012 *Body Knowledge, Identity and Communities of Practice*. Tucson, AZ: University of Arizona Press.

Wendrich, W. and Cappers, R., 2005 'Egypt's Earliest Granaries: Evidence from the Fayum', *Egyptian Archaeology* 27 (Autumn 2005): 12–15.

4

The sustainability of English traditional willow basketmaking

Mary Butcher MBE

In 1977 I was learning traditional willow basketmaking in East Kent. I was excited by my growing mastery of traditional technique but also by its ancient nature. Alwyne Hawkins made me aware that we were both part of that long continuum of basketmakers who wove what was needed as people had been doing for centuries. He had a keen sense of that history and the regional details of techniques for local, regional or national forms. Later, learning with apprenticed professionals from London, Fred Roger and Ted Tween, and from Norfolk, Colin Manthorpe, reinforced in practical ways the many and various forms and their relationship to local industries, each dependent on a range of adaptable techniques. The future of sustainable basket production has, in part, depended on these being transmitted to future makers. Active preservation through teaching enables that transmission, of tacit knowledge as well as physical process.

In the early nineteen seventies it seemed that woven structures might again be needed in quantity. Oil was thought likely to become scarce, a threat to production of plastic containers rapidly replacing those traditional baskets once used in so many industries. Current research deems plastics to be so hugely detrimental to the environment, with demonstrable damage to our oceans and other habitats, that they are being replaced as quickly as manufacturers can do it. Nuances of this research may suggest certain plastics are sustainable for multi-use, affecting habitats and species less, though that is not yet clear. Sustainable containers of natural materials for a diverse range of uses are still available although it seems unlikely that former large-scale production will be seen again. An upsurge in interest in basket manufacture would be a welcome and relevant sustainable response.

The age-old learning 'on the plank' from the workshop Governor, no longer exists here, short courses and time with one maker being the only option. There is danger that more complex techniques may vanish. Our square work tradition, no longer widely learnt, needs a place in a new craft climate, providing useful and long-lived containers of any size. Our strongest UK method, unique to us, uses thick base edge sticks, pierced at intervals so that slyped side stakes can be inserted then bent up. Now regarded as difficult, it is a precise knack like any other but best worked under foot. Classes, working on tables and not easily bending to the floor, make this difficult although a table-top jig of some sort would help. Such baskets have great strength, take rough handling and were once essential to movement of supplies. They should be part of a maker's repertoire.

Our second form of square work involves cutting scalloms, thinned lengths at the thick end of the rod used to tie it onto a framework. Cut slightly differently from those on the Continent or Ireland, they were used here for domestic ware, cradles and shoppers, having a neat and attractive appearance. This versatile system deserves to be taught here more widely (Fig. 4.1).

Nellie Pilcher, an East Kent craftsperson who took over domestic basketmaking in East Kent during the Second World War, adopted a system where basket side stakes are woven in at intervals along the base and then bent up for the sides (Fig.4. 2). It is easier to master than the pierced stick method and highly serviceable in many situations. It is not for larger work or baskets given hard wear, as the bending up of the stakes gives potentially vulnerable 'elbows'. For domestic use it

FIGURE 4.1 *Lyn Darby, 2018, scalloms attaching the sides of an oval basket to the base. Photograph: Lyn Darby.*

FIGURE 4.2 *Tricia Fraser, 2018, thicker rods woven into a square base before becoming side stakes. Photograph: Tricia Fraser.*

works well and can be used with our blunt corners or corner posts. It is simple to master so is more frequently taught, risking the disappearance of our traditional method.

Our English traditional oval base is also unique, found elsewhere only in one small area of the South Netherlands. It is an interlaced un-pierced structure of great strength and adaptable to any size of work (Fig. 4.3). It is technologically ingenious, an elegant solution to the problems of oval structures developing torque, and, once learnt, is quick to make. Provided it is sufficiently crowned it can take enormous weights and so was used frequently in agriculture and other industries. Our second woven oval base, with a split slath used in lighter baskets, is twined in one direction then in reverse. That terrible twist is removed but the base is far from elegant and was rarely used in professional workshops. The superior Continental French randed method spread here in the 1980s and 1990s, using a weave alien to us previously.

Other unique aspects of our repertoire, the blunt corners on some square work, the exact way corner posts are added for sharp right angles, have their place in the skill set and deserve preservation. They may be necessary for future basket uses, avoiding the need to reinvent.

FIGURE 4.3 *Mary Butcher, 2018, English traditional oval base, made as a demonstration sample. Photograph: Mary Butcher.*

FIGURE 4.4 *Terry Bensley, 2008, scalloming on a ring for a Suffolk eel trap. Photograph: Mary Butcher.*

Willow basketmaking changed radically with the introduction here of French and Polish techniques, differing in detail from ours, maybe more refined but without that raw robust quality that attracted me to baskets in the first place. I do not regret that introduction, but the way in which they are increasingly taught as replacements alarms me. Our needs have been different in past times and may well be again, so I feel it important to keep the full range of possible techniques alive. I also regret that newer basketmakers may not know if they are working French or English methods. That basis of historical knowledge is also being lost.

Many of our traditional forms are very rarely made now as basket usage has changed radically. Industry uses other transport as agricultural, rural and domestic life have all changed. Yet basket animal traps, for fish or mammals, are potentially important for future food supplies and for animal number control related to conservation. Often basket type and technique are linked, the scallom method used for a classic Norfolk eel trap being extremely efficient at tying large rods to a thick ring to provide the inner cone of the trap. I have not seen this highly regional but efficient way of working scalloms elsewhere (Fig. 4.4).

Sustainability of traditional basketmaking is highly dependent on an available, good quality crop, grown in sufficient quantity, as technique and material are interdependent. Recently insufficient willow has been grown commercially in the UK with growers selling out before the next autumn cut. There are rising numbers of basketmaking sole traders using willow and needing supplies and an extraordinary rise in production of willow sculptural projects. Funded by arts organisations, education establishments and local councils, many are community engagement and local initiative schemes, using a substantial proportion of the crop each year.

In 1977 there were about twelve farming families in Somerset growing willow on the Levels, at least one in Norfolk, several along the Trent Valley, one or two in Lancashire round Mawdesley and others elsewhere. Now we are down to three large businesses. P.H. Coate and Son, Musgrove Willows and The Somerset Willow Company[1] each keep a proportion of their crop either for their own basketmakers or for a local basket firm, good collaboratively and economically. That leaves relatively little for smaller businesses and projects that must buy in their raw material.

Jonathan Coate runs an almost two-hundred-year old willow-growing business, based on *Salix triandra* Black Maul, with smaller quantities of Champion Rod and many others. Susceptible to rust fungi, some are no longer viable as herbicides and insecticides become increasingly restricted, so major changes have been implemented. Hand cutting and planting, slow processes, are replaced by fast mechanical methods, introducing options. Recent willow beds can be planted with a mixed crop. Belgian Red, Flanders Red, Dicky Meadows, and others providing a good harvest of beautifully coloured rods, are harvested for fifteen years and then grubbed up. New beds are planted elsewhere with varieties chosen to suit site conditions, levels of disease, and climate. It is a responsive and flexible way of providing quality willow.

Until about twenty years ago the three *Salix triandra* varieties, including Black Maul and Whissender, traditional basket willows of the Levels since the 1850s, and Noire de Villaine, made up the bulk of Musgrove Willows crop. The first two drop their leaves by 17 November, a date familiar from my early basketmaking days, so harvesting and processing began well before Christmas. Noire de Villaine, a hard willow, excellent for white preparation by pitting or cutting later, has a January leaf drop, usefully spreading the cutting season. Willow of second quality was steamed, turning it dark brown for rough work hurdles, softer from the steaming but with imperfections hidden by the colour, largely going to piece-work basketmakers.

Changing willow-growing conditions and basketmakers' needs have resulted in Musgrove's monocultures being interspersed with varieties of *Salix purpurea*, particularly Brittany Green. These finer willows, with wonderful bark colours, for lighter weight, more decorative baskets, whether functional or not, fit with our changing practices. Heavier traditional work still has material available, while the small business or hobby basketmaker is able to play with colour, pattern and decorative appearance. Now good quality willow is steamed, Noire de Villaine being rich, dark chocolate, very beautiful, no longer a disguise for second quality material.

Musgrove Willows plan to be self-sufficient in two or three years. Foreign imports are no longer economically viable and although *Salix Americana* has been imported in recent years there are difficulties ahead. The processing season is changing with climate change, autumn coming later, and weather extremes are a serious threat to the Levels. Flooding is still a real possibility. Many of the sprays currently used against both insect and fungal attack are banned, it becoming necessary to vary and increase the range of varieties grown, avoiding monoculture. Crops must be checked weekly at the height of the growing season to avoid blanket spraying. *Salix Americana*, not much grown in England so far, but relatively disease free, is to be introduced, along with a new osier for sticks, the traditional stick willow being no longer vigorous. Such flexible practices are difficult with a crop that can last thirty years.

Somerset Willow Growers developed to support Darrell Hill's long-established family business, the Somerset Willow Company. Originally willow came largely from Stan Derham but following his retirement in 2007, Darrell and farming partner Richard Rogers took over the business, establishing new beds to increase supply. An increasing workforce and larger storage facilities mean that the Somerset Willow Company has a guaranteed supply, with willow in variety available to others.

Permanent large workshops are now rare. Those sole traders with land plant their own willows for convenience and control of their supplies, avoiding the dilemma of demand outstripping commercial production, a recent problem in summer months. Mixed cultures, as a way of preventing disease spread, are the norm, the resulting willow being spray free where possible. Those willows with specific characteristics: coloured barks; long and thin rods; those for a particular soil and position; or tolerant of less favourable climates can be selected and intermixed. Makers may need to supplement their own crop from commercial growers but can plan their purchasing.

In spite of these small beds willow basketmakers are highly dependent on one area of the country, the Somerset Levels, and a handful of major growers. This could be considered risky, being as we are, subject to so much change. Climate change predicts weather extremes of heavy rainfall, dry hot summers or both. Possible changes to the Common Agricultural Policy (CAP) subsidies, that have been available to farmers, make for uncertain times. These changes have unknown effects, growers currently responding by extending acreage under willow production where possible to avoid costly imports and the threats of changing pests and diseases.

Tradition changes and always has, being largely market led. Markets have changed and will continue to do so. Active preservation of traditional techniques does not mean stagnation. Being open to new structures and weaves arising from our ancient skills, or combining or replacing them with newer methods, allows for the exploratory, both in the functional basket or more expressive form.

Willow sculpture was brought to our notice in 1991, thanks to many surprising structures at *New Forms In Willow*, (Ness Gardens, Cheshire), causing us all to look again at willow work. John McQueen, David Drew, Brit Smelvar and many others opened our minds to new scales of work, a shock of new forms and unconventional weaves. It was revelation from Europe, the USA and the

UK, changing our perception of what 'basket' meant. Willow sculptural work appeared in magazines, the daily press and on television. It attracted a lot of attention. Willow growers responded to change in customer demand for the longer willow now needed in quantity for outdoor work. Projects developed by art organizations or for supervised work in schools frequently demanded work at short notice and outside the normal cutting season. Waiting for fully dry willow was not an option, growers now sending stuff out green, fresh cut but with a soft bark, or half dry to avoid soaking or shrinkage in the finished work. Large quantities of our willows are used in these ways leaving less for the basketmaker, another cause for concern.

Contemporary baskets, sculptural work and some installations are often based on strong, well-executed traditional technique, this adding to their success. We now also benefit from the influx of European and other techniques carried widely by those of us who have travelled and taught. It is a rich palate to draw on and long may it remain, but we must not neglect our own strengths, our traditional technical expertise. These are immensely valuable to us and to a wider community as basketmaking inevitably changes. In the late 1960s the fashion designer Jean Muir noted that 'we, as a nation, are in danger of regarding technicians with contempt. The idea is not everything. The execution is just as important . . .'.

Despite decline, transformation and adaptation, basketmaking has re-emerged with a new vigour. There is a new determination to draw upon the achievements of the past and on the diverse creativity of many cultures to produce exciting forms. Enthusiastic new audiences now enjoy both traditional and contemporary baskets and sculptures. We must keep our ancient techniques, basket forms and natural materials to support these developments.[2]

Notes

1 www.englishwillowbaskets.co.uk; www.musgrovewillows.co.uk; www.willowgrowers.co.uk. (Accessed 12.06.19)
2 I would like to thank those basketmakers and willow growers who have given generous help with information or image: Joanathan Coate, Lyn Darby, Tricia Fraser, Ellen Musgrove, Richard Roberts. The views expressed are my own.

Bibliography

Butcher, M. (ed.) 1999 Contemporary International Basketmaking. London: Merrell Publishers.
Fitzrandolph, H. and Doriel Hay, M. 1977 [1926] The Rural Industries of England and Wales, Vol. 2 Osier-Growing and Basketry and Some Rural Factories. West Yorkshire: EP Publishing.
Macalpine, W. J., Burns, H., Hammerin, A., Shield, I. F., Butcher, M., Davies, O., and Bertram, G. 2018 Cultivation and Use of Basket Willows – a guide to growing basket willows. London: The Basketmakers' Association.
The Basketmakers' Association, https://basketmakersassociation.org.uk (accessed 12.06.19)
The Worshipful Company of Basketmakers, www.basketmakersco.org (accessed 12.06.19)

5

Drawing out a tune – from head to hand

Tim Johnson

Drawing is a tool that I use in a variety of ways depending on context and intention. In my making process drawing can be a diagram for instruction, a process and documentation of observation, a visualisation of design conversation, an exploration of structure and generator of implied possibilities as well as a spontaneous expression of gesture and declaration of existence.

When I make drawings, inspecting and rehearsing traditional basket and textile structures, the hands-on process of mark-making clarifies my understanding of working with materials. As I pencil

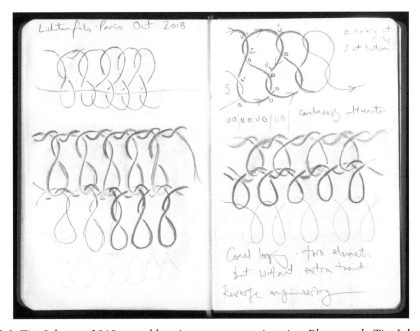

FIGURE 5.1 *Tim Johnson, 2018, camel looping – reverse engineering. Photograph: Tim Johnson.*

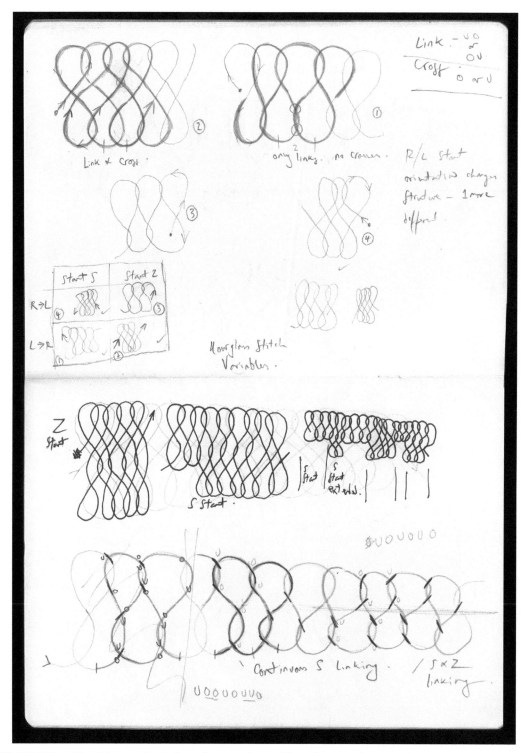

FIGURE 5.2 *Tim Johnson, 2018, hourglass stitch variables. Photograph: Tim Johnson.*

FIGURE 5.3 *Tim Johnson, 2018, looped esparto bag (detail). Photograph: Tim Johnson.*

FIGURE 5.4 *Tim Johnson, 2017, looping samples. Photograph: Tim Johnson.*

the lines describing knots, twists, interlacings and overlappings, another process is happening. An analogy could be if I were a folk musician (rather than classical with a written score) – in my mind the tune is playing and the hands deliver through the instrument. My delivery could be through the pencil as a drawing or with the same thought process through weaving with materials. The delivery of the music, drawing or basket is an approximation of the tune or pattern played in one's head and its quality and accuracy will depend on the skill and focus of the artisan, the quality of tools and the particular properties and selection of available material. Flexible willow rod, combed grass or split rush are woven into place, fixing the pattern. As work progresses a continuous assessment of the object being made, in relation to intention, informs the making process; adjustments of technique and material are made accordingly.

Spontaneity and creativity also play a part in the making, not only in being open to an acceptance of discordance between intention and delivery but also in a willingness to create without a tune – to improvise in the moment and to converse with the material in hand. A challenging dichotomy presents itself for traditional and contemporary makers, for the traditional to deliver the tune with fluency, speed and accuracy but with little divergence and for the contemporary maker perhaps to play without a tune at all, to improvise without reliance on a pattern but still to make something coherent, with presence and a 'rightness' of design. Of course, many makers see themselves neither as strictly traditional nor contemporary, preferring a personal placement of their makings which combines intentions from both. As a matter of degree, a traditional maker will innovate and a contemporary maker will adhere to known patterns when useful.

In my own making process tradition plays an important role in suggesting possibilities; through research and practice new structures present themselves. Specifically, when I am studying traditional objects I will try and understand them, as well as I am able through drawing and making, and then allow the possibilities of structural variations and hybridisation of techniques to lead to new opportunities of expression. These, when combined with material researches and shifts in scale and function, offer endless choices.

A strand of my current research explores animal muzzles and regalia. Perhaps because of their specific and demanding function, muzzles include a variety of unusual textile structures including ply split braiding and darning, multi-strand looping and unusual knotting structures. This contrasting palette of possibilities inspires my curiosity and I hope to make work both rooted in tradition while shifting by degree to innovation.

The accompanying illustrations, (Figs. 5.1 to 5.4), show some of my drawing and woven research into looping structures related to north African camel muzzles, bilums from Papua New Guinea and other looped objects from my collection.

6

Material values

Lois Walpole

The materials I use in my work are not just a vehicle for weaves and stitches and patterns. They are the primary inspiration for the work because of the message with which they silently imbue it.

Traditionally, basketmaking has been a practical investigation of what was possible using the freely available materials in the maker's immediate environment. Prior to the industrial revolution, available materials for basketmakers came from plants, but we now have a wide choice of freely-available materials in our immediate environments, most of which are destined for landfill. By using both manmade and natural materials that I collect from my personal environment, I believe I am continuing in the sustainable tradition of autonomous basketmakers everywhere. Conversely, I feel that if I buy materials, I am adopting the practices of commercial basketmaking, which forgot about sustainability long ago.

When I started making baskets in London in 1982 almost all my materials were purchased, some like rattan having a substantial carbon footprint because they were imported from South East Asia. Once in my possession I made their environmental footprint much heavier by altering them with chemical dyes, paints and varnishes. In the early nineteen-nineties, a growing unease about this chain of events led me to research rattan production methods, which confirmed my inquietude. Not only was it being shipped long distances, but some of the harvesting and processing methods were far from ecologically or environmentally sound. Rattan is a climber and its canes were being stripped out of virgin tropical forests by felling the trees that they climbed up. The canes were then 'cured' by boiling them in used diesel oil by workers with no masks or gloves and with bare legs and feet. The final stage of processing was to treat the machined canes with fungicide so that there was no risk of them going mouldy on the long sea journey in an enclosed container. Rattan wasn't the only problem at that time as I had also discovered that commercially-grown willow monocultures in Europe required the assistance of pesticides and herbicides.

These issues, combined with impatience about the lack of spontaneity that resulted from having to pre-order and dye my materials and curiosity about techniques used in other parts of the world, led me to begin using things like cardboard, strapping tapes, Tetra Pak® cartons and plastic bags (Figs. 6.1 and 6.2). These I gathered from the streets around my home in East London or from the weekly food shopping. In so doing I discovered that they had lots of advantages over bought materials. Firstly, they were free, which allowed me to be more creative than I was with

FIGURE 6.1 *Lois Walpole collecting materials, Spitalfelds, London, late 1980s. Photograph: Lois Walpole.*

FIGURE 6.2 *Lois Walpole, 1997, handbag for Paul Smith womenswear (recycled Tetra Pak®). Photograph: Lois Walpole.*

materials I had to pay for. Secondly, they were often very colourful which meant there was no need to dye or paint them and thirdly, they had their own histories. For a while I used a 'pick and mix' of both recycled and purchased materials.

At the same time, through exhibiting, I had begun to meet makers such as David Drew, Markku Kosonen and John McQueen, who used only the materials they grew or harvested from the wild. In doing so they were not only making superb work by controlling the quality of their materials but also respecting the tradition of basketmaking and making a very clear statement through their work about sustainability. I had also learned about Ed Rossbach, who, when teaching at the University of California (1950–1979), encouraged his textile students to make three-dimensional work, so making connections between basketry structures and textile techniques. He also made baskets out of recycled materials that were quite shocking at the time for their originality. Thanks to these people I began to realise that the materials I used in my work mattered as much as the forms or the weaving.

So, when I finally took the decision in 1992 to stop buying materials it came as a great relief. Using only found and recycled materials fitted perfectly with my growing disenchantment with consumerism and its profligate waste of materials in the chase for profit. I also realised that using materials that were considered to be of no value would speak far more clearly and with more force about what I saw as an appalling waste of resources than anything I could actually say about it. I began to use a lot of materials that arrived with food bought from the supermarket because at the time there was no organised system for recycling these; the Tetra Pak® cartons quickly became a favourite. To me it seemed astonishing that once you bought a carton of juice or milk and took it home and opened it, it was only a matter of hours before it was in the bin and destined for landfill. Yet, this beautiful, colourful, strong, flexible and waterproof material, made of six layers of paper, plastic and aluminium, that had required so many human and material resources for its manufacture, was still in perfect condition. As time has passed and recycling has become more highly developed, I have moved onto different 'waste' materials that are not being recycled and, since 2012, I have been working almost exclusively with 'ghost gear' that I have gathered from beaches in the Shetland Islands (Fig. 6.3).

The commercial fishing industry, either deliberately or by accident, deposits tons of ropes and nets in the oceans along with a lot of other stuff like crates, wellies, empty plastic chemical bins, rubber gloves, brooms, nets, buoys and hard hats, collectively now known as *ghost gear*. Certain beaches trap it and others don't but where it is trapped it eventually becomes part of the landscape, tying itself in knots around rocks and being forced by waves into crevices where it becomes part of the topography. Not only are these ropes and other debris dangerous for marine life but they are also a wasted resource. I have found up to 15 metre lengths of almost new, expensive, braided, polypropylene rope. Even where the ropes are chafed on the outside once they are unravelled there is often a core of shiny new material inside.

My mother's family came from Yell (one of the Shetland Islands) and my great-grandfather crofted at Midbrake overlooking the beach at Breckon. From what my grandmother told me of her life there, as one of his thirteen children, I know that if he had found all these materials lying on the beach he would have made use of them in a thousand ways around the croft and would probably have used some to stitch his kishies.

FIGURE 6.3 *'Ghost gear' on Breckon beach, Isle of Yell. Photograph: Lois Walpole.*

Traditional basketmaking in Shetland is now all but dead. Fortunately, we have Ewen Balfour, the guardian of kishie-making knowledge, and we have a video that Lise Bech and the Scottish Basketmakers Circle made of Lowrie Copeland making one, but there are few people alive now who made them to use on their crofts. It was in this knowledge that I went to the Shetland Museum store and looked at lots of old kishies as well as flakkies, maishies, cuddies, boddies, skeklers' outfits, hobbles, brushes and a duckie. I also saw a picture of a hovi (Baldwin, 1982[1]), perhaps its only representation – there are none in the Shetland Museum – and I read about strae-beuts (straw boots), though have never seen a picture of them. There is something terribly poignant about handling some of these beautifully made things knowing that the knowledge for making them has gone. Yes, we can guess at how it was done but anyone who makes baskets knows that there is always some little thing that you can only learn by watching someone else making one. If I had never seen Ewen or Lowrie make a kishie I don't think I would ever have thought of using my buttocks or my teeth to maintain tension on the weave!

I brought all these real and metaphysical elements to my studio and produced a body of work that used only found materials from the islands, both manmade and natural (Figs. 6.4 to 6.8). Where I have used basketry techniques, they are only those that were part of the tradition. Interestingly the polypropylene ropes have lent themselves exactly to the same techniques that had been previously employed with oat straw, bent (marram grass) and floss (field rush) in traditional Shetland basketry. The first showing of 'Weaving Ghosts' took place in the Shetland Museum in 2016.

In 2017 I was invited to take part in the *Woven Communities* project in schools in Shetland to teach pupils how to turn ghost rope into a basket. I wanted them to use material that they recognised and that they could easily go and find for themselves, without having to ask their parents for money. I also wanted them to see this material as part of the choice of materials

FIGURE 6.4 *Lois Walpole, 2017,* Andrew, *kishie, oat straw and found rope. Photograph: Lois Walpole.*

FIGURE 6.5 *Lois Walpole, 2017,* Shellfish Crates 3 ways (no.2), *bowl, found shellfish crates and rope. Photograph: Lois Walpole.*

FIGURE 6.6 *Lois Walpole, 2017,* Buoy Bags, *handbag and basket; found buoys, rope, catch and crab cage hook. Photograph: Lois Walpole.*

FIGURE 6.7 *Lois Walpole, 2017,* Ropeback, *chair; found rope and driftwood. Photograph: Lois Walpole.*

FIGURE 6.8 *Lois Walpole, 2019,* North Atlantic Drift, *in* Weaving Ghosts *at Broadway Gallery, Letchworth. Found rope, plastic, wood, pottery, grasses and leaves. Photograph Lois Walpole.*

that they had freely available to them along with floss, bent and oats, thus not as something undesirable and untouchable but as something they could profit from as their forebears would have done.

As I write, 'Weaving Ghosts' is heading for its sixth venue. I would like to think that in some small way my use of ghost gear has helped add to the growing awareness of its ubiquity. Certainly, the beaches of Yell are much cleaner than they were two years ago and soon I will happily have to move onto other materials.

Note

1 Baldwin, J. R. 1982 *Caithness: A Cultural Crossroads.* Edinburgh: Scottish Society for Northern Studies.

PART TWO

Basketry as maths, pattern and engineering

Introduction
Stephanie Bunn

The relationship between basketwork and mathematics is arguably bound up with basketry's embodied techniques and practices, which develop and express informal geometric and numerical mathematical knowledge, from proportion, symmetry and spatial relationships to quantity, strength and time passing.

Such diverse techniques build rhythmically through repetition, creating patterns in the work, emerging at the interface of the maker's strength and that of the material. The force or tension captured in the ensuing folds, twists and knots holds the basket together, creating form and structure. For mathematical educationalist Ricardo Nemirovsky, the techniques and gestural moves in basketwork (and other crafts) articulate a form of bodily and mathematical understanding, where tangible geometric relationships are produced and revealed through movement, touch and engagement with the material, manifest also in the form of the finished basket. Maths, Nemirovsky suggests, has a physicality that can be explored through crafts such as basketwork – a significant insight in a world where learning has become increasingly abstracted and digitised.

The structural strength created through hand-twisting fragile plant materials such as straw or grass together is discussed by Ian Ewart in regard to Keshwa bridge construction, a feat of textile engineering renewed on an annual basis in the Andes. Artist Geraldine Jones also reveals the geometric aspects of basketwork through her looped wire structures, drawing on similar techniques to those used in Borneo looped-cane basketry. While she did not engage with mathematics as taught abstractly at school, she says, the practical engagement with materials and technique in basketwork has given meaning to geometric relationships, in similar vein to the mathematical patterns incorporated into African basketwork discussed extensively by Paulus Gerdes (1999).

Patterns and rhythms in basketwork link to time, counting and number as well as to space and form, and are thus both qualitative and quantitative. These temporal and spatial aspects of basketwork are synthesized in the spiral forms of many basket bases, which parallel plant and animal growth patterns (including pine cones, sunflower seeds, nautilus shells. . .), as discussed by D'Arcy Wentworth Thomson, (1992). Like baskets, they grow, expanding in space from one end only – the centre – over time, and thus inevitably have this structure.

Artist Mary Crabb, reveals how the temporal, rhythmic aspect of basketry may embody memory. In *Significant Figures*, each knotted or twined strand is counted, commemorating the years passed since the death of her grandmother's former boyfriend, Cecil, in the First World War. Her knotted baskets quantify time. Andean *khipus*, knotted wool cord boards from the past as discussed by Hyland, have similarly been used to record reckonings such as debt. Hyland develops the numerical potential of *quipus* to consider how the direction of twine in the wool and its colour might also have had a narrative quality. The link between number, pattern and colour in basketwork is explored further by Hazelgrove-Planel in regard to 'mathematical literacy' through her experience of learning plaiting in Vanuatu. Here, colour gives a multi-layered dimension to patterning and geometric understanding.

Finally, Küchler reveals the relevance of knots and other forms of binding, as used in the topological branch of mathematics, for incorporating the capacity of social and political phenomena for self-organisation. She shows how binding in the Pacific is not so much symbolic, or representational, as revelatory of emergent social and political forms of order as diverse as kinship and kingship.

Bibliography

Gerdes, P. 1999 *Geometry from Africa*. Washington, DC: The Mathematical Association of America.
Thompson, D. W. 1992 *On Growth and Form*. Cambridge: Cambridge University Press.

7

On the continuities between craft and mathematical practices

Ricardo Nemirovsky

A pilot initiative exploring how to unveil and nurture new continuities between craft and mathematical practices has been a two-day Basketry and Anthropology workshop entitled *Tinkering with Curves*, that we organized at the University of St Andrews in April 2018, In partnership with three professional basket weavers (Geraldine Jones, Hilary Burns and Mary Crabb). A fourth basketmaker (Tim Johnson) participated in the workshop. The core idea was to use basket-weaving materials and techniques to create curves of different kinds and to investigate their variations. Participants included anthropologists, artists, architects and graduate students. By weaving willows, ropes and wires, participants crafted, with the support of the professional weavers, diverse pieces exhibiting families of curves. Figure 7.1 shows some of them. The subsequent presentation and discussion included topics such as curvature, smoothness, shadows and the poetics of curved lines.

Continuities between craft and mathematical practices must traverse old cultural-historical gaps secluding mathematics to intellectual and mental realms, devoid of physicality and materiality,

FIGURE 7.1 Pieces woven in the *Tinkering with Curves* workshop. Photograph: Stephanie Bunn.

and craftsmanship to affective and bodily techniques, lacking abstraction and theory. Do these continuities exist? How can we explore them? Mathematical analyses of decorative patterns, folk dances or music scores can be found in various strands of literature, and yet it is unclear whether these studies illuminate continuities with mathematics. Such uncertainty is fostered by the realization that these studies are not necessarily sources of new insights or developments in mathematics or crafts, arts and performances, beyond the notion that artisans and performers often unconsciously enact mathematical patterns.

A true continuity should be a source of inspiration for *both* craftsmanship and mathematics. A particular basketry practice from the South Pacific islands illustrates this point. 'All their baskets, small and large, are triangularly sixty-degree (three-way) woven, while all the basketry of all the rest of the world is square, or ninety-degree (two-way) woven.' (Buckminster Fuller 1981, 88). Figure 7.2 shows a pair of diagrams helping differentiate two-way and three-way weave. A triangular weave is stronger and more stable because horizontal strips are prevented from sliding upwards at points A and downwards at points B.

The stability of a triangular weave is threaded with the stability held by three struts joined by articulated joins on a plane (see Figure 7.3a). In contrast to the case of a quadrangle (see Figure 7.3b) — or of any figure joining more than three struts — each angle in the triangle is opposed by a single rigid strut, which ensures that these angles cannot change.

The fact that a triangle of sticks has a stability that no other planar figure has is a cornerstone of work in architecture, engineering and mathematics. It is deeply connected to the results that any three non-collinear points define a plane, and that a triangle is the simplest figure that can separate an inside region from its outside on a plane. These results can be generalized to any number of dimensions: the simplest stable structure that separates inside/outside in 3D space is a tetrahedron, formed by four triangles (see Figure 7.4)

The stability of a tetrahedron is derived from the stability of each triangle opposed to a vertex. Intertwining the strength and stability of three-way baskets with the ones of articulated triangles is an endless source of questions, which can inspire work in both, basket-weaving and mathematics. One can investigate, for instance, what kinds of spherical or oval balls can be woven triangularly, such as the ball shown in Figure 7.5. Basketry examples would have the potential to pose new

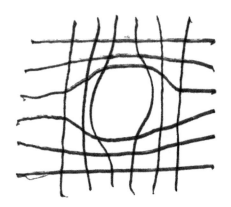
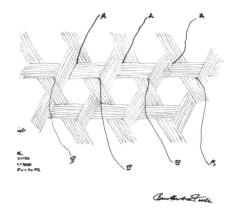

FIGURE 7.2 *Perpendicular and triangular weave, taken from* Critical Path *(Buckminster Fuller 1981, 89).*

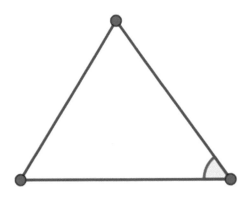

FIGURE 7.3a *Three struts connected by articulated joins on a plane.*

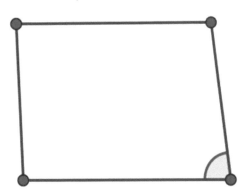

FIGURE 7.3b *Four struts connected by articulated joins on a plane.*

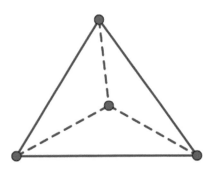

FIGURE 7.4 *The tetrahedron is the simplest figure bounding an interior region in 3D space.*

FIGURE 7.5 *Ball woven by Geraldine Jones.*

mathematical questions and mathematical insights could help imagine possibilities in basketry. This is what makes the search for continuities consequential. Furthermore, besides innovations in basketry and mathematics, continuities between them can help us grasp the cosmic and poetic significance of both practices.

Among philosophers working to elucidate the origins of geometry, Husserl envisioned the world of craft practices as an ancient ground in which geometry came to be:

> in the life of practical needs certain particularizations of shape stood out and that a technical praxis always aimed at the production of particular preferred shapes and the improvement of them according to certain directions of gradualness. First to be singled out from the thing-shapes are surfaces—more or less 'smooth,' more or less perfect surfaces; edges, more or less rough or fairly 'even'; in other words, more or less pure lines, angles, more or less perfect points.
>
> HUSSERL 1989, 178

The gradual approximation to an unattainable archetype, such as polishing towards perfectly smooth surfaces or sawing near perfectly straight cuts, gave grounds to conceive of ideal shapes always differing from physical models and yet, related to them. While measuring the perimeter of a wooden circle cannot obtain the exact length of a corresponding ideal circle, it must not be far from it; furthermore, polishing the wooden disc and using more accurate measurement techniques would get even closer to it. Husserl (1970) argued that modern developments of science and mathematics have worked to forget these origins striving to purify[1] mathematics by detaching it from everyday worlds of practical and ethical concerns; in other words, continuities between craft and mathematical practices had been central during the ancient origins of the geometry, but afterwards they were hidden down into an abyss separating them.

These persistent efforts to purify mathematics appeared to restrict the tangible and bodily basis of our mathematical intuitions to the work of children and uneducated adults and led to the formulation of learning trajectories going from the 'concrete' to the 'abstract', depicting mathematics learning largely as a gradual dispossession of bodies, gestures, and performances towards distilled and decontaminated thoughts. The result is somewhat paradoxical: during mathematical work the presence of feelings, gestural movements and interactions with materials, including diagrams, are inescapable but all of these disappear from public accounts and published proofs. A background of life with materials and diagrams recedes onto an unspoken underground, supplanted by definitions presented as free-floating statements that can stand on their own. This suggests that Husserl's historical intuition about the centrality of craft practices for the ancient origins of mathematics has not gone away. Life with materials has always been and is crucial to mathematical development, but, subject to a process of discursive purification, it has been veiled out of sight. Unveiling this ground is necessary in order to trace continuities between craft and mathematical practices. I pursue this disclosure by striving to unpack the notion of *conversation with materials*.

'Conversation with materials' is a phrase associated, in my recollection, with the work of Jeanne Bamberger and Donald Schön (1983, 1992). The gist of its meaning, as I understand it, can be grasped in opposition to the conception of hylomorphism – a term derived from the Greek words matter (*hulê*) and form (*eidos* or *morphê)* – for the interplay between form and matter. According to the hylomorphic framework that can be traced back to Aristotle and ancient Greece, material objects are pieces of matter or substance – largely passive or inert – shaped by the active and external imposition of forms. Hylomorphism, which postulates an asymmetry between conformist matter upon which a design is inflicted or caused, has influenced widespread and prevalent images of fabrication, education and medicine. Simondon (2015) has elaborated an influential critique of the hylomorphic framework.

> A hylomorphic model, Simondon concludes, corresponds to the perspective of a man who stands outside the works and sees what goes in and what comes out but nothing of what happens in between, of the actual processes whereby materials of diverse kinds come to take on the forms they do. It is as though, in form and matter, he could grasp only the ends of two half-chains but not what brings them together, only a simple relation of moulding rather than the continuous modulation that goes on in the midst of form-taking activity, in the becoming of things.
>
> INGOLD 2013, 25

Conversations with materials points at an alternative to hylomorphism by portraying the interplay between matter and form-taking activity as akin to the interaction between conversants jointly improvising, mutually thought-provoking and learning, as they pursue open-ended conversations that keep drifting from anticipated courses of action. Understood in this way, the notion of crafting as a conversation with materials is obvious to any craftsperson: far from imposing preconceived forms on passive materials, craftspeople are shaped by the materials as much as they shape materials, through an intertwinement suffused by improvisation, surprise, and mutual responsiveness.

Conversations with materials have had a marginal presence in the modern history of mathematical practices, particularly compared to the clearly predominant conversations with diagrams. Folding has been an example of a peripheral but mathematically significant conversation with materials (Friedman 2018). Ancient Greek mathematicians chose two instruments, straightedge and compass, as the only means apposite to use for the development of theorems in geometry besides textual ones. '[Euclid] however, employed a fourth tool without accrediting it – this was the surface upon which he inscribed his diagrammatic constructions' (Buckminster Fuller, cited in Krausse and Friedman 2016). The materiality of surfaces amenable to sustain perdurable inscriptions, such as parchment, papyrus and paper, is capable of sustaining powerful conversations, which include folding. A remarkable outcome of folding a piece of paper is that it obtains a straight line. The straightness of a folded crease is an expression of the materiality of paper interwoven with skillful actions of hands and fingers over time. That skillful actions and material engagements are temporal processes is a crucial element in the course of conversations with materials. Thinking of lines as emerging from acts of drawing or folding intertwined with active materials that resist, guide, entice or block, rather than preexisting entities that appear already formed or completed without history and genesis, has profound implications in all realms of life (Ingold 2007), including mathematics:

> We find experimentally that two lines cannot go through the same point at the same time. One can cross over or be superimposed upon another. Both Euclidian and non-Euclidian geometries mis-assume that a plurality of lines can go through the same point at the same time.
>
> BUCKMINSTER FULLER, cited in KRAUSSE and FRIEDMAN 2016, 3–4

Try to draw two straight lines with a pencil in each hand: close to the time of the intersection one of the pencils will block the other one from reaching the overlapping intersection point. An equivalent result is obtained with two folds since they cannot be folded simultaneously around the intersection. Occasionally, folding became a powerful metaphor for the foundations of mathematics, such as in this remark by Leibniz:

> the division of the continuum must not be considered to be like the division of sand into grains, but like that of a sheet of paper or tunic into folds. And so although there occur some folds smaller than others infinite in number, a body is never thereby dissolved into points [. . .] It is just as if we suppose a tunic to be scored with folds multiplied to infinity in such a way that there is no fold so small that it is not subdivided by a new fold [. . .] And the tunic cannot be said to be resolved all the way down into points; instead, although some folds are smaller than others to infinity, bodies are always extended and points never become parts.

> LEIBNIZ, cited by FRIEDMAN 2018, 385

Folding has also been a source of new insights and developments across mathematics and crafts. The work of David Huffman – a computer scientist who became a practitioner of origami – illustrates this continuity: 'One of [his] discoveries was the critical "pi condition." This says that if you have a point, or vertex, surrounded by four creases and you want the form to fold flat, then opposite angles around the vertex must sum to 180 degrees' (Wertheim 2004 June 22). The aftermath of Huffman's work includes not only new theorems, but also the development of new origami approaches, including the use of curved folds (e.g. https://blog.kusudama.me/2017/09/24/origami-tools-curved-folding/). It is critical that this work is not a matter of applied mathematics; in other words, it is not about using certain mathematical results to design innovative pieces of origami, but about working out continuities originating new mathematics and origami. In one of their papers about the mathematics of folding, two mathematicians expressed such merging of mathematics and paper folding as they invited the readers to perform an experiment:

> draw a curve on a sheet of paper and slightly fold the paper along the curve. A word of practical advice: press hard when drawing the curve. It also helps to cut a neighborhood of the curve, for it is inconvenient to work with too large a sheet. A more serious reason for restricting to a neighborhood is that this way one avoids self-intersections of the sheets, unavoidable otherwise.

> FUCHS and TABACHNIKOV 1999, 28

I focused on folding to illustrate the presence of conversations with materials in mathematical practices and how they have fostered continuities with craft practices. Various other examples could have been chosen for this purpose, such as the historical roles of linear perspective for the emergence of renaissance art and projective geometry, or the use of mechanical devices to draw curves during the sixteenth and seventeenth centuries for both, design and study of mathematical functions. Contemporary instances, such as fractals, molecular synthesis and system dynamics, suggest that conversations with materials tend to be less marginal in mathematics than they used to be. Conceivably, as compared to the mathematical ethos of a century ago with its almost exclusive orientation towards formalism, nowadays mathematics is gradually embracing materiality (de Freitas and Sinclair 2014) and movement (Ferrari 2019).

Through initiatives such as 'Tinkering with Curves', we envision the creation of studios in which participants engage in craft and art projects, explore mathematical themes, and share experiences in partnership with mathematicians, craftspeople, artists, architects, anthropologists and educators.

Note

1 I use the term 'purification' in ways that are akin to how Latour (1993) uses it in *We Have Never Been Modern*.

Bibliography

Bamberger, J. and Schön D. A. 1983 'Learning as Reflective Conversation with Materials: Notes from Work in Progress', *Art Education* 36 (2): 68–73.

Buckminster Fuller, R. 1981 *Critical Path*. New York: St. Martin's Press.

de Freitas, E. and Sinclair, N. 2014 *Mathematics and the Body. Material Entanglements in the Classroom*. Cambridge: Cambridge University Press.

Ferrari, G. 2019 'Mathematical thinking in movement'. PhD, Università di Torino.

Friedman, M. 2018 *A History of Folding in Mathematics. Mathematizing the Margins*. Basel: Birkhauser.

Fuchs, D. and Tabachnikov, S. 1999 'More on paperfolding', *The American Mathematical Monthly* 106 (1): 27–35.

Husserl, E. 1970 *The Crisis of the European Sciences and Transcendental Phenomenology*. Evanston, IL: Northwestern University Press.

Husserl, E. 1989 'Origin of geometry, *Origin of Geometry: An Introduction*. Lincoln and London: University of Nebraska Press.

Ingold, T. 2007 *Lines: A brief history*. London: Routledge.

Ingold, T. 2013 *Making: Anthropology, archaeology, art and architecture*. Abingdon: Routledge.

Krausse, J. and Friedman, M. 2016 'Folding and Geometry: Buckminster Fuller's Provocation of Thinking'. In W. Schäffner and M. Friedman, *On Folding: Towards a New Field of Interdisciplinary Research*. Bielefeld: Transcript Verlag, 139–174.

Latour, B. 1993 *We Have Never Been Modern*. Cambridge, MA: Harvard University Press.

Schön, D. A. 1992 'Design as reflective conversation with the materials of a design situation', *Research in Engineering Design* 3 (3): 131–147.

Simondon, G. 2015 *La Individuación*. Buenos Aires: Cactus–La Cebra.

Wertheim, M. 2004 'Cones, Curves, Shells, Towers: He Made Paper Jump to Life', *The New York Times*, 22 June.

8

Friction:

An engineer's perspective on weaving grass rope bridges

Ian Ewart

Introduction: The grass rope bridge

In a remote area of the Peruvian Andes, 120 miles southeast of the regional capital Cuzco, a rickety rope bridge sags and sways precariously over a deep gorge. Beneath is a muddy raging torrent, sure to sweep away any unfortunate traveller careless or unlucky enough to fall in. This is the so-called 'last remaining *keshwa chaca*', a design of bridge dating back at least 500 years to the time of the Inca Empire. Crossing the Apurimac river (the 'Great Speaker') near the villages of Huinchiri and Percaro, it has survived only through the ongoing work of the local communities who come together in an annual festival to cut down the old decaying bridge and build a new one, recreating the traditional design. The lightweight construction means that it is only suitable for people and llamas, so in 1968 a new steel bridge was installed a few hundred metres away to take the increasing number of vehicles in the area (Gade 1972). But far from being an anachronism, or even simply a tourist attraction (which it most certainly is) the *keshwa chaca* is now, and always has been, a nexus of social regeneration and reinforcement.

This type of bridge was common throughout the high Andes in the early seventeenth century, astonishing the Spanish Conquistadors as they went about their ruinous plundering (Poma de Ayala 1936 [c.1615]). The reason why the bridges were seen with such amazement was the fact that they were woven anew each year entirely from the locally abundant *qqoya* grass. Today the annual ceremony still takes place - each of the local communities produces an agreed amount of rope for the bridge, usually based on 40 arm-lengths per household (Finch 2002). Making the rope is a technical business, literally passing through many hands before it is finished. The grass is first softened by pounding and soaking, often carried out by children, and then spun into pencil diameter cordage by adult women. Once sufficient grass cord has been produced, which McIntyre estimates

FIGURE 8.1 *The* Keshwa Chaca *crossing the Apurimac River in the Peruvian Andes. Image courtesy of peruwildtreks.com.*

to be about 22,000 feet in length (about 7km), this is then passed on to the men, who twist bunches of 24 cords into ropes of about 25mm diameter. These are then further combined into the two main types of cable: a 2-rope twisted hand-cable and a 3-rope plaited deck-cable (McIntyre 1973; Finch 2002). Gade, in reviewing the sixteenth century Spanish sources, says that 'the older men braided the cables, leaving the younger men with the more laborious job of stretching them across the channel.'(1972: 98). The larger ropes are gradually pulled tight and fixed together with grass cord, before the bridge is finished with a brushwood-matting deck.

Friction (part 1)

When I started my PhD in 2008 and was in the early throes of reading and thinking about different bodies of literature that would ultimately support my thesis (Ewart 2011), I read a recently published book by Anna Lowenhaupt Tsing. It was called *Friction: An Ethnography of Global Connection* with the word 'Friction' in bold red above a photograph of deforestation by fire taking place in Indonesia. It was relevant to my studies for two reasons. Firstly, it was set in the Indonesian province of Kalimantan (the Eastern part of the large island of Borneo), which was relatively close to the area where I did my own anthropological fieldwork, in Sarawak (the Malaysian province on the western side of Borneo). Secondly, it described an ethnographer's view of a changing world, which to some extent mirrored my own interests in the adoption of new engineering practices and materials by a remote community. Tsing's *Friction* remains one of my favourite books, ranging from the shocking tragedy of the ecological disaster taking place in Indonesia, to the extraordinary stoicism of the local people who see the world and their own lives changing, determined to save something for posterity.

My interest was piqued further by the use of the term 'friction'. As an engineer, I was aware of the concept of friction as physical force acting between two surfaces, so was curious to see how this could be translated from the physical to the social sciences. Tsing's book, as the subtitle tells us, is a nuanced examination of globalization, considering the process from many angles rather than just that of the apparently dominant (Euro–American) culture. 'Instead, a study of global connections shows the grip of the encounter: friction', and 'speaking of friction is a reminder of the importance of interaction in defining movement, cultural form, and agency.' (2005: 5–6). As a cross-disciplinary term, 'friction' is quite appealing to the anthropologist, replacing the two physical surfaces with two cultural surfaces and metaphorizing some of the characteristics of friction, such as heat and resistance, to become people 'rubbing each other up the wrong way', or the idea of global trade flowing freely and thus being 'frictionless'.

The social sciences in general, and anthropology as a discipline in particular, sometimes struggle to explain quite complex views of the world. Belief systems that are alien to us can be difficult to comprehend, while the mundane everyday life that we experience can be equally hard to see for its greater significance. It gets no easier to understand when the solution comes from academics agonizing over competing theoretical approaches or writing dense monographs. So resorting to familiar metaphors is a useful way to explain and think through social issues. However, although it might be a useful metaphor for anthropologists, friction is also an engineering term, and can demonstrate the possibilities of investigating the world around us through technical production. We can build on the 'anthropology of technology' literature of the 1990s (e.g. Lemonnier 1993), and the 'design anthropology' of the last decade (e.g. Gunn et al. 2013), to say nothing of the work of many (especially French) scholars of the mid twentieth century (e.g. Leroi-Gourhan 1993 [1964]). Admittedly, disciplinary boundaries are formidable, since anthropology traditionally seems to draw more aspiring scholars from the humanities than the natural sciences, but that leaves plenty of scope for the future.

Friction (part 2)

Before discussing why engineering friction (as opposed to its metaphorical namesake) is worthy of anthropological study, I will first explain what it is. Having said that, I am aware that at this point a sizeable proportion of my readers, when faced with the prospect of something mathematical will be seriously thinking about skipping forward either to the next pictures, or even worse to the next chapter. To counteract this impulse, I will draw on another author, Tim Ingold, and particularly his use of objects and materials in his work as prompts for thinking. The sub-discipline of anthropology that I am particularly interested in has been called 'Material Culture Studies' and involves studying the way that social and cultural relations are mediated by objects/things and materials. This involved some rather esoteric debates about the usefulness and meaning of terms such as 'materiality', or the distinction between a thing and an object, to which Tim contributed most generously. In one such article he illustrates his thoughts by using a specific object to demonstrate the changing nature of materiality, suggesting it is not a fixed property but an ongoing story, exposed to the flow of the world around us (Ingold 2007; see also Miller 2007). The material object he used was a wet stone, and it was with this in mind that I fixed upon a material of my own with which to entice you: an A4 piece of paper. Or rather, two pieces of paper, which will serve to illustrate some of the principles of friction and cause me to reflect on the nature of friction as a material property.

To do so, please humour me by finding two pieces of plain A4, taking the first piece of paper and laying it horizontally on your table in front of you ('landscape' orientation). Then lie the second piece of paper end-to-end beside the first; next slide it over the first by about one third, so the two pieces appear to form one extended horizontal sheet, overlapping in the middle. Now tightly roll the two overlapping pieces of paper lengthways: working away from you is easiest, so you end up with one long thin tube. Finally, to prevent it from unrolling, squash it flat. What you have now is the start of a paper rope. To demonstrate the power of friction, grab one end of your paper rope (squashed roll) in each hand and pull hard!

At this point there are generally three possible outcomes: one, the two pieces of paper pull apart easily and you frown, slightly bemused; two, you pull hard and manage to pull them apart with a struggle; three, you pull as hard as you can and cannot pull them apart. In fact, you may end up ripping the paper while still leaving the rolled/squashed joint intact. When I have tried this with groups of students, very few if any manage to achieve the last of the three outcomes and are immediately suspicious that I have tricked them in some way. Of course, there is no trick, it is all down to the friction between the two pieces of paper. And here's where the maths comes in: the *frictional force* (F) acting against your attempt to pull the paper apart is quantified as the *product* (i.e. numbers multiplied together) of the *coefficient of friction* (μ) between the two surfaces, and the *normal reaction* (R) between those two objects.

As an equation, we would write: $\mathbf{F = \mu \times R}$

You can think of μ as a measure of how slippery the surfaces are, and R as the amount of force pushing them together. If the frictional force exceeds the inherent strength of rolled paper, then you will rip rather than separate the two pieces of paper. If on the other hand, your rolling was not tight enough (the value of 'R' is relatively small), or you chose particularly slippery paper ('μ' has a lower value), then your frictional force is reduced and the two pieces of paper will slide apart unscathed. With a little practice, you will be able to roll together two pieces of paper tightly enough so that you will not be able to pull them apart, and you too will be able to impress your friends and family (or students) with this demonstration of the power of friction!

An anthropology of friction

How then can this be useful when thinking about the *Keshwa Chaca* described in the opening of this paper? If we think about the annual recreation of the bridge, then it is easy to reflect on the socio-cultural significance of what is happening: each household contributes to a larger communal effort; the status of the bridge has changed from common transport infrastructure to regional icon; the economic benefits of appealing to the new breed of adventure traveller; the bridge festival as an opportunity for social enactment and engagement, etc. But there is also the physical act of production, and it is this that particularly interests me. Now we are armed with some basic knowledge of engineering friction, we are in a much better place to consider how and why this rope has been made. The first point to note is that the *Keshwa Chaca* is in the high Andes, well above the treeline – the highest point at which trees will grow. This is obvious from early Spanish illustrations, (Pomo de Ayala 1936, 356), which show only bare mountain peaks. As a structural element, a stout trunk would be immediately useful in making the simplest of bridges, what is known as a beam bridge, by laying it so that it reaches either side. In this region, such large trees are not locally available, so sourcing them as a construction material would be physically difficult and probably require political wrangling to transport over long distances and through different administrations. What does grow in abundance is *qqoya* grass, a type of tough and long-stemmed grass. However, this is not obvious as a bridge-making material, and as we saw with our paper rope, strength varies according to the exact method of production. A very strong rope only needs one weak point to become a very weak rope.

It is quite difficult to explain in words a physical action. Even in the simple paper rolling exercise I described above, I am convinced that my attempt to write down in a limited number of words what is in fact a very simple physical action will confuse a fair proportion of those who try it. This will become apparent when I try to explain how rope is made from grass for the *Keshwa Chaca*. There are a number of videos of the bridge and its annual reconstruction, such as the Youtube video added by Atlas Obscura in 2015 (see chapter endnote for URL) that show this, although often without a great deal of detail. The grass is woven by taking small handfuls of grass stalks and separating them into two loose bundles. The two bundles are squeezed between the hands as the hands are rubbed together, one moved towards the body and the other away from the body. This action causes each of the two bunches to twist their stalks together, while at the same time they are wrapped around each other forming a cord. The whole sequence takes a fraction of a second and requires no deliberate thought on the part of the women doing the weaving, continuing as she does to continue laughing and talking to her neighbours. Once a certain length of the stalks has been twisted together, the weaver has to introduce more grass, ensuring that the length of overlap provides sufficient friction to bind the strands when put into tension, just like our experiment with the two pieces of paper.

We could use friction as a metaphor for the way that the annual bridge ceremony brings communities together or creates conflict, maintains identity or allows easy movement through the landscape, and it might work well as a heuristic device. But I think we can learn more about the *Keshwa Chaca* by considering friction as an engineering phenomenon. Understanding the basic components of frictional forces – the coefficient of friction (how slippery the surfaces are), and the normal reaction (the force pressing the surfaces together) puts a different perspective on the grass rope as a socio-technical artefact. We can see friction as a material property that the bridge engineers have learned to manipulate to their advantage as part of their technical production. The processing described in the introduction (soaking, pounding etc.) and the weaving actions described above, have come about over generations through engagement with the grass and a sensitive understanding of the properties that it reveals as a material. With a better sense of the way that frictional forces have been harnessed to create this extraordinary bridge, we can gain a greater depth of insight, and appreciation for the skills developed by these communities than would be possible if we remained ignorant of the engineering behind it.

FIGURE 8.2 *Women weaving grass rope during the construction of the* Keshwa Chaca. *(Image courtesy of Ric Finch).*

Bibliography

Atlas Obscura. 2015 *Keshwa Chaca – The last Incan rope bridge.* Youtube video. Available at: https://www.youtube.com/watch?v=pvo4iLDAERg (accessed 13 March 2019).

Ewart, I.J. 2011 'An Anthropology of Engineering'. Unpublished DPhil thesis, University of Oxford.

Finch, R. 2002 'Keshwa Chaca, straw bridge of the Incas', *South American Explorer* 69: 6–13.

Gade, D. W. 1972 'Bridge types in the central Andes', *Annals of the Association of American Geographers* 62 (1): 94–109.

Gunn, W., Otto, T. and Smith, R. C. (eds) 2013 *Design Anthropology: Theory and practice.* London and New York: Bloomsbury.

Ingold, T. 2007 'Materials against materiality', *Archaeological Dialogues* 14: 1–16.

Lemonnier, P. (ed.) 1993 *Technological Choices: Transformation in material cultures since the Neolithic.* London and New York: Routledge.

Leroi-Gourhan, A. 1993 [1964] *Gesture and Speech.* Cambridge, MA: MIT Press.

McIntyre, L. 1973 'The Lost Empire of the Incas', *National Geographic Magazine* 144 (6): 729–787.

Miller, D. 2007 'Stone age or plastic age?', *Archaeological Dialogues* 14: 24–27.

Poma de Ayala, F. G. 1936 [*c.*1615] *El primer neuva corónica y buen gobierno (codex péruvien illustré).* Paris: Institut d'Ethnologie, Université de Paris.

Tsing, A. L. 2005 *Friction: An Ethnography of Global Connection.* Princeton, NJ: Princeton University Press.

9

Basketry and maths:
Some thoughts and practical exercises

Geraldine Jones

Basketmakers are probably amongst the last group of people to consider themselves mathematicians. I failed my 'O' level Maths and never realised when I first began to make baskets how interested I would become in the connections between the two disciplines. I've been using mathematics in basketry from the first calculated measurements required to make round and oval willow basket bases through to the more random geometrical sculptural structures which I now make using woven looped wire rope.

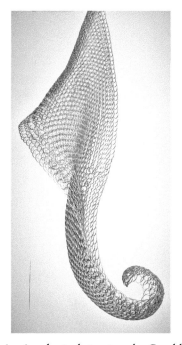

FIGURE 9.1 *Natural spiral occurring in a looped structure by Geraldine Jones.*

Early basketmakers would have relied upon an instinctive understanding of mathematics, as the simple bases of stake and strand baskets were produced long before any recorded mathematical calculations existed. Examples of early (pre-1AD) round basket bases would have called for an assessment of the number of base sticks and a visually measured spacing of uprights, showing how a practical division and segmentation of a circle preceded the concept of inches and centimetres.

Every basket, from stake and strand willow basketry through to hexagonal flat bamboo weaving has its own mathematical integrity, dictated not only by the maker but also by the material. Geometrical forms will be produced more naturally and exactly when weaving with evenly-sized, flat bands of split cane and bamboo rather than irregular and tapering willow sticks. The basketmaker's aim is to produce a basket of pleasing proportions through a symmetry of design and an appropriate division and spacing of all elements.

More complicated mathematical surprises occur naturally when experimenting with various weaves, techniques and materials. For example, the geodesic domes of Buckminster Fuller resonate with the hexagonal basketry weave, and the connection is demonstrated clearly in studies of indigenous weaving in Africa by Paulus Gerdes, a former Professor of Mathematics in Mozambique. (https://csdt.rpi.edu/culture/legacy/african/hex/intro.html)

FIGURE 9.2 *Circular looping workshop. Photograph: Stephanie Bunn.*

I came across the following forms by chance when trying out ideas:

1 Intertwining two 7-strand willow plaits will create a helix when put together.

2 A sphere can be formed by joining two hemispheres constructed using a looping technique. The first row forms a continuous circle of 8 loops, the next row increases to 16 loops. Larger spheres are formed by an 8 loop increase for each following row. The worksheet diagrams above show the first 2 rows. I use stainless steel wire rope for this work.

3 By applying a calculated row-by-row increase in the number of loops following a Fibonacci sequence of numbers (0, 1, 1, 2, 3, 5, 8, 13 etc) to a piece of weaving, I ended up with a spiral pattern (see Fig. 9.6). I am working now to create shell spirals with an interior core.

Recently, I have been experimenting and running workshops to expand this looping technique.

The pattern was first transcribed by Shuna Rendel from a finely woven 'fez stand' of natural materials, see Figures 9.3a&b, which she attributed to the Yemen region. Shuna inspired the worksheets developed in Figures 9.4 and 9.5. Examples of similar 'looping' techniques have been found in Borneo, where it is recognised as 'cycloid' weaving.

My own looping work has been made using stainless steel wire rope. I am intrigued by the formation of spirals and the looping technique lends itself to the application of Fibonacci sequences with unexpected results. Looping could have been the simplest and earliest form of weaving, following on naturally from the discovery of twisting strands to produce rope.

Looped baskets and bags are also successfully made in Papua New Guinea and Australia using soft, shorter materials such as grasses in a continuous weave, the weaving material being

FIGURE 9.3a *Fez stand.*

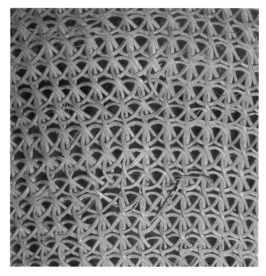

FIGURE 9.3b *Fez stand detail (both images courtesy Shuna Rendel).*

CIRCULAR LOOPING

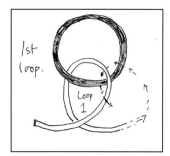 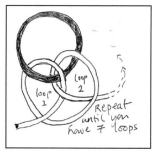 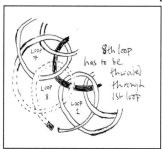

Ist row of looping around the ring. To make the first loop the length of wire will travel in front of the ring, then behind it, then behind the loop that has just been made, leaving the short end behind to join eventually with the 8th loop. The second loop does the same but after going behind the ring it has to travel IN FRONT of the previous loop before going behind itself and moving on to the third loop

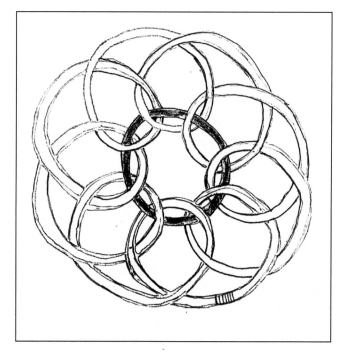

FIGURE 9.4 *Circular looping worksheet 1.*

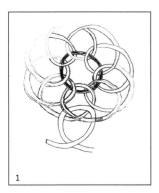
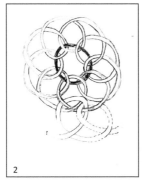
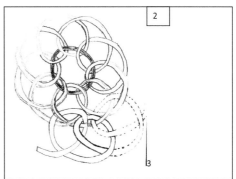

2nd ROW. INCREASING to 16 loops.
Make a loop through one of the loops in the first row, following the path shown above in diagram 1.

The 'increasing' loop is made next, in the link between the loops of the first row, see above diagram2.

The third loop is made in the same way as the first loop but will pick up the second loop before crossing in front of the first row. Continue in front of the second loop and behind itself (loop 3) before beginning the 4th loop.

Repeat this pattern until you have connected the 16 th loop with the 1st.
 (tip; copy exactly the pattern of the existing, corresponding loops)
Rearrange sizing if necessary then crimp the two ends together.

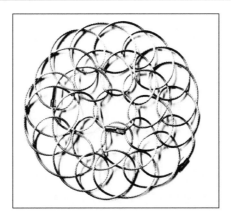

Geraldine Jones, Salt Cellar Workshops, Porthleven, Cornwall, geraldine@basketryandbeyond.org.uk / 07773124241

FIGURE 9.5 *Circular looping worksheet 2.*

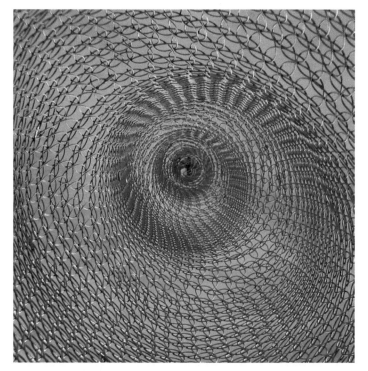

FIGURE 9.6 *Looped wire shell spiral form by Geraldine Jones.*

produced by rolling and twisting fine stems and seamlessly adding new stems to lengthen the strand as the work progresses. Thus, there is one continuous length from the beginning to the end of the basket. (see for example Maureen Mackenzie's *Androgynous Objects* and Lissant Bolton's *Basketry and Belonging*)

Bibliography

Bolton, L. 2011 *Basketry and Belonging: Indigenous Australian Histories*. London: British Museum Press.
Gerdes, P. https://csdt.rpi.edu/culture/legacy/african/hex/intro.html
Mackenzie, M. 1991 *Androgynous Objects*. Reading and Melbourne: Harwood Academic Publishing.

10

Counting, number, loops and lines . . .

Mary Crabb

I am a textile artist and basketmaker with interests in engineering and maths. As a STEM Ambassador for maths with a background in primary teaching and museum education, I am drawn to problem-solving, the challenges that making provides and its capacity to link mathematical thinking with creating. I am developing my work to combine a curiosity in the links between basketry and textiles, to connect with my interest in the past and to use my hand-skills to

FIGURE 10.1 I Will Remember Him *by Mary Crabb.*

communicate mathematical concepts, such as number and time, in a means that others can sense and understand.

My recent work, *Significant Figures*, is a response to my custodianship of a photograph of Cecil, my grandmother Elsie's boyfriend, killed in action in 1916. By taking the facts, figures and numbers of Cecil's story, I have made artefacts that reflect significant numbers as well as the people involved.

I Will Remember Him is a visual and tactile record of the remembrance and time passing from 1916–1992. The time marked is from the date of Cecil's death until Elsie's death over seventy-six years later. Made from twisted strips of Bible paper, with a hidden handwritten text secreted in the twist, each circular motif is woven, or twined, to contain the exact number of days for the year it represents.

The making of each motif involved thinking about the practicalities of working with the materials, the technique and the numbers. Starting with 365 and 366, the numbers in a year and leap year, I had to design a 'symbol' to represent a year that could easily be repeated. The twisted Bible paper had to be cut into lengths, 26 for each motif that could be doubled to provide 52 loose ends, or warps. Weaving in a circle would enable continuous rounds to be completed and extra twines to be added. 7×52=364.

An additional one or two twines would equal 365 and 366. (7×52)+1=365; (7×52)+2=366.

My work with maths

For a recent collaboration with *Woven Communities*, I was thinking about the connection between looping/linking/knotless netting and curves. One textile technique that I've always been intrigued by is double looping – the figure of eight or hourglass looping which is found in some *bilums* (see for example Figure 10.2).

A *bilum* is a looped bag known for its use in Papua New Guinea. Worked without tension the bag is expandable and stretches to carry its load. The loops can be formed over a gauge to produce an even stretch and weave. This prompts consideration of whether a *bilum* is looped in a round or a spiral. In *The Maker's Hand,* Collingwood makes a study of four *bilums* from Papua New Guinea. The examples are noted as each having a calculated length of thread, with a start and finish to each round, concluded with a knot (Collingwood and Cripps 1998). Using a thread or long corded plant material (making the cordage as the work progresses would alleviate the need for knots), it is worked in rounds or rows, and built up in layers.

Looking at the figure of eight loop reminded me of a curve I had studied some time ago at University. I looked at the Lemniscate of Bernoulli in relation to Watt's Parallel Motion, in particular to where the crossing over of the curve is, and the movement of a point changes from linear to radial. That's not really important. It made me think about some linkages I'd made for the assignment and the movement of a point along a curve, and how several curves could be repeated and linked to form a structure.

Here are the linkages, I made, just to illustrate the curve (see Figs 10.3.a and b).

Although this curve is not continuous and is discrete, what would it look like if the curve were stretched out to become continuous? Perhaps like the figure of eight weave in a *bilum* basket?

FIGURE 10.2 *Detail of* bilum *(Courtesy Tim Johnson Collection).*

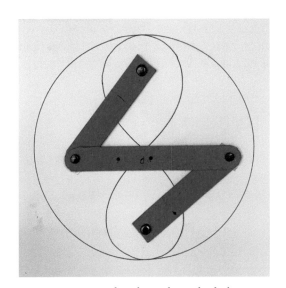

FIGURE 10.3a *This shows how the linkage can be used to draw both a circle and the figure of eight, with the pen placed at P.*

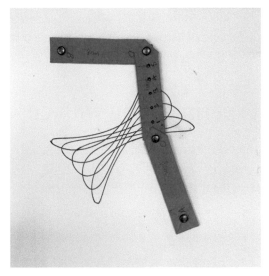

FIGURE 10.3b *This shows what happens when you move the point (P).*

Think of this like spinning the wheel of a static bicycle and following a point on the rim. Then follow the same point on the rim but ride the bicycle along a straight line. The point changes from a closed circle to a continuous curve.

Consider this in the context of handwriting and the development of an individual letter compared with a joined letter, (I used to teach this transition to my primary classes.) Take for example the

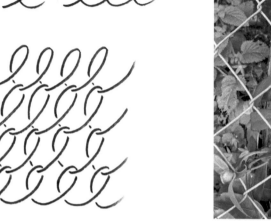

FIGURE 10.4a *Handwriting loops.*   **FIGURE 10.4b** *Chain link fence.*

letter *e*. It is formed with a line, with a beginning and end, but in the context of a line of joined *e*, it becomes a continuous line of loops. Connect a row of loops and you have a fabric or basket weave.

A commonly seen example of loops and lines is in a chain link fence. The material is rigid and under tension, but what would it look like if there was no tension? Would the line become a curve?

Experimenting with curved forms

The corn dolly rattle spiral design is a great introduction to developing geometric forms through playing with numbers and turns. It offers room for experimentation with the forms and curves that occur. By playing with the number it results in some interesting patterns. If you start at the beginning:

1 rod – does not create a weave

2 – creates a wrapped rod, so perhaps a point

3 – creates a spiralling line along the length of the rod, with a cross section of a 2- sided shape, but could be thought of as a line

4 – an equilateral triangle

5 – a square

6 – a regular pentagon

7 – a regular hexagon

etc.

So, the number of sides in the shape is always one less than the number of rods.
The vertical growth of the spiral is faster as the number of rods increases.

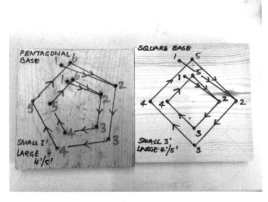 

FIGURE 10.5a *Two formers.*   **FIGURE 10.5b** *Former with willow plait in place.*

Above are the formers I've worked on, but the weave can be worked in the hand too. Figure 10.5a shows two formers. The former on the left uses six willow rods and weaves a regular pentagonal base. On the right, is the former for a square base using five rods. Figure 10.5b highlights the spirals formed by the weave when the willow plait is viewed from above, one spiral for each rotating vertex.

The placing of each rod in relation to the other rods in the set dictates the form of the final object. Stacking the rods above each other results in a vertical form, taking the rods to the outside enables the base shape to increase. Placing on the inside results in the base shape decreasing in size. The willow plait in Figure 10.5b shows the base square decreasing in side length with each turn, finishing at a point.

It would be interesting to see if the placing of the rods could be played with to create irregular shapes and changes to the growth of the spiral.

FIGURE 10.6 *Range of plaited objects, including vertical and conical forms.*

Bibliography

Collingwood, P. and Cripps, D. 1998 *The Maker's Hand*. London: Bellew Publishing.

11

Extracts from 'Imagining the body politic: The knot in Pacific imagination'[1]

Susanne Küchler

. . . The knot as mode of being, thinking and binding

Knots are found across almost any domain of life in need of binding. While the humanities have little to offer in understanding the knot, its study has been subsumed under the field of topology and as such is central to mathematics (Adams 1994). Topology in mathematics achieved prominence with the recognition of the importance of 'organic', non-mechanical space-time in understanding apparently 'chaotic', not rule-governed, phenomena which surround us. Knots, from the perspective of science, capture the capacity of phenomena for self-organisation, from cells to the weather, and thus appear in manifold interconnected and generative forms (see Ho 1998).

The anthropological investigation of the knot has been hindered, rather than helped, by its seeming ubiquitous presence as a mode of binding. An anthropology of the knot became possible only recently with publication of MacKenzie's study of net bags in Papua New Guinea (1991) which looked at the knot through the lens of the loop, a variant technique of binding which produces the unseverable, expandable open meshwork, characteristic for net bags. Implicit in her study of looped net bags is a tale of contrasting knowledge technologies, one amplifying a continuous line, the other a planar surface, that effectively separate non-Austronesian-speaking cultures of mainland New Guinea from the Austronesian speaking cultures of island Melanesia and Polynesia (cf. Hauser-Schäublin 1996).

Studies such as Ascher's work on the *quipu* (1981, 1991), a system of knotted cords used by the Incas to store information, or Zaslavsky's work on numeration systems in Nigeria and Kenya (1973), position the investigation of the knot within the field of ethnomathematics; others have examined the knot as a mapping device, relating its mnemonic function to spatial configuration (Silverman 1998).

We can take from their work an insight into the revelatory capacity of bound form, for its capacity to emulate both being and thinking, and use this insight to look again at artefacts that have never been considered in relation with each other.[2] Tightly bound, planar surfaces of knotted artefacts are commonly found in early nineteenth-century collections of island Melanesia and Polynesia. Famous examples include the Hawaiian sacred cord (Valeri 1985: 296), the figural images of Tahitian *to'o* made from tightly bound sennit cord (Babadzan 1993), Tongan bark-cloth patterned by rubbing *tapa* over knotted fish-nets, sand drawings and dances of Malekula, whose patterns are composed of knots (Layard 1936), clubs from the Marquesas, 'soul-catchers' from the Cook Islands, and Kiribati armour, to name a few.

Common to these various forms is an acknowledgement of a double-edged nature:[3] as the technical means of 'binding', the knot is also the artefact of wrapping. Knotted effigies effect both the sacrificial 'death' of the gods, holding their powers at bay, while simultaneously securing the continuing protection offered by them to the living (Gell 1998: 111–113). Yet while wrapping has received the attention it deserves, 'binding' and its technical and conceptual foundation in the knot has been given comparatively scant attention, the exception being Valeri's detailed account of its place in Hawaiian kingship (1985), which I will draw on in this paper.

The knot is ascribed more than functional value in the Pacific, becoming the object of meditative thought, holding together through binding not two *things* but two *concepts*: that of the visible, and that of the invisible whose momentary entanglement facilitates temporal concepts of genealogy and remembrance. The conceptual and visual elaboration of knots in Austronesian effigies expresses the fiction of a conjunction of two bodies, one individual, natural and mortal, the other representing a supra-natural and immortal entity or principle. Knotted effigies, such as the Hawaiian sacred cord or Tahitian *to'o* thus fashion a 'body politic'. In the Pacific, such effigies give rise to a polity of ranked images which is mirrored in the hierarchical structure of the natural body of man.[4]

To illustrate the logical force of difference and conjunction, of rank and textured bond, fashioned by the figural knot in the Pacific, I draw on three ethnographic examples from island Melanesia and Polynesia: the Hawaiian sacred cord central to the sacrifice of the Hawaiian king as described by Valeri (1985: 295–300), the Tahitian *to'o* described by Babadzan (1993) (Fig. 11.1), and New Ireland *malanggan* (Fig. 11.2). These examples have the virtue of documenting the visually and conceptually distinct articulation of binding in the creation of effigies in three adjacent, yet, in terms of political organisation, distinct, cultural areas . . . [aiming] to illuminate how ritually sanctioned order is conceptualised from within the mundane and material matters of knots in all cases.[5]

On knots and knot-spanning surfaces

There are two insights developed in knot-theory that will help in examining the ethnographic case studies below. The first is that, while there is a large number of distinct knots, such as the trefoil or the figure of eight knot, each can undergo deformations known in knot-theory as *projections*. The second lies in the observation that the *surface* or the space around the knot, which is everything but the knot, with the knot lying within or beneath the surfaces which make it visible to the eye, is essential for understanding and distinguishing knots.

Mathematically speaking, therefore, all the surfaces that we look at live in the complement of the knot. This just means that the knot usually appears to us as a planar surface which, when aligned in a series, constitutes a visually impenetrable plane. This projectable and surface-creating nature of the knot distinguishes it most clearly from the looped string for which it is most frequently mistaken (cf. MacKenzie 1991; Hauser-Schäublin 1996). Looping is a technique most artfully exemplified in the open meshwork of the Papuan net bag. Here it is the line that is emphasized in the technique of looping which avoids self-intersecting string to create an expandable container. While there are projections or surfaces of knots, seen as transformations of a specific type of knot, loops are serially repeated rather than resulting from acts of transformation.

Moreover, as the knot is contained within the negative space created by surfaces, it lends itself to be applied to the conceptualisation of sculptural form. Within the Pacific, the tightly knotted cordage of Tahitian *to'o* and the richly incised curvilinear planes of *malanggan* carvings represent two logical applications of knotting in the creation of the figural. But we shall see that, whereas the *to'o* (Fig. 11.1) visually celebrates the impenetrability of the plane, the *malanggan* (Fig. 11.2) renders the contained negative space of the knot visible in the hollows of its surface.

The negative space thus produced is strictly self-referential in that it does not represent spaces of imaginary or past experience. As virtual space, the knot-spanning surface acts synthetically in bringing together, like mathematical formulae or architectural plans, experiences from a number of domains; rather than just articulating already-existing knowledge, the knot as artefact is thus capable of creating something 'new' – a momentary integration of distinct domains of experience which may be a reason for the symptomatic use of the knot as contractual object.

The knot thus represented in sculptural form epitomises what Levinson (1991) recently called 'knowledge technology', responsible for externalizing non-spatial, logical problems in a distinctly spatial manner. He distinguishes internalised technique, reproducing what one already knows or has learned to know, from a technology designed to produce knowledge through associative understanding. The translation of a non-spatial conceptual problem into a spatial one involves, therefore, the creation of visual analogy. The analogical force of the figural, however, has largely been ignored. Navigators, hunters, ocean fishers, trackers and traders must operate with complex mental maps, and with various systems of dead reckoning to locate current positions on the map, and reach their destination or prey. Less practical spatial models are cosmologies, mental models of the universe, where spirits, ancestors, moral and spiritual qualities, together with terrestrial and celestial phenomena are conceived of as all having their proper place in some three-dimensional scheme. It is however questionable whether such holistic spatial models are expressed in ritual, myth, art and architecture, or whether the spatial concepts that are given analogical force in figurative form entrap thought (cf. Gell 1996).

We could make the hypothesis that artefacts conceived as knot-spanning surfaces work not just in externalising the existing knowledge acquired through experience, but serve to order such knowledge in a way that, like diagrams, maps or charts, they create new knowledge. Yet how can an object that is figured as a knot be seen *as* knowledge without seeing knowledge *in* it, or, in other words, how can such figures serve as incantation and not as interpretation of knowledge?

We find it so hard to abandon this theory of the referentiality of form because of its embeddedness in a web of cultural assumptions of which the most crucial, and perhaps least questioned, pertains to the nature of spatial conception. There are many reasons to think that spatial conceptualisation is central to human cognition. Spatial understanding is perhaps the first

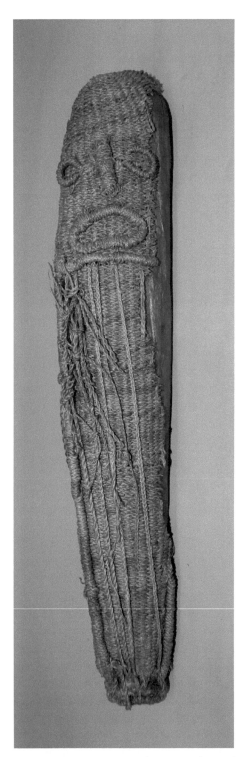

FIGURE 11.1 To'o. *God image of wood with sennit, found in the Society Islands, Tahiti, 1881. British Museum Q81.OC.1550 (Creative Commons).*

FIGURE 11.2 Malanggan *mask, Papua New Guinea, New Ireland. Nineteenth or early twentieth century. Bern Museum (Creative Commons).*

major intellectual task facing a child, but, above all, spatial thinking informs our conceptualisation of many other domains, such as time, social structure, music, mathematics and emotions (Levinson 1991: 8). Spatial conceptualisation is of interest when examining cultural relativity, as it appears constrained by the nature of the phenomenal world as well as by human physiology with its visual system and upright posture. Post-Newtonian theory of space right through to contemporary cognitive science has taken these environmental and cognitive constraints as evidence of the natural and universal conception of space from a 'relative, egocentric and anthropomorphic' point of view (ibid.).

The universality of this conception of space as proceeding from the human body was recently questioned by Wassmann, who argues that the Yupno of Papua New Guinea use three different reference systems at the same time, conceptualising space as decentred in everyday life (1994). Recent computer modelling is also able to visualise spatial conception as decentred since it allows us to transform the same object from a reference system in two-, to one in three- and four-dimensional space. The spatial properties of an object are no longer confined to the perceptual and relative relationship to the human body, but have become the material remains of mental arithmetic. This decentreing of spatial conception, in fact, was facilitated by 'knot-theory' which provided the mathematical tool for tracing the behaviour of solids in shifting reference systems.

The capacity of the knot to fashion decentred spatial cognition, an incantation of knowledge rather than an interpretation, is of paramount importance for understanding how knotted effigies can visually and conceptually effect a 'body politic' that seems at once phenomenal and yet also mystical in nature. The images that appear in and around the space of the knot are a mirror of society, while constituting simultaneously a system of reference for spatial cognition that is independent of particular points of view. Alternatingly formed and dissolved in processes of tying and untying, knotted effigies call for the spatio-temporal conception of a body politic which mediates the contradictory nature of gods whose powers need to be arrested while being kept at a safe distance.

Binding and body politic in the Pacific

Pacific studies of kingship and sacrifice give us an insight into the humanizing of figures that effect the vision of a divine body from within their own remains. Of these, it is the now classical study of Hawaiian kingship and sacrifice by Valerio Valeri which offers poignant reference to the knot (1985: 296–300).

In Hawaii, a sacred cord ('aha) acted as reference point to genealogy, representing not just the king's relationship with the gods, but also the connecting force that 'binds together all other genealogies, since it is their reference point and the locus of their legitimacy and truth' (ibid. 296). The cord of Hawaiian kingship was not inherited – the undoing of the king's sacred cord dissolved the social bond embodied by the king. The strands obtained from the undoing of the cords were woven into caskets in which the bones of the king were enshrined (ibid. 298).

During the king's reign, the weaving of the cord which celebrated his installation was re-enacted repeatedly as the central organizing rite of the sacrifice of the king. The metaphoric or real 'twisting' of the strands that make up the *'aha* cord was enclosed and thereby removed from sight in the space where the knot resides, containing and thus arresting the divine powers which come to form the mystical body of kingship.[6]

The Hawaiian sacred cord effected a contiguous relation with divinity, in that it did not represent through resemblance, but through an associative or contiguous link. As undifferentiated as are the knots that make up the cord, so kingship in Hawaii appeared to possess a unifying force. In Valeri's words (1985: 296–297) 'the king's "cord" (*'aha*) is in fact also the 'association' or 'congregation' (*'aha*) of nobles. The cord becomes the community; the link that connects the king with the social bond itself'. In braiding his sacred cords, the king braids social relationships, or, as Valeri puts it, 'binds men with his cords' (ibid. 298). The king's title reflects the idea that he is the 'binder', since *'haku'*, 'ruler', also means 'to weave', 'to put in order', 'to compose a chant'.

Valeri extends the political function ascribed to weaving or binding to the poetic function of chants which are collectively composed by those whom the king tied to himself, and therefore become a bond that, bound in the memory of all, binds them all (ibid. 299). The 'weaving' of the chants, like the weaving of the cords, is thus 'also an intellectual weaving, since social relations are reconstituted by the reproduction of the ideas that are their correlate and justification' (ibid.). Since it can be used to tie and untie, according to Valeri, the cord evokes social bond, memory, but also transformation, as is made evident in string games which are used 'to represent mythical transformations or even to produce ritual ones' (ibid.). The unvarying element of two opposing states (tied and untied) contained in the cord permits the representation of the passage from one to the other – from the inaccessibility of divine nature to its state in myth and ritual, or from sickness to healing in medical rites.

The Hawaiian sacred cord is given *processual value* in being assigned a temporal and performative role responsible for linking the invisible and the visible. It is not what the cord looks like that is important. It is the processes of binding and opening to which the cord is subjected which constitutes the mystical, corporate body of kingship. This effectivity of the binding of the cord as the core of Hawaiian body politic resonates across the Pacific, yet is not articulated everywhere in the same manner. Thus, while much of what has been said about the Hawaiian cord can also be said about my second example, the Tahitian *to'o,* in this case the bound representation of the link with the gods fashions a polity of ranked images which form the conceptual foundation of society.

Alain Babadzan (1993) describes the *to'o* as a composite object, in general made of a piece of hard wood, in elongated shape like a stick or club, of about several centimetres in length to 1.80 metre for the most important piece. This stick remains completely invisible, because the wood is covered in a tight binding of sennit cordage called *'aha,* like the Hawaiian sacred cord. The binding is made of plaits of cords from the fibres of the coconut tree and/or different layers of wrapped up *tapa,* the whole comprising feathers of different colours, but mainly red feathers, that are placed either outside the *to'o,* or between the wooden frame of the object and its different layers of wrapping. The mummy-like object is decorated on the outside with roughly delineated facial features and limbs made out of sennit cordage.

While the *to'o* were thought of as a specific representation of the god 'Oro, they did not all represent the same deity, nor exclusively the principal gods alone. A great number of images existed, each owned by a family, a blood line, a clan, a district, and even a whole island. The images were ranked according to size. The correlation between the polity of images and social rank was given regular and formal expression in a ritual called *pa'iatua,* which, translated, means the 'gathering and undressing of the gods'. This ritual consisted of three stages, mirroring the cycles which compose the agricultural calendar, each stage being defined in relation to the manipulation of the *to'o*: 1. The unwrapping of the *to'o,* effecting the death or departure of the gods; 2. The exchange of feathers as the 'sharing' of the remains of the gods; 3. The re-assemblage or 'renewal' of the *to'o* invoking the return of the gods and the period of abundance.

A close relation existed between this last stage and the treatment of the corpse at funerary ceremonies which witnessed the presentation of precious fabrics used as a wrapping for the corpse. Babadzan also remarks (ibid. 120) on the similarity between the practice of the wrapping of *to'o* and funerary practices outside of Tahiti such as the Cook Islands as well as with the Polynesian bundle gods, all consisting of the wrapping of corpses in matting given as funeral presents which then were tied into a parcel with numerous rounds of sennit cord. The rewrapping of the *to'o* was thus also considered responsible for the summoning of the god under a shape evoking that of a deceased covered in his funeral costume, thus 'travelling in reverse the whole journey which normally leads men to ancestrality' (ibid. 121). Because the renewed *to'o* borrows the shape of a body withered by time and appearing as a corpse, in fact as the 'remains of the gods', the renewal of the *to'o* foreshadows the expulsion of the deity and the renewal of the cycle with the subsequent moulting or rotting of the *to'o* and its consequential undressing.

The processuality of tying and untying implicit in the knot while clearly important is, however, secondary to the question of control over the execution of the rite and the placement of the *to'o* in the funerary enclosure. Here, the knotted surface emerges as container whose manipulation allows for the incorporation as well as the expulsion of forces deemed beyond control. Owning a *to'o* as artefact that can be stripped and reclad in its cordage is thus likened to owning access to the remains of the gods and of the dead, while keeping them for the most time at safe distance.

The similarities between the Tahitian *to'o* and *malanggan* of New Ireland is striking, given that we are dealing with societies on either side of the Polynesian/Melanesian cultural zone. Like the *to'o,* the *malanggan* renders the knot visible in sculptural form, yet in contrast to the *to'o,* the knot as the seat of ancestral power is not fully contained in the *malanggan,* but visible as negative space surrounded by surfaces that literally span across the knot. The ritual work required to contain the knot and thereby secure the continuing link between the visible and the invisible, which is apparent in the *to'o* in the ranking of its images according to size, is heightened in the *malanggan* as the principle governing the ranking of its images according to the volume of negative space. Here it is not the size of the figure alone which determines the prestige assigned to proprietary rights extended to its image, but the degree of incision as well as the position of the image in a ranked polity of images of startling complexity. While also stressing the process of knotting, as in Hawaii, and the prestige derived from the control of the process, as in Tahiti, the rendering visible of this process in the images of *malanggan* aesthetizises the value assigned to ritual work. The ranked polity of *malanggan*-images mirrors social rank in so far as images can be bought, lent or sold within and between clans, blood-lines, and districts, yet it is overtly the visual and conceptual quality of an image that provokes attempts to partake of the image and thus to become part of a fluid and expanding network of relations of labour and loyalty.

The term *malanggan* refers to an array of figural images invested with the divine powers of the god *moroa. Malanggan* are carved from wood, woven from fibre or moulded from clay, yet of these, only the carved and painted figures were collected since the 1870s and today form one of the largest western museum holdings of a still contemporary and flourishing tradition.

Visually and conceptually, these carved figures recall a body wrapped in images that draw attention to bodily folds, contours and shape. The emerging fretwork takes the forms of instantly recognisable motifs found in abundance in the physical and animate environment of the island culture which produces them. In carved and painted planes, we can identify birds, pigs, fish and seashells, depicted with an accuracy and attention to detail that they appear almost life-like; the same can be said for the figure set within the fretwork which appears to stare at the beholder with eyes that could hardly be more vivid. . . Motifs appear enchained, as figures stand inside the mouth of rock-cods, framed by diverse fish that bite into limbs and chins, birds that bite into snakes, snakes biting into birds, and pig skulls that appear to metamorphose into birds. Inner shapes appear enclosed by outer frames in ways which contest the apparent reality of what is depicted.

In search for meaning we direct our eyes away from the hollowed spaces clustering between figure and frame. Yet it is in these hollowed spaces, in what is rendered absent through incising, that we find a surprising clue of what a *malanggan* is: what we are looking at are complex knot-spanning surfaces reminiscent of the string figures which form a beloved pastime across the Pacific. Finding a knot in the hollowed spaces of the wood distinguishes ritually effective artefacts from those which are considered 'mistakes" – the space framed by the enveloping planes of the carving calls to mind the heap of wood-chips left at the back of the carver's hut, called *rotap,* literally 'salty rubbish', likened to the dead, uprooted trees which drift ashore once a year during the rainy season from the direction of ancestral land and to the smell of women in the early stages of pregnancy.

The knot, which is visible as negative space, reflects upon containment as both desired and yet inherently dangerous. Any contact with the traces of the knot in any of its forms has to be combated with ritual cleansing to avoid the person being "caught' and thus falling ill with usually fatal consequences. The deadliness of the knot is associated with the 'killer vine' (*ru*) which twists itself around trees with such force that they eventually succumb and fall. Killer vines are found in small patches of primary rain forest that lie close to river sources or springs, tightly twisted around gigantic trees, which are known as the dwellings of 'skin-snatchers', beings who kill humans by taking skins and appearing in human disguise as tricksters. Like in Hawaii, illness ascribed to the trickster is cured by metaphorically cutting a vine twisted around the patient's body.

The knot as a trap renders it effective as means for recapturing the life-force which was set free during ritual work tracing bodily decomposition and the dismantling of social relations associated with the deceased person. Like artefacts made from tightly bound cordage, *malanggan* effects rather than represents the relationship between the living and the ancestors, because its surface quite literally recalls the space rendered absent within which the knot resides. In contrast to the Hawaiian cord, however, the relation with the world of spirits evoked through the encompassment of the knot is conceived in terms of spatio-temporal processes rather than in terms of genealogical connection, because the carving and rotting of *malanggan* coincide with the pulling ashore and release of ancestral power which mark the agricultural calendar of New Ireland.

The characteristic feature of knowledge created as witness to a contractual relation is its association with place. The act of witnessing links people with a place that begins to act as a nodal point even when, or possibly because, the object and its relational field are rendered invisible soon after the display. That contractual relations are inseparable from the act of witnessing and thus have to be reactivated means that the place of reference is not fixed, but movable, creating regional systems of an expansive and distributed kind. In other words, the ability of the artefact, which is conceived as a knot-spanning surface, to decentre spatial description may be seen to be carried over into the description of social relations. As a result, such relations may appear inherently fluid, notwithstanding the ego-centred and relative narratives of anthropological modelling.

The artefact as knot visualises this place-making capacity through its inherent *voluminousness*, which may be found in the negative space around an object or in the void implicit in its form. Knots, as we have seen, exist in this void, since they can be made visible, and thus comprehensible, by activating the surface of the knot taking away the knot itself. All we see are these rubber-like, inherently deformable surfaces within which voids take on shape and become cognizable as place. From a New Ireland perspective, it is in these voids, that is in the space of the knot, that ancestral power is made to reside; the greater the incisions, the greater the power to the figure and to those capable of realizing it. From a Tahitian perspective, the voluminous quality of the knot is visualized also in terms of size – the bigger the artefact, the more powerful were regarded those who bound it, yet here the surface created by the tightly knotted cordage appears as a continuum, rather than as a body cavity full of holes and joints. Like a wrap, this continuous surface conceals only to reveal place as the source of power, while the folds of the skin-like surface reveal place-making power within its folds.

The knot's differential articulation, as process of binding, as artefact of wrapping or as second skin or surface that protects has been shown to bring forth visually polities of images whose specific relational constitutions are mirrored in the ranked and hierarchical conception of social relations. Cords, bound effigies or wooden carvings of the Pacific are not just illustrating a culture style, a way of thinking already in existence, but may be seen as the carriers of specific analogical thought upon which new forms of social relations came to be built. While certainly not conclusive or complete, this paper aims at stimulating reconsideration of the body politic and allied relations of hierarchy by locating their logical force in the mundane and textured nature of binding.

Notes

1   The original was first published in *L'Homme, Revue française d'anthropologie* (January–March 2003): 206–222. Although focused on knots, the author extends discussion to include many forms of binding, including looped meshwork, twined and wrapped effigies, and plaited armour.

2   For a further discussion of the relation between binding, being and thinking, see Küchler 1999, 2001.

3   For a further discussion of the relation between binding, being and thinking, see Küchler 1999.

4   The distinction between the 'body mystical' and the 'body natural' is a genuine European distinction, though Burkhard Schnepel (1995) has recently traced its impact on accounts of royal ritual in Southern Sudan and East India. His fascinating comparison in the conception and use of effigies in the European, African and East Indian data points to their decisive role in the shaping of the body politic.

5   A topic such as the 'body politic' cannot of course be discussed without reference to the literature on personhood and its articulation in Melanesia and Polynesia (e.g. Mosko 1993; Strathern 1988; Sahlins 1983). Discussions of Strathern's notion of the Melanesian 'divisual' 'fractal' person versus

Sahlin's theory of the Polynesian 'expansive person' have retained an abstract tenor which this chapter aims to counterbalance by arguing that the very processes of decomposition which allow relations composing a person to become apparent are visually and conceptually made manifest in knotted artefacts. The relevance of the knot for an understanding of social relations in both Polynesia and island Melanesia gives credence, moreover, to Mosko's argument on the complementarity of Polynesian and Melanesian models of personhood and hierarchy.

6 I will follow Valeri in abstaining from the temptation to provide a symbolic interpretation of the cord.

Bibliography

Adams, C. 1994 *The Knot Book: An Elementary Introduction to the Mathematical Theory of Knots.* New York: W. H. Freeman & Co.

Ascher, M. 1981 *Code of the Quipu: A Study in Media, Mathematics, and Culture.* Ann Arbor, MI: University of Michigan Press.

Ascher, M. 1991 *Ethnomathematics: A Multicultural View of Mathematical Ideas.* Pacific Grove, CA: Brooks/Cole Pub. Co

Babadzan, A. 1993 *Les Dépouilles des dieux: essai sur le religion tahitienne à l'époque de la découverte.* Paris: Éditions de la Maison des sciences de l'homme.

Bonnemaison, J. 1994 *The Tree and the Canoe: History and Ethnography of Tanna.* Honolulu: Hawaii University Press.

Carrier, J. & Carrier A. 1990 'Every Picture Tells a Story: Visual Alternatives to Oral Tradition in Ponam Society', *Oral Tradition* 5: 354–375.

Damon, F. H. 1990 *From Muyuw to the Trobriands: Transformations along the Northern Side of the Kula Ring.* Tucson, AZ: University of Arizona Press.

Duggan, L. 1989 'Was Art really the Book of the Illiterate?', *Word and Image* 5 (3): 227–251.

Francis, G, with Brent Collins 1993 'On Knot-spanning Surfaces: an Illustrated Essay on Topological Art'. In Michele Emmer, ed., *The Visual Mind: Art and Mathematics.* Cambridge, MA: MIT Press, 57–65.

Gell, A. 1996 'The Thrill of the Line, the String, and the Frond, or why the Abelam are a Non-cloth Culture', *Oceania* 67 (20): 81–106.

Gell, A. 1998 *Art and Agency: Toward an Anthropological Theory of Art.* Oxford: Oxford University Press.

Ho, Moe-Wan 1998 'The New Age of the Organism', *Architectural Design* 129: 44–51.

Küchler, S. 1993 'Landscape as Memory: the Mapping of Process and its Representation in a Melanesian Society'. In B. Bender, ed., *Landscape: Politics and Perspectives.* Oxford: Berg, 56–83.

Küchler, S. 1999 'Binding in the Pacific: Between Loops and Knots', *Oceania* 69 (3): 145–157.

Küchler, S. 2001 'Why Knot? Towards a Theory of Art and Mathematics'. In C. Pinney and N. Thomas, eds, *Beyond Aesthetics. Essays in memory of Alfred Gell.* Oxford: Berg, 57–79.

Layard, J. 1936 'Maze-Dances and the Ritual of the Labyrinth in Malekula', *Folklore* 41: 123–170.

Leach, E. R. 1954 *Political Systems of Highland Burma. A Study of Kachin Social Structure.* Cambridge: Harvard University Press.

Levinson, S. 1991 'Primer for the Field Investigation of Spatial Description and Conception', *Pragmatics* 2 (1): 5–47.

MacKenzie, M. 1991 *Androgynous Objects: String Bags and Gender in Central New Guinea.* Philadelphia, PA: Harwood Academic Publishers.

Mosko, M. 1993 'Rethinking Trobriand Chieftainship', *Journal of the Royal Anthropological Institute* 11 (4): 763–786.

Munn, N. 1983 'Gawan Kula: Spatio-Temporal Control and the Symbolism of Influence'. In Jerry Leach and Edmund Leach, eds, *The Kula: New Perspectives on Massim Exchange*. Cambridge: Cambridge University Press: 277–308.

Sahlins, M. 1983 'Raw Women, Cooked Men and Other Great Things of the Fiji Islands'. In P. Brown and D. Tuzin, eds, *The Ethnography of Cannibalism*. Berkeley, CA: University of California Press, 72–93.

Schnepel, B. 1995 *Twinned Beings: Kings and Effigies in Southern Sudan, East India and Renaissance France*. Goteborg: IASSA.

Semper, G. 1856 *Uber die formelle Gezatzmassigkeit des Schmickes und dessen Bedeutung als Kunstsymbol*. Berlin: Alexander ("Schriften zur Kunsttheorie" 3).

Silverman, E. K. 1998 'Traditional Cartography in Papua New Guinea. In Donald Woodward and George M. Lewis, eds, *The History of Cartography: Cartography in the Traditional African, American, Arctic, Australian, and Pacific Societies*. Chicago, IL: Chicago University Press, 422–442.

Strathern, M. 1988 *The Gender of the Gift: Problems with Women and Problems with Society in Melanesia*. Berkeley, CA: University of California Press.

Summers, D. 1989 'Form: Nineteenth-Century Metaphysics and the Problem of Art Historical Description', *Critical Inquiry* 15: 52–87.

Valeri, V. 1985 *Kingship and Sacrifice in Hawaii*. Chicago, IL: Chicago University Press.

Wassmann, J. 1994 'The Yupno as Post-Newtonian Scientists: The Question of what is Natural in Spatial Descriptions', *Man* n.s. 29 (3): 645–667.

Wölfflin, H. 1941 *Gedanken zur Kunstgeschichte, Gedrucktes und Ungedrucktes*. Basel: B. Schwabe & Co.

Zaslavsky, C. 1973 *Africa Counts: Number and Pattern in African Culture*. Boston, MA: Prindle, Weber & Schmidt.

12

Secret strings:
The sounds of fibre and ply

Sabine Hyland and William P. Hyland

A stuffy minivan, crammed with people and supplies, carries me and my husband far above from Lima's coastal mist into the sun-filled mountains 12,000 feet above sea level. Hours later, as the van climbs ever higher, raising clouds of dust on the dizzying hairpin turns, our hostess stops to point out to us curious shapes in the towering rock formations. We exit the van to examine the natural figures in the stone – a condor, a turtle, even a fox whose tail is a red mineral streak on the cliff face. In the endless blue sky we spot a lone condor gliding on the air currents. Our hostess informs us that this is a good omen; the condor is a messenger for the mountain gods – called *apus* – and is carrying the news of our presence to the watching peaks.

Below us lies our destination – the remote Andean village of Collata, population three hundred. A scattering of adobe houses with no running water, no sewage, and electricity for only a couple of homes, entering the village feels like stepping into another world. Our visit has been timed to coincide with the annual assembly of the village peasant community. We spend the next few hours making formal presentations to the indigenous officers, requesting permission to study two rare and precious objects that the community has guarded for centuries – bunches of twisted and coloured cords known as *khipus*. After dinner, the man in charge of the community treasures, a middle-aged herder named Huber Brañes, brings to our house the colonial chest containing the *khipus* along with goat hide packets of original seventeenth- and eighteenth-century manuscripts – the secret patrimony of the village. In the ensuing days, we would learn that these multicoloured *khipus* were narrative epistles created by local chiefs during a time of war in the eighteenth century. But that evening, exhausted yet elated, my husband Bill and I simply marvel at the shimmering colours of the delicate animal fibre cords – crimson, gold, indigo, green, cream, pink and shades of brown from fawn to chocolate.

The Inkas and other ancient Andean peoples had used *khipus* to record numerical accounts, as well as histories, biographies and even letters sent from one regional administrator to another. In its heyday, there would have been 100,000s of *khipus* in the Inka Empire, conserved in both imperial and local archives. Most Inka *khipus* recorded numerical accounts; accounting *khipus* can be easily identified by the knots tied into the cords, which represent numbers, even if we don't

FIGURE 12.1 *Collata* khipu *cords*.

know what those numbers mean. More elusive are the narrative *khipus*; discovering a narrative *khipu* that can be deciphered remains one of the holy grails of South American anthropology. If we could find such an object, we might eventually be able to read how native South Americans viewed their history and rituals in their own words, opening a window to a new Andean world of literature, history, and the arts.

Today there are about one thousand two hundred *khipus* in museums around the world, but no one knows anymore how to 'read' them. Until recently, scholars believed that *khipu* use died out in the Andes soon after the Spanish conquest in 1532, lingering only in the simple cords made by herders to keep track of their flocks. Yet in the 1990s, anthropologists found that a few communities in the Central Andes continued to make and interpret *khipus* up until the early twentieth century. Although the inhabitants of these villages are not still able to 'read' the cords, this handful of recently created *khipus* holds out the promise of new insights into this mysterious communication system. *Khipus* preserved in their original village context are incredibly rare; each one provides new knowledge that one day may allow us to decipher these enigmatic texts.

Bill and I had been granted 48 hours to photograph and take notes on the two Collata *khipus* – a daunting task, given their complexity. As we begin working the next morning, it becomes clear that these two *khipus* are unlike any that I have ever seen before. They possess a much greater range of colours and colour combinations than any accounting *khipu* I had studied previously. I ask Huber and his companion, who had been assigned to watch us, what types of animal fibres were present in the cords. Their answers reveal another surprising level of sophistication. The 487 pendant cords of the two *khipus* are made of fibres from six different Andean animals – vicuña, deer, alpaca, llama, guanaco and vizcacha (the latter a common rodent hunted for food). In many cases, the identification of the fibre can be made only through touching the cords – brown deer hair and brown vicuña wool, for example, may look the same but feel very different. My interlocutors insist that the difference in fibre is significant, and Huber even calls the *khipus* a 'language of animals'. They request that I handle the *khipus* with my bare hands, and teach me how to feel the fine distinctions between the various animal fibres. Curiously, there are no knots, suggesting that these might be two long-awaited examples of narrative *khipus*.

As I questioned elderly men in Collata about the *khipus*, they revealed to me that the *khipus* were 'letters' – '*cartas*' – written by local leaders during their battles on behalf of the Inkas in the eighteenth century. Until a few years ago, the *khipus'* existence was a fiercely guarded secret amongst the senior men, who passed on the secrets of the colonial archive to younger men when they reached maturity. Their disclosures confirm a recent finding by scholars that *khipu* 'letters' played a major role in a 1750 rebellion in the Collata region. The text of one of these eighteenth-century *khipu* missives survives, written out in Spanish by a local colonial official, even as the original *khipu* has disappeared. It recalls how the intended recipient had double-crossed his fellow rebels – a straight-forward story, but a narrative nonetheless. If the Collata *khipus* encoded narratives, as the evidence suggests, why did local people use *khipus* instead of alphabetic literacy, which they knew as well?

Surely one reason for retaining *khipu* literacy in remote corners of the Andes was the desire for a form of writing that was opaque to colonial tax collectors and other authorities. The Collata *khipus*, for example, were created as part of a native rebellion in 1783 centred in the two villages of Collata and nearby Casta. Felipe Velasco Tupa Inka Yupanki, a charismatic merchant from Lima who peddled religious paintings in the mountains, declared the revolt against Spanish rule in the name of his brother the Inka Emperor who, he claimed, lived in splendour deep amid the eastern rain forests. Testimony from captured rebels specifies that Tupa Inka Yupanki demanded warriors to lay siege to the capital of Lima, with the goal of placing his brother – or more likely himself – on the throne of Peru. In January 1783, he spent two weeks in Collata, stirring revolutionary fervour, and appointing the Mayor of Collata as his 'Captain of the People'. Dressed in a lilac coloured silk frock coat, with lilac frills at his neck, black velvet breeches, white leather boots with steel buckles and a white tri-cornered hat, Tupa Inka Yupanki must have cut a striking figure as he accepted the homage of the Collata farmers and herders. His attack on Lima had scarcely begun when a confederate betrayed him by reporting the conspiracy to the regional Corregidor. A small band of Spanish troops captured Tupa Inka Yupanki and his associates, and, despite a fierce ambush by rebels from Collata and Casta, successfully carried him to prison in Lima. There he was tortured, tried and executed. Reading through the trial notes, it's clear that the most damning evidence against him were letters detailing the conspiracy, written on paper in Spanish and found among his possessions. Likewise, his main lieutenants carried alphabetic letters that discussed their efforts to raise troops, and that railed against Spanish crimes in the Andes; these Spanish letters provided unassailable proof of guilt. Spanish authorities never found comparable written letters against the rebel leaders in Collata, despite plentiful witness testimony implicating them in the rebellion. The Collata leadership completely escaped prosecution, all the while guarding their war *khipus* in their cherished archive. We don't know how long the tradition of narrative *khipus* lasted after the 1783 revolt, but do know that Andeans carried on making accounting and ritual *khipus* to shield their records from the prying eyes of outsiders.

How did the Collata *khipus* encode messages through colours and animal fibres, with no characters or letters? Out of the 487 pendants in the two *khipus*, there are a total of ninety-five unique pendants, or symbols, in terms of colour, animal fibre and ply direction (that is, whether they are twisted like the middle stroke of an *S* or a *Z*). This falls within the normal range of symbols (80 to 800) for writing systems that are logo-syllabic; in other words, of systems whose signs represent either entire words or single syllables. According to village authorities, one of the *khipus* (Khipu A) was composed by the primary lineage, ALLUKA. Given that the manuscript letters preserved in the village archive ended with the signatures of the authors, I wondered whether we can match the final cords of this *khipu* with the lineage name:

Khipu A ending sequence
Dark brown *wanaku* (S) = **A**
White/dark brown, llama/*wanaku* (wrapped) (Z) = **LLU**
Blue llama (S) = **KA**

Ankas was the Huarochiri Quechua term for 'blue'; the phonetic value 'ka', the first syllable beginning with a consonant, might possibly relate to the colour's name.

Do the proposed equivalences between the final cords of Khipu A and the syllables of ALLUKA allow us to decipher the ending cords of Khipu B?

Khipu B ending sequence:
Dark brown *wanaku* (S) = **A**
Blue llama (S) = **KA**
Golden brown vicuña (S) = **?**

The Quechua term for the golden-brown hue of the third cord is *Paru*, likened to ripening corn. This creates the word A-KA-PAR(U) or YAKAPAR, the name of one of Casta's only two lineages, conforming to the pattern of a lineage name at a khipu's terminal end. This accords with the history of the villages as the twin centres of the 1783 Huarochiri revolt, and with Collata's oral history about the *khipus*. This proposed decipherment suggests that at least some narrative *khipu* pendants possess standard syllabic values.

Other signs represent entire words or ideas; for example, the brush of bright red deer hair at the beginning of one of the *khipus* indicates that the *khipu* is about warfare. This discovery marks the first time that any *khipu* has been found to be logo-syllabic. The Collata *khipus* are an entirely new form of logo-syllabic writing, one that communicates sounds through three-dimensional animal fibre cords that must be felt as well as seen. However, these phonetic *khipus* raise a host of questions. Were these logo-syllabic *khipus*, which date to the eighteenth century, a relatively localised phenomena influenced by contact with alphabetic writing, or do they have far-reaching roots into the pre-Columbian Andean past? Do the other types of *khipus* that were used in the Central Andes until the twentieth century, such as those for accounting and for funerals, share semiotic features with the phonetic *khipus*? What are the epistemological implications of a three-dimensional writing system, in which the sense of touch plays as important a role as sight, and how does this expand our understanding of what 'writing' is?

Although these *khipus* were hidden in the past, away from the prying eyes of outsiders, village authorities in Collata and the other Central Andean communities where I have done fieldwork are now eager for recognition of their valuable cultural heritage. With my assistance, the Collata village council has created a packet of information about their *khipus* for use in the village school. As one community official wrote to me, 'it is imperative that our children know the value of their cultural heritage here in Collata so that they will not abandon their village when they grow up'. On 24 June 2017, which is the official feast day of the village, the village council and the President of the Collata Peasant Association formally inducted a Spanish translation of my *Current Anthropology* report on their *khipus* into their treasured archive.

The extraordinary *khipu* texts of the Central Andes, including the logo-syllabic animal fibre cords, are a proud testament to the intellectual achievements of Native American peoples.

Bibliography

Arnold, D. 2014 'Textiles, knotted *khipus*, and a semiosis in common'. In D. Arnold and P. Dransart (eds), *Textiles, Technical Practice and Power in the Andes*. London: Archetype Publications.

Brokaw, G. 2010 *History of the Khipu*. Cambridge: Cambridge University Press.

Brown Vega, M. 2016. 'Ritual practices and wrapped objects', *Journal of Material Culture* 21 (2): 267–272.

Cereceda, V. 1986 'The Semiology of Andean Textiles'. In J. V. Murra, N. Wachtel and J. Revel (eds) *Anthropological History of Andean Polities*, pp. 149–173. Cambridge: Cambridge University Press.

Conklin, William 2002 'A *Khipu* Information String Theory'. In J. Quilter and G. Urton (eds), *Narrative Threads*, pp. 53–86. Austin, TX: University of Texas Press.

Curatola Petrocchi, M. and de la Puente Luna, José (eds) 2013. *El quipu colonial*. Lima: PUCP.

Dransart, P. 2014 'Thoughts on productive knowledge in Andean weaving with discontinuous warp and weft'. In D. Arnold and P. Dransart (eds), *Textiles, Technical Practice and Power in the Andes*. London: Archetype Publications.

Femenías, B. 1987 *Andean Aesthetics*. Madison, WI: Elvehjem Museum of Art.

Franquemont, C. 1986 'Chinchero Pallays'. In A. Pollard (ed.), *The Junius B. Bird Conference on Andean Textiles*. Washington, DC: The Textile Museum.

Garcés, F. and Bustamente Rocha, M. 2014 *Lutrina Timpu*. Cochabamba, Bolivia: Universidad de San Simón.

Garcés, F. and Sánchez, W. 2015 *Textualidades*. Cochabamba, Bolivia: Universidad de San Simón.

Garcés, F. and Sánchez, W., 2016 'Inscripciones y escrituras andinas', *Boletín del Museo Chileno de Arte Precolombino* 21(1): 115–128.

Hyland, S. 2014 'Ply, markedness and redundancy', *American Anthropologist* 116: 3: 643–648.

Hyland, S. 2016 'How khipus indicated labour contributions in an Andean village', *Journal of Material Culture* 21 (4): 490–509.

Hyland, S. 2017 'Writing with Twisted Cords: The Inscriptive Capacity of Andean Khipu Texts', *Current Anthropology* 58 (3): 412–419.

Hyland, S., Ware, G. A. and Clark, M. 2014 Knot direction in a khipu/alphabetic text from the Central Andes. *Latin American Antiquity* 25: 2: 189–197.

Justeson, John S. 1976 'Universals of language and universals of writing'. In A. Juilland (ed), *Linguistic Studies Offered to Joseph Greenberg*, pp. 57–94. Saratoga, CA: Anima Libri.

Lau, G. 2014 'On Textiles and Alterity in the Recuay Culture (AD 200 – 700), Ancash, Peru. In D. Arnold and P. Dransart (eds), *Textiles, Technical Practice and Power in the Andes*. London: Archetype Publications.

Loza, C.B. 1999 'Quipus and Quipolas at the Museum für Völkerkunde, Berlin', *Baessler-Archiv, Neue Folge*, XLVII: 39–75.

Mackey, C. 2002 'The continuing khipu tradition'. In J. Quilter and G. Urton (eds), *Narrative Threads*, pp. 321–347. Austin, TX: University of Texas Press.

Molina, T de (Gabriel Téllez). 1973–4 *Historia general de la Orden de la Nuestra Señora de las Mercedes*. Manuel Penedo Rey, ed. 2 vols. Madrid: Provincia de la Merced.

Murúa, M. de. 1987 *Historia general del Perú*. Manuel Ballesteros, ed. Madrid: Historia 16.

Pärssinen, M. 1992 *Tawantinsuyu: The Inca State and Its Political Organization*. Helsinki: SHS.

Pimentel N.H. 2005 *Amarrando colores: La producción del sentido en khipus aymaras*. La Paz: CEPA, Latinas Editores.

Platt, T. 2015 'Un Archivo campesino como 'Acontecimiento de Terreno': Los nuevos papeles del Curaca de Mach;, *Americania (Seville)*: 158–185.

Radicati di Primeglio, Carlos. 2006 *Estudios sobre los quipus*. Lima: Universidad Nacional de San Marcos.

Rappaport, J. and Cummins, T. 2011 *Beyond the Lettered City*. Durham, NC: Duke University Press.

Sala i Vila, N. 1995 'La rebelión de Huarochirí de 1783'. In C. Walker (ed), *Entre la retórica y la insurgencia*, pp. 273–308. Cuzco, Peru: CBC.

Salomon, F. 2001 'How an Andean "writing without words" works'. *Current Anthropology* 42(1), 1–27.

Salomon, F. 2004 *The Cord Keepers*. Durham, NC: Duke University Press.

Salomon, F. and Niño-Murcia, M. 2011 *The Lettered Mountain*. Durham, NC: Duke University Press.

Salomon, F. and Urioste, G. I. 1991 *The Huarochiri Manuscript*. Austin, TX: University of Texas Press.

Salomon, F., Brezine, C. J., Chapa, R. and Huayta, V. F. 2011 'Khipu from Colony to Republic'. In E. H. Boone and G. Urton (eds), *Their Way of Writing*, pp. 353–378. Washington, DC: Dumbarton Oaks.

Silverman, G. P. 2008 *A Woven Book of Knowledge*. Salt Lake City, UT: University of Utah Press.

Spalding, K. 1984 *Huarochiri*. Stanford, CA: Stanford University Press.

Splitstoser, J. 2014 'Practice and meaning in spiral-wrapped batons and cords from Cerrillos'. In D. Arnold and P. Dransart (eds), *Textiles, Technical Practice and Power in the Andes*, pp. 46–82. London: Archetype Publications.

Szeminski, J. 1987 'Why Kill the Spaniard?' In S. Stern (ed.), *Resistance, Rebellion, and Consciousness in the Andean Peasant World*, pp. 166–192. Madison, WI: University of Wisconsin Press.

Tello, J. C. and Próspero, M. 1923 'Wallallo: Ceremonias gentílicas', *Inca*, 1: 475–549.

Uhle, M. 1897 'A Modern Kipu from Cutusuma, Bolivia', *Bulletin of the Free Museum of Science and Art* 1 (2): 51–63.

Urton, G. 2003 *Signs of the Inka Khipu*. Austin, TX: University of Texas Press.

Urton, G. 2005 Khipu Archives. *Latin American Antiquity* 16 (2): 147–167.

Urton, G and Brezine, C. 2011 'Khipu Typologies'. In E. Boone and G. Urton (eds), *Their Way of Writing*. Washington, DC: Dumbarton Oaks.

13

Exploring mathematical and craft literacies:

Learning to read and learning to make patterned baskets in Vanuatu

Lucie Hazelgrove-Planel

If we are to understand basketry techniques and not become enchanted by the technology (Gell 1992), first-hand experience of the technique and direct experience of the materials are essential. Doing fieldwork and learning how to plait patterns and designs into pandanus baskets in Vanuatu, I became aware that there are different ways of thinking about, knowing or 'reading' patterns and that this affects how they are made and worked in plaited pandanus basketry.

This is where, for me, the concept of mathematical literacy becomes useful. As discussed below, mathematics at its core is a method and an approach; it is much more than a study of numbers and the ways that these can be manipulated. Comprehending plaited pattern work in order to reproduce it, the focus of this chapter, similarly requires more than an external reading of the designs. Basketry practices are therefore at the intersection of our concepts of numeracy (mathematics) and literacy (reading with understanding) and I think the concept of mathematical literacy can help us understand and recognize the thought processes involved in plaited basketry.

This relatively new interpretation of the term 'literate' pushes it beyond its etymological background linked to 'letter' – and thus read/write – and instead emphasizes skills and knowledge about a particular subject or activity (Merriam-Webster 2018). The focus is not on a person's knowledge, but on their ability to put this knowledge to use to navigate different social and technological contexts (UNESCO 2005, 147–50). This is a skills and context-based understanding of literacy, in line with the New London Group's concept of 'multi-literacies', where the focus is on multi-modal meaning-making through linguistic, visual, audio, gestural and spatial practices (Cope and Kalantzis 2009, 166).

In regard to maths, mathematical literacy is therefore an understanding of elementary mathematics – concepts of structure, order and relations of spatial and measurable objects – and its practical use (Gardiner 2008). Basketmakers' ability to mentally deconstruct plaited patterns in order to understand their underlying structure is therefore a prime example of literacy in mathematics. In effect, craftwork involves its own forms of literacy, which I demonstrate below by drawing from my initial mistakes in learning plaiting work.

Plaiting baskets

The Pacific Islands have a long history of creating with plaited pandanus and have maintained the importance of these skills locally, producing a diverse handicraft industry that spans across this 'sea of islands' (Hau'ofa 1994). Within Vanuatu alone, different islands continue to work a range of different techniques, creating recognisably different styles and developing new basketry trends. Women's basketry in the country is celebrated as a vital form of contemporary cultural heritage (Bolton 2003, Kelly 1999) and as an important income generating activity (Geismar 2005). Women who work basketry are in turn celebrated for their creativity, skill and productivity in working these materials. Many ni-Vanuatu plaited baskets feature complex, eye-catching patterns worked on the oblique into the fabric of these textiles and many basketmakers enjoy the challenge of developing new patterns and styles, driving national fashions as they do so (Hazelgrove-Planel 2019).

Living on Futuna Island in the South of Vanuatu over 2014–15 while conducting anthropological fieldwork, I regularly joined women as they worked pandanus in their yard; cleaning and rolling pandanus leaves, straightening them in preparation for plaiting, or occasionally, picking up unfinished baskets and continuing the plaiting work. One day Pamali, a highly skilled pandanus worker and daughter of the local Pastor and his wife, asked me to work a brightly patterned *boks* basket (see figure 13.1), so named because of the inner box that structures this basket type. She gave me a quick demonstration and handed me the basket, going back to working on a mat she had been commissioned for. Pamali had already started work on the exterior walls of the basket she gave me, where the coloured pattern is worked, and so I had a sizeable section to use as a reference point.

Working the pandanus ribbons, I tried to follow the colour sequence I was aiming to achieve. I compared what I was doing to identical sections of the pattern elsewhere on the basket and used the sequence of colours as my guide. Following the colour work, I was trying to reproduce a system of criss-crossing red bands on a brown background; what I thought was the key to the pattern both visually and in terms of its construction. It was not, however, I later noticed, what Pamali had emphasized when showing me how to work the pattern. Pamali, like others who showed me how to work patterns, taught me through plaiting a section of the pattern herself. She hadn't drawn attention to the colour work – had in fact ignored it – and had instead given a practical demonstration of the rhythmic workings of the pattern.

My attention during Pamali's demonstration had been misdirected: I was focused on the coloured pattern and not the underlying structural pattern. The coloured pattern is an additional dimension to the pattern, but distracts, rather than aids in comprehending the structure of the

FIGURE 13.1 *Working the* boks *basket with the four-pointed star pattern and using the overall coloured pattern as a guide to work out the twill. With this method, I saw that all of the white and the red pandanus ribbons coming from the top right of the image would pass over and under the same sequence of ribbons from the bottom of the image (i.e. over 5 under 1, over 5 under 1). I had greater difficulty with the brown pandanus ribbons, where the sequence changed.*

FIGURE 13.2 *Completed pattern work on a* boks *basket. This is the four-pointed star pattern.*

plaited pattern. The structural pattern is seen through a rhythmic sequence of movements effected by the pandanus ribbons. For an oblique plaiter, understanding this rhythmic movement means embodying the pattern. Embodying the pattern means that a rhythm can be maintained, which is important for the work to be effective and regular (Bunn 1999, Franquemont and Franquemont 2004, Lindsay 1996.)

Demonstrations are, moreover, important in the process of learning, as when we see the bodily movements of another, the brain simulates and imagines the bodily movements for itself, thus gaining experience of the physical actions (Marchand 2008, 263–4). I had demonstrated my lack of skill in oblique plaiting (and knowledge of the use of demonstrations) by approaching the pandanus pattern visually and not as a plaited construction, surveying it from a distance rather than following the path of movement (Ingold 2007a, 91), which in this case was the rhythmic movement of pattern.

To work the pattern and to understand its construction, I had to disregard colour, the additional but more visible aspect of the pattern, and instead look at it in terms of the oblique line of rows I was working with. I had to think of the pattern in terms of the rhythmic path of movement in a set of rows worked on the oblique around the basket.[1] Thus, rather than following the twill[2] of individually coloured ribbons along the length of the basket from its base, what matters is the twill techniques in the movement of construction, see figure 13.3.

For locals on Futuna Island, the different twill techniques are named elements of construction, used to think about and think through plaited pattern work. Names for twill techniques on Futuna are in the local Futuna-Aniwa language, whereas names for most of the overall patterns are in Bislama.[3] In practice, pandanus workers describe their plaited patterns amongst themselves in terms of these different twill construction techniques. They adapt their language according to the situation and use pattern names that describe the whole pattern visually when talking with people unfamiliar with the techniques. The pattern in figure 13.1 can therefore be described to a visitor according to its visual aspect as *sta* (star) in Bislama, or to a local as a sequence of *rotoa* and *ngufe*, the two twill types that together form the overall pattern. *Ngufe* is a section where several

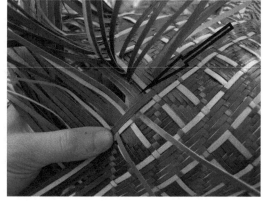

Figure 13.3 (a&b) *Two paths of movement. On the left is the path of construction, following a set of rows on an oblique line. On the right is the path of colour.*

ribbons are worked following the same twill sequence, while *rotoa* is an incremental increase or decrease in the twill. This use of language demonstrates that pandanus plaiters have a way of thinking about their patterns that is not commonly understood by people not literate in the technique.

Craft literacy

I began this chapter by suggesting that understanding the techniques of a craft demystifies it and makes it no longer enchanting. This is not to say that the beauty of the artefact or technique (Bunn 2018), and the skill of the craftsperson (Sennett 2008) cannot still enchant. On Futuna, people appreciate and take pride in the plaited pandanus work made on the island. Those who work pandanus have a keen sense of the different abilities and interests of pandanus workers. Some, like Pamali, have gained a reputation for being incredibly fast workers, while others, such as Nai, are known for their innovations. One skill that is frequently mentioned is the ability to reproduce patterns and baskets after seeing only the final form: *'hemi luk save nomo'* (she only has to see it to know) was a comment often made about women like Sepoa, Pamali or Saloki during my fieldwork. These women can understand and embody the twill techniques of construction of a pattern without having to see the rhythmic movement of the pattern as it is made by someone else.

Someone who 'only has to see a pattern to know it' is clearly both knowledgeable and skillful. While Sepoa, Pamali and Saloki are exceptionally skilled, this phrase is useful more broadly as it reveals what skill means in this context. In Bislama, *save* (to know) has its roots somewhere between the English 'savvy' and the French *savoir*. It is a wonderfully all-encompassing term that means 'can', 'to understand' and 'to know'. It therefore embraces both the embodied *savoir-faire* or 'knowing how', necessitating understanding, and the propositional *savoir*, 'knowing that', located in the mind (Ryle 1984). What is interesting about the phrase '*hemi luk save nomo*' then is the multiplicity of understandings achieved through seeing something, a patterned basket in this case. These ways of knowing allow someone to find meaning and interpret what they see. There are clear similarities between this and reading.

As in my example of learning to plait a pattern with Pamali above, a person is literate in a craft such as plaiting if they can understand what they see and interpret it in order to reproduce or use this knowledge in a practical context. They can mentally separate the visual whole of a pattern into its underlying structural parts and reproduce this physically in a basket. It may take several attempts, but the person's understanding of the inner workings of the craft technique, of how patterns are constructed and the importance of the direction of movement within this, allows them to create a physical reproduction of what they have in mind.

Craft literacy in this sense is the ability to (re)compose and (re)construct new patterns. It is a way of thinking that is particular to that craft technique. I argue that it is a physical example of mathematical thought as it is built upon an understanding of different structures and the relations between them. Literacy in a craft is therefore a deep comprehension of the craft technique, an in-depth understanding of the inner workings of pattern work and, crucially, the technology of the craft. Using the term craft literacy I think defends the value of craft as a technology and, crucially, demystifies it.

Thinking about plaited baskets

Basket patterns on Futuna Island are in fact deliberately made to confuse the gaze and to conceal the workings of a pattern from other pandanus workers. They are made to fascinate, catch the eye and to enchant, following Gell (1992). The basket pattern seen in figures 13.1 to 13.3 is a prime example of this technique as the structural pattern together with the additional coloured pattern combine to create several images. The overall pattern can therefore be perceived in several alternating ways: in terms of the dominant red bands bordered by white stripes on a brown background; as a series of interlocking four-pointed red stars; or by its structure, as a series of rectangles delineated by brown lines. Figure 13.4 shows the same pattern worked with different colour combinations to highlight these different possibilities.

The use of dyed pandanus ribbons in such a pattern serves to highlight different aspects of the pattern and so women experiment with their use of colour to this goal. A greater number of colours emphasizes the criss-crossing diagonal stripes whereas fewer colours draw out the stars and the rectangular pattern. The careful use of colour to create figure-ground reversals distracts people from seeing the underlying twill structure of a pattern and so the makers of such patterns demonstrate their power by their control over what is seen (Wagner 1987). Thus, the square base of *rotoa*, one of the core twill structures of the four-pointed star pattern, is more clearly seen in the undyed basket in figure 13.5. It may be noticed that even without dye, this *rotoa* pattern plays with the figure-ground reversal technique.

As previously noted, women who work these plaited patterns approach them not by visually surveying the whole pattern but by following the construction techniques and the rhythmic movement needed to create the pattern. This disconnect is similar to that described by Ingold in comparing our reading of printed and handwritten texts:

> Unlike his medieval predecessor – an inhabitant of the page myopically entangled in its inked traces – the modern reader *surveys* the page as if from a great height. . . he moves in terms of area. In so doing he occupies the page and asserts his mastery over it. But he does not inhabit it.

INGOLD 2007A, 92

The distinction between *inhabiting* the page – or basketry technique – and *surveying* it is crucial. In an overview, we miss the lines and paths of movement from which shape emerged; the lifelines through which the thing breathes and grows. In plaited pandanus work, it is therefore no surprise that pandanus workers look beyond the colour work to see the techniques and the flows of movement. Pandanus workers switch between the two modes of seeing, between surveying and inhabiting plaited pandanus forms and this provides them with greater insights. An oblique plaiter's ability to 'see through' surface colours to see the underlying structural components of a pattern requires a particular way of thinking that I consider to be an example of craft literacy.

FIGURE 13.4 *Variations on a pattern. These baskets all feature the four-pointed star pattern. The use of colour creates different visual effects, but the underlying twill structure is the same in all of the baskets.*

FIGURE 13.5 Rotoa *pattern worked on an undyed basket.*

Mathematical literacy of craft

There is no universally agreed upon definition of mathematics but rather a series of what may seem like rather vague statements, each proposed by the different schools of thought: logistic, formalist or intuitionist. Mathematics is therefore considered a form of logic, a study of the structures and properties of symbols, or an abstract, inductive construction and classification of phenomena (Black 1933). More generally, Sawyer defines mathematics as 'the classification and study of all possible patterns. . . [that is] *any kind of regularity that can be recognized by the mind'* (Sawyer 1982[1955],12). For the purpose of this discussion, I situate myself somewhere between the constructivism of intuitionism and Sawyer's view of underlying structures.

When pandanus workers in Vanuatu work with and make sense of patterns they are exploring the properties of forms and sequences of movement. They use twill structure to create a range of shapes, exploring the various forms, such as *rotoa*, and how these can be extended or reduced. They consider the relationship between different shapes, combining *rotoa* and *ngufe* in different orders. They create rhythm and movement through sequences of these shapes and techniques and study the possibilities available to them in their craft. Moreover, pandanus workers on Futuna favour twill structures which allow figure-ground reversal: they therefore play with form, creating multiple visual designs out of a single twill technique, as in figure 13.5.

Furthermore, in their work, pandanus plaiters work with multiple layers of meaning – working simultaneously with structural patterns and coloured patterns. In *Art and Agency*, Gell (1998, 77) explains that seeing and understanding a pattern means registering how it is constructed, understanding the relationship between parts and a whole and the translations that have been applied to them. He is interested in surface decorations. On Futuna Island, pandanus workers therefore see in several dimensions: they see what is visible, for example colour, and they see the underlying structure. They see the bodily movement needed for the construction of a pattern. Oblique plaiters move between the visual surface and the technology required to create it, interpreting what they see and translating this into what the body does. In plaiting patterns, craft workers have to be confident at manipulating plaited structures and techniques.

If mathematical literacy means having an understanding of simple mathematics and being able to put this to use, then basketmakers in Vanuatu demonstrably fulfil this condition. The contexts they work within are not those of formal mathematicians, but the exercises they work on have the same form. Basketmaking is a process where models are created and explored and its relationship to other models are analyzed. Basketmakers moreover put this into practice, giving their models physical forms. Their chosen technology is plaiting, but their ways of thinking are mathematical.

Notes

1 The path of movement, or process of construction, in oblique plaiting is to work several rows simultaneously, which means working several rows (up to about 14) along the oblique line. In contrast, in crafts like weaving or knitting, which are also worked in rows, the path of movement generally follows just one row at a time to form a perpendicular structure.

2 The twill is the sequence in which the pandanus strips pass over and under each other.

3 Bislama is one of the three national languages of Vanuatu.

Bibliography

Black, M. 1933 *The Nature of Mathematics*. London: Routledge and Kegan Paul Ltd.

Bolton, L. 2003 *Unfolding the Moon: Enacting Women's Kastom in Vanuatu*. Honolulu: University of Hawai'i Press.

Bunn, S. 1999 'The Importance of Materials', *Journal of Museum Ethnography* 11: 15–28.

Bunn, S. (ed.) 2018 *Anthropology and Beauty: From Aesthetics to Creativity*. Abingdon: Routledge.

Cope, B. and Kalantzis, M. 2009. 'Multiliteracies: New Literacies, New Learning', *Pedagogies: An International Journal* 164–195.

Franquemont, C. R. and Franquemont, E. M. 2004 'Tanka, Chongo, Kutij: Structure of the World through Cloth'. In D. K. Washburn and D. W. Crowe (eds), *Symmetry Comes of Age: The Role of Pattern in Culture*, pp. 177–215. Seattle: University of Washington Press.

Gardiner, A. 2008 'What is Mathematical Literacy?', *Proceedings of the 11th International Congress on Mathematical Education (ICME)*. Monterrey, Mexico.

Geismar, H. 2005 'Reproduction, Creativity, Restriction: Material Culture and Copyright in Vanuatu', *Journal of Social Archaeology* 5 (1): 25–51.

Gell, A. 1992 'The Technology of Enchantment and the Enchantment of Technology'. In J. Coote and A. Shelton (eds), *Anthropology, Art and Aesthetics*, pp. 40–63. Oxford: Clarendon Press.

Gell, A. 1998 *Art and Agency: An Anthropological Theory*. Oxford: Clarendon Press.

Hau'ofa, E. 1994 'Our Sea of Islands', *The Contemporary Pacific* 6 (1): 148–161.

Hazelgrove-Planel, L. 2019 Weaving Through Life: An Ethnographic Study of the Significance of Pandanus Work to the People of Futuna Island, Vanuatu. Unpublished PhD Thesis, University of St Andrews.

Ingold, T. 2007a *Lines: A Brief History.* London: Routledge.

Kelly, S. K. 1999 *Unwrapping Mats: People, Land and Material Culture in Tongoa, Central Vanuatu.* PhD thesis, London: University College London.

Lindsay, S. 1996 Hand Drumming: An Essay in Practical Knowledge. In M. Jackson (ed) *Things as They Are: New Directions in Phenomenological Anthropology*, 196–212. Bloomington: Indiana University Press.

Marchand, T. H. J. 2007 Crafting Knowledge: The Role of 'Parsing and Production' in the Communication of Skill-Based Knowledge among Masons. In M Harris (ed), *Ways of Knowing: Anthropological Approaches to Crafting Experience and Knowledge*, 181–202. New York: Berghahn Books.

Marchand, T. H. J. 2008 'Muscles, Morals and Mind: Craft Appreticeship and the Formation of the Person', *British Journal of Educational Studies* 53 (3): 245–271.

Mauss, M. 1979 *Sociology and Psychology: Essays.* Translated by Ben Brewster. London: Routledge and Kegan Paul.

Merriam W. 2018 *Literate.* Accessed 8 June 2018: https://www.merriam-webster.com/dictionary/literate#h1.

Ryle, G. 1984 *The Concept of Mind.* Chicago, IL: University of Chicago Press.

Sawyer, W. W. 1982 [1955] *Prelude to Mathematics.* New York: Dover Publications, Inc.

Sennett, R. 2008 *The Craftsman.* New Haven, CT: Yale University Press.

UNESCO 2005 *Education for All: Global Monitoring Report 2006.* Paris: UNESCO.

Wagner, R. 1987 'Figure-Ground Reversal Among the Barok'. In L. Lincoln (ed), *Assemblage of Spirits: Idea and Image in New Ireland*, pp. 56–62. New York: George Braziller.

PART THREE

Gathering knowledge: Basketry as a medium of memory, belonging and evocation

Introduction
Victoria Mitchell

Although the traditional materials of basketry are easily perishable, and material remains are therefore limited in quantity and extent, much evidence exists to indicate its extensive continuity and unassailable ubiquity. Basketry is now widely collected by museums, for example, and knowledge of basketry, including the cultural narratives and social identities it embodies, are increasingly disseminated in the 'public' domain; what were once local basketry traditions (and in some locations still survive as such) can be compared, distinguished, analysed and generally 'made known' as a network of relationships rather than as confined to local roots. In addition, knowledge of basketry is articulated through verbal records, oral testimony, archaeological traces, photographs, prints and paintings, for example.

Contemporary basketry artists are often adept at drawing on this wide range of sources in their innovative reworkings of and experimentation with materials and forms, such as represented here by Caroline Dear (Parts 1 and 3) and Joe Hogan (Part 3), who draw on both local testimony as well as on more widely distributed contexts in their endeavours. That both of them write about their work as well as making it is also significant – the voice of the maker is beyond compare as a fount of that which otherwise might not or would not be communicated. For Hogan, oral testimony and embodied knowledge of traditional ways of working is formative of his own basketry and is additionally recounted through the written word. Dear similarly reflects on ways in which the intangible becomes tangible; basketry, even in the form of a long-discarded puffin snare, carries memories of the people and peoples for whom it was significant which can be recalled through acts of making in the present.

While baskets conveniently contain goods to be carried it is also the case that basketry, in the breadth of knowledge which it articulates, additionally functions to carry stories and modes of wisdom-making, many of which are rooted in the deep past and allude to culturally poignant symbolic narratives in the present; for all it's apparent simplicity, it can serve as a locus of power and a container of complex history and heritage. John Mack's focus on 'baskets of wisdom' in the accession rituals of royalty amongst the Kuba peoples highlights the function of containment, in this instance as a form of mythological concealment for which possession of the basket is 'the guarantor of access to the fundamental things of royal inheritance'. Beyond the individual maker, such baskets are invested with the ancestry, wisdom and potency of the people at critical times of royal succession.

Although the spirit of ancestry is woven into the layered fabric of reference in Lissant Bolton's account of curating the British Museum's exhibition *Baskets and Belonging: Indigenous Australian Histories* it is above all a sense of place or 'country' that emerges as the most potent locus of narrative. Place evokes belonging, not only for the location of materials but also with respect to the identity of those who gather or gathered them for the basketry that hence carries and tells the story of that belonging. The effect of historical circumstances on place is also an intrinsic aspect of the narrative that emerges, and is one which the exhibition unfolded with care, with reference not only to collectors who make such exhibitions possible but also to the contemporary makers who have revitalised this sense of belonging in imaginative ways.

The distinctiveness of place and the unfolding of layered narratives are also central to the basketry traditions and practices recounted in different ways by Hugh Cheape for Atlantic Scotland and by Stephanie Bunn for Scotland as a whole. Both authors note the way in which plant fibres were sought after, processed and adapted for specific and varied basketry uses, reflecting the care and ingenuity that was practiced in adapting to the often-challenging environment of Scotland. Both accounts draw on oral accounts or 'hearsay' and on artefacts that have been collected or photographed, but whereas Cheape draws extensively on historical contexts and written, often literary evidence, Bunn has a worked with members the Scottish Basketmakers' Circle and others to capture an 'on location' example of basketry culture as it is now, poised between a disappearing past and an energetic renewal of interest in the present. That is a story in itself.

14

Snare and enfold

Caroline Dear

Memory is enfolded into an object when we handle the material to make it. The touch of the hand and the essence and smell of the material intertwine. The memory of making is embedded within the skill, the knowledge of the material is encoded within the making.

As part of the *Cuimhne* symposium and exhibition at An Lanntair Arts Centre in Stornoway on the Isle of Lewis, I made a contemporary snare inspired by the puffin snare in the accompanying exhibition. The puffin snare, on loan from the Highland Folk Museum in Newtonmore, was collected by I.F. Grant from St. Kilda. My memory snare, in contrast, is a collaborative piece made to celebrate the traditional skill of rope-making and to ensnare people's memories of rope (Fig 14.1).

The museum puffin snare comprises a central two-ply rope (at present this material is unidentified) of about one metre long with forty snoods of fine horsehair rope coming off both sides. Originally, a small rock was bound at each end and these were wedged into crevices at a place known to be favoured by puffins. The puffins were trapped by their own inquisitive nature, as observed by the Kearton brothers on St Kilda in 1896. 'He pulled several of the nooses about with his beak, and after a while grew bolder. Poor bird! His inquisitiveness cost him something; for in the course of his investigations one of his feet slipped through a noose, and when he came to lift his leg he discovered he was a prisoner.' (Kearton 1899, 109). Many birds were caught this way in a single haul, 'In Martin's time the natives caught forty or fifty birds a day with a snare' (ibid.112). He is referring to Martin Martin from Skye, who was the first to document traditions from the Western Isles and St Kilda.

In contrast the memory snare is made with a central rope of soft rush with many thin rope nooses made of grass (*Fescue*) and moss (*Polytrichum*) and the ends bound with moss bundles.

FIGURE 14.1 *Caroline Dear, Puffin snare, pen and ink drawing, 2018.*

FIGURE 14.2 *Looking at memory snare labels. Photograph: C. Dear.*

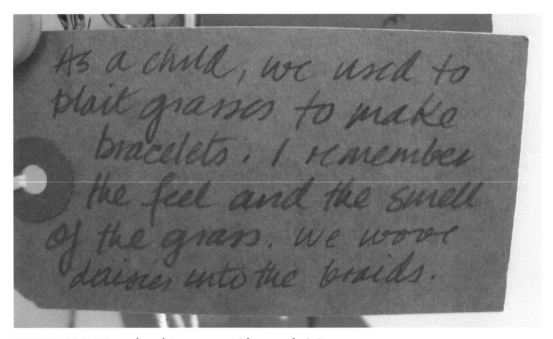

FIGURE 14.3 *'We used to plait grasses . . .' Photograph: S. Bunn*

FIGURE 14.4 *Making rope for the snare. Photograph: C. Dear.*

This snare acts to gather and celebrate people's personal rope memories. I taught participants how to make rope by hand, using the method traditionally employed in Lewis, and while making rope, I asked people about their own memories of ropes. Conversations developed around rope; its past and present uses; personal memories; and the evocative power to connect. Each person wrote out their own memories and attached these to a snare. Over the course of the symposium the snare filled up with personal memories, forming not only a document of the event and making visible intangible links to the past, but it was also honouring and valuing these individual memories.

As an artist I am interested in making the intangible tangible. Using traditional skills, making objects, or through the direct process of interaction and conversation, these fragile threads then become visible. Memories become tangible, materials link people to place, traditional skills connect us to the knowledge that we didn't know we had, smell rekindles vision and touch lights up emotion.

Some rope memories ensnared at *Cuimhne*, Stornoway 23–24th April 2018:

> 'Last summer my dad showed me where to cut the marram grass on the machair and how to bind it for making a *bann*.'

> 'When I was a child we used to twist and plait grasses to make ropes, and then made necklaces and bracelets from them, I remember the feel and smell of it.'

> 'In days of deep grief, I made wool into rope and wove it across my room and wove it into a new life.'

> 'My *seanair* had a wooden boat and we would go out fishing together, I remember enjoying the touch of the rope we used to tie the sheet up as well as the line we'd use to fish.'

> 'A never-ending roll of binding twine scenting my childhood, it was used for tying everything and lived in every shed as we moved from place to place.'

> 'My neighbour used to be a cowboy in Argentina; he used old bits of rope to lasso things in our garden.'

FIGURE 14.5 *Memory snare/Puffin snare. Photographs: C. Dear.*

'I remember noticing the fishing boats in Stornoway harbour, those coming from the outer lying areas had mooring ropes made of heather, which floated.'

'My father had a lorry and used rope to secure his loads of timber – so for me rope was always blue in colour and stank of oil and grease and your hands got black when you used them.'

'As a child, many years ago, I used a long hemp rope for skipping – I remember it sore on my legs.'

'Stornoway's rope walk is just a few hundred yards away and where rope used by my seafaring ancestors was made.'

Memory snare

How to catch a memory?

1   Make a short length of rope from grass or rush. Try to find out how to do this in the traditional way.

2   While making, think about the feel of the material in your hands, the movement of your hands and the plant material you are using.

3   Do you have a particular memory relating to rope?

- making some as a child
- tying a special knot
- learning to bind
- plying rope or thread
- combining different thicknesses

- gathering materials to make rope
- learning a skill using rope

4 Recount your memory, story or anecdote as you work.

5 When your rope is finished write your memory down on one of the paper strips and attach this to the short length of rope you made, 'the snare'.

There are spare ropes for you to use if you don't want to make your own. Please feel free to attach lots of memories to your rope, snare.

Bibliography

Dwelly, E. 1994 *The Illustrated Gaelic–English Dictionary*. Glasgow: Gairm.
Kearton, R. and C. 1899 *With Nature and a Camera*. London: Cassell.
Martin, M. 1994 *A Description of the Western Islands of Scotland circa 1695*. Stirling: Birlinn.

15

Irish woven communities:

A glimpse into the Irish indigenous basketry tradition

Joe Hogan

My introduction to the indigenous baskets of Ireland came about when my near neighbour, Tommy Joyce, came armed with a bundle of willow rods and, having found a suitable spot in the field behind our house, showed me how to make a donkey creel. This was the primary basket in this area of Connemara in the west of Ireland. Two creels were placed on a wooden yoke and straw straddle mat and used as donkey panniers for bringing peat, or 'turf' as it's usually called in Ireland, down from mountain bogs. The creel was used for any task where a basket for storage or carrying would be useful, so each hill farm in this area would have had several creels in use.

We had moved to the area a few weeks previously to attempt a life of basketmaking, gardening and small-scale farming. When Tommy called to our house to welcome us, he mentioned that he himself was a basketmaker and that he would show me how to make a creel when his rods had seasoned a bit. He had harvested the rods from his own willow bed, or 'sally garden'. Each farm in the area had a small willow bed of this sort so that the rods needed for making the necessary farm baskets could be harvested annually.

So it was, on a fine April day in 1978, that Tommy marked a rectangle in the area of smooth grass he had chosen and began by pushing the strongest rods into the ground to begin making a creel. This basket, it should be explained, is made upside down, with the weaving proceeding around the uprights, the uprights being then folded over to form the base. The opening weave, the mouth-wale, is quite complex and was used not only for creels, but also for *currachs* or coracles and was, I was to discover, unique to Ireland and areas of Scotland and Wales.

Thus, began my journey of discovery into the world of the traditional baskets of the Irish countryside. This was a wonderful and exciting insight into a world of skills which I had barely known existed and it certainly fostered in me a love and an appreciation of basketmaking which has deepened over the years. I remain deeply grateful for the mentoring and encouragement I have received from different basketmakers from this time. This kind of giving is rarely a direct exchange, and I would wish to be as helpful as possible to others who are finding their way in this craft now. When one unearths a hidden world like this, one develops a better understanding of the people who practiced these skills, the ease with which they felt at home in their place on this earth, and the wide range of skills they had. The idea of useful and meaningful work was understood by almost everyone and people took great pleasure in their work and in doing it well. Having spent a few years in an urban setting and having seen young people unemployed and disaffected, seeing people engaged in their work like this had a profound effect upon me.

The creel Tommy had shown me was only one of several different styles of creel. Thus, in the limestone area of the Burren, where hazel grew freely, creels, though similar in shape to the Connemara creel, were made from hazel. There was also a creel with a hinged bottom, known as a *pardóg* (Fig 15.1). This was used to transport manure and the load could be released to fall on to the ground. Creels in parts of Ulster had rounded bottoms reflecting, perhaps, a Scottish heritage, since this is a feature of many Scottish creels. Most creels had double stakes, ensuring the basket was very robust and strong, but some were single staked, especially those designed to be carried by a person.

Another basket in widespread use in this area was the *skib*. This was a flat circular basket used for straining, and then serving, potatoes. In many cases this took the place of a table and acted as a communal serving dish. This shape is very much associated with the west coast of Ireland, in particular the counties of Galway and Mayo. After use, the *skib* was washed and hung up on a wall

FIGURE 15.1 *Hinged bottomed D-shaped hazel creel known as* pardog *by Joe Hogan.*

FIGURE 15.2 *Grid base* skib *with inner* skib *by Joe Hogan.*

and this practice gave rise to a more recent fashion of using the *skib* as a wall decoration. The one shown here (Fig 15.2) has an inner basket which was used as a container for a bowl of milk into which the potatoes were dipped as they were being eaten. When I make *skibs* I use different varieties of coloured willows to enhance their decorative quality.

In other regions of the country a frame basket known as a *sciathog* (pronounced ski-ogue) had the same use, and again there were regional variations. Most began with two central ribs but an interesting variation shown here (Fig 15.3) begins with one central rib. This *sciathog* was made by Alison Fitzgerald, a superb maker of frame baskets. A closely related basket, which uses a similar type of framework, was the Ulster potato-harvesting basket. There were, of course, potato-harvesting baskets made throughout the country but these Ulster baskets were made in their thousands around Lough Neagh and this is one of the few instances where a traditional basket style came to be made commercially in large basketmaking workshops. They were sent for sale to other potato growing regions, particularly in the east and midlands of Ireland.

There was a wide variety of baskets used for fishing. Along with professionally made herring crans used on commercial fishing trawlers, the baskets to which I am referring here are those used by small-scale fishermen and most of these were made by the fishermen themselves. There were baskets used for holding baited long lines and, although all were low, shallow-shaped baskets, there was a marked variation in how they were made. In the north-east, these were frame baskets, similar in construction to a *sciathog,* but in the west of Ireland and the Aran Islands

FIGURE 15.3 Sciathog *by Alison Fitzgerald.*

a low basket with a flat base and pointed end known as a *ribh* was used. There were also baskets used for catching eels and crabs.

One of the most interesting fishing baskets, to my mind, is the Connemara lobster pot (Fig 15.4). These pots were still in use in the early 1980s around Killary Harbour near where I live. I managed to get one from a man called Festy Mortimer, one of the last fishermen makers. He pointed out to me that it had been made of wild willow, a variety known locally as 'black sally' (*salix caprea, salix cinerea, salix aurita* or their crosses). Although this willow was brittle and the rods often broke, it was chosen because the wood was much harder than that of the normal sally rod (common osier or *salix viminalis*). Thus, it would last at least three seasons in the water before rotting as opposed to only one, or at best, two seasons. The lobster pot had a special weave, an elaboration of common pairing, which ensured the weave could not readily slip up and down. This contributed hugely to its strength and longevity. By the late 1970s, knowledge of this weave was all but lost and the sides of most pots were simply paired. But makers still used the real lobster pot weave when joining in new rods and there were enough clues in the pots to allow me to rediscover it. I have found the lobster pot weave useful in many situations where strength is required and I am delighted to have added it to my language of techniques.

In the south-west of Ireland, there was a very beautiful bell-shaped lobster pot, similar in style to those made in Brittany and in Cornwall. In fact, as described by Tomás O Croimthán in *The Islandman*, the fishermen of the south-west learned lobster pot making from French fishermen from about 1890 onwards as they had not previously tried to catch them. On the exposed and

FIGURE 15.4 *Connemara lobster pot by Joe Hogan.*

windswept north-west coast of Mayo there was very little willow growing, so fishermen harvested common heather (*caluna vulgaris*) from mountain slopes and cliffs where it had not been grazed by sheep. There it had an opportunity to grow to long lengths for making pots. (Fig 15.5). Heather was certainly not an easy material to weave but the pots had remarkable longevity in the water and thus the extra trouble was justified.

Whereas using heather was exceptional, straw was widely available throughout the Irish countryside. Although probably most commonly used for making the straddle mats used in conjunction with donkey creels, it was also used for making hens nests, baskets for storing grain and food and for seed-sowing baskets. There were two quite distinct techniques. Hens nests were made by a plaiting technique, a method also used for the straddle mat, mattresses and storage baskets. Oat straw was usually the preferred material for this technique though rye straw was occasionally used. Seed-sowing baskets were made by sewing rows of straw, one on top of the other, a technique often referred to as *lipe* or coilwork. For this, more rigid straw such as wheat could be used and split bramble for sewing. This technique is practiced in some form in almost every basketmaking culture in the world, but was used in quite a particular way in Ireland. Straw was also widely used for making ropes. It was twisted using a winder known as a *thraw-hook*, a task for two people. The more skillful task involved feeding the straw evenly into the rope. These ropes, known as *sugáns,* were used for seating chairs, securing thatch and numerous other jobs around the farm.

FIGURE 15.5 *Detail of heather lobster pot.*

In my experience of exploring Irish basketwork, I would say that no living tradition remains static. When a traditional skill is thriving then skills are being honed and improved but when a skill-base is in decline then the level of skill one sees rarely does justice to that making culture when it was in its prime. I have heard people remarking that a particular basket was too perfectly made to represent a tradition. This type of thinking assumes that a snapshot of a skill-base in decline gives a representative picture and I very much doubt if that is the case. Most properly motivated makers want to make the best basket possible for them to make. Sometimes constraints, such as poor material, lack of skill or insufficient time, may prevent them from making a basket as well as they would like, but the goal of the good craftsperson is nonetheless to aim for a high standard of work.

For me, the discovery and exploration of the rich tradition of Irish indigenous techniques has deepened my understanding of what respect for a place and the materials found there can bring to one's making. The poet Anne Michaels advises us to 'find a way to make beauty necessary, find a way to make necessity beautiful'. I think almost all indigenous basketry traditions throughout the world accomplish this. They take local materials and with a profound understanding of the potential of these materials transform them into beautiful and necessary objects. In places where these baskets are no longer considered necessary this is a loss to that material culture. The baskets can still, however, be appreciated for their beauty and skill and also for the light they shed on a way of living in harmony with the world around us. In my own case, I now make more sculptural baskets than functional ones but the technical solutions and a great many of the techniques I use come from the indigenous tradition of this country.

Bibliography

Estyn Evans, E. 1967 *Irish Folkways.* London: Routledge
Hogan, J. 2001 *Basketmaking in Ireland.* Co. Wicklow: Wordwell
Ó Croimthán (Crohan), T. 1978 *The Islandman.* Oxford: Oxford University Press

16

The primordial basket

John Mack

Discussions of the order in which different crafts and technologies have made their appearance in human history will always be hindered by the lack of consistent evidence of datable organic materials from the deep past. There is, as a result, no 'fibre' age with its basketry and weaving practices to set in the sequence of inorganic materials and associated technologies which otherwise delimit the pervasive scientific model of technological and cultural progress. But the emphasis on certain durable materials – stone, bronze and iron – as cultural markers is, in any case, at odds with the direction some material culture studies have taken recently. Tim Ingold has argued in a number of publications (2000, 2007, 2010) for an approach which emphasises what he has termed a 'textilic' model of how things come to be made. The focus is on process rather than product. It is innovative in following the course of the interactions of the maker with their materials, working forwards through the act of making rather than backwards. It thus contests an approach which regards the object as if it were robotically reproduced, embodying a predictable intentionality that can be recovered.

Some disciplines are better equipped than others to chart the alternative course. Archaeology, as the primary route into the study of prehistory, is challenged from the start in having to begin not just from found things, but often from the fragmentary remains of things. The bits have to be brought together and reimagined, remaking the whole object from which to then work backwards to the circumstances of its original creation. The implication is that the reconstructed object is, as all objects are assumed to be, the realisation of an intellectual model which is mechanically recreated in the process of its making, and which is therefore recoverable. An alternative 'textilic' model already implies applicability to the weaving of fibres and the ways in which form arises in being built up organically through the skilled engagement of a maker with their materials. As metaphor, however, it is also a useful and radical way to think about processes of making in general, whether the materials are organic or inorganic.

This absence of fibre technologies in western scientific discourse about the remote past, it is argued here, is not necessarily replicated in other ways of constructing the past in other cultural traditions. The objects to be considered in this chapter are not fragmentary, nor have they fallen out of use. Rather they are things which continue to be made and which have a recognized place – indeed, in some cases a primary one – within an ongoing regime of value in which they contain not just prized 'things' but non-material phenomena, such as restricted forms of knowledge and potent sources of insight. The examples discussed are baskets from west central Africa whose significance is established in various cycles of myth. The essay begins by discussing their occurrence amongst the Kuba peoples before widening out to explore related examples in the wider equatorial forest region.

In 1908 the Hungarian-born ethnographer Emil Torday visited Mushenge (Nsheng), the capital of the kingdom of the Kuba peoples in the south of what is now the Democratic Republic of the Congo (DRC). As an accomplished linguist - and being possessed of an engaging personality - he was able to gain exceptional access to the Kuba ruler (*nyim*) and his court. The outcome of his work there was what has become a foundational text on Kuba culture (Torday and Joyce 1911) and the formation of one of the most comprehensive documented collections of the art and material culture of the area, most of which is now in the British Museum (Mack 1990). In neither his writing nor the collections do baskets feature significantly, though other fibre arts (notably, raffia weaving and embroidery) are more conspicuous. Most attention has focused on Kuba woodcarving, much covered with elaborate geometric patterning. Amongst these, the most celebrated objects are a series of figures of individual kings (*ndop*), three of which, described by Torday as 'portraits', are in the British Museum. But, as with the naming of the technological ages of prehistory, the absence of significant attention to basketry in particular is deceptive and at odds with other evidence of Kuba thinking about its place in the history of their culture.

An immediate indication of the pervasiveness of fibre-derived references is the number of interlocking patterns carved on a wide range of wood surfaces that seem to be derived from textiles, mats and baskets – such as the sequence of patterns and their variants known as *imbolo* (Torday, 1925: 219, Figs. 23, 24) (Fig. 16.1). Beyond that, as persuasive a collector – and as diligent a fieldworker – as Torday was, there remained one important class of basket which went unremarked. These are the so-called 'baskets of wisdom' of which there are usually two at any one time, one of which remains as part of the inheritable property of royalty and a second which is made for an incumbent king and is buried with him when he dies. One of the baskets has a looped attachment above the lid and it is this which is handed down to successive kings. Its significance within the royal treasury is explained in a cycle of myths, versions or equivalents of which are found more widely in this part of the DRC and surrounding areas.[1] The Kuba myth in various forms relates the origins of the Kuba state. It concerns the Kuba equivalent of Adam, a figure known as Woot, who is identified as having created the Kuba peoples through an act of incest. Once this was discovered, he was obliged to flee and carried with him a basket – the prototype of the basket of wisdom – in which was contained the accumulated knowledge by which chiefs exercise prudent governance and the associated regalia and magical devices in which

FIGURE 16.1 *Variations of the* imbolo *design found on many Kuba carved objects and assumed to be derived from methods of interlocking fibres in basketry, textiles and mats. Democratic Republic of Congo. (After Torday, 1925: 219, Figs. 23, 24).*

it is invested. On taking flight, the basket with its cargo of the vital attributes of kingship was hidden in a tree, left there to be collected by Woot's favourite son who belonged to his chosen section of the Kuba polity (Vansina 1978, 24). However, instead of the son for whom it was intended, it was discovered by a Pygmy, a trickster figure, who in turn passed it to the ancestor of a different section of the Kuba, the Bushoong, who thereby took (and retain) the right to elect the paramount ruler of the Kuba.

Possession of the basket is, in effect, the guarantor of access to the fundamental things of royal inheritance. This passing on of the 'basket of wisdom' remains a central part of the installation rites of kings, though its actual contents are a secret known only to a few privileged courtiers who act as the guardian of the baskets and the ruler, who is permitted a peek inside during the process of his investiture. (Mack 2019, chapter 2: 'The Death of Kings'). Thereafter, the baskets are displayed on formal occasions and the *nyim* might typically lean on the basket during sessions of the royal court, supported physically and mystically by its presence (Fig. 16.2). Arguably, in terms of Kuba conception the basket is of considerably more importance than the famous sculpted figures of

FIGURE 16.2 *Parts of the Kuba royal treasury including the two 'baskets of wisdom'. Democratic Republic of Congo. (AP.0.0.26217 Royal Museum of Central Africa, Tervuren, Belgium; photo: L. Achten, 1927).*

kings which Torday and others were permitted to collect. The *ndop* has a significant role in the interregnum between the death of one king and the installation of a successor, but subsequently it would be placed in storage with the figures of previous rulers (Vansina 1972). The baskets, in contrast, retained a central and ongoing importance in ensuring the continuing vitality of the kingdom, their concealed contents rendering them inalienable.[2]

A related series of myths amongst the Luba in the south-east of the DRC also attributes a leading role to baskets in the creation and continuity of royal power, but it is more explicit about its hidden contents. Again, an act of incest is the prelude to the founding of kingship with the same ambiguous implications; and there is a similar story about the switch of kingship from one intended incumbent to another with ensuing risks of conflict. In the genesis myths of the Luba a 'sacred basket' contains the head and the genitals of the original ruler who is killed on account of his cruelty. The inheritance of such baskets was part of an enchainment which linked rulers to the sources of power of their predecessors, as amongst the Kuba. An account recorded in the 1920s in a missionary source reports that in the past the body of a deceased ruler would be allowed to rot until the head could be removed by being screwed off (the spilling of blood by cutting being judged inappropriate in the case of royalty). It would then be smoked and dried out before being added to the basket of royal relics (Burton 1961: 19). Until then the fact of the death of a chief or king would not be acknowledged and only when the basket was ready, with its newly prepared skull inside, would a successor be announced.

A number of common features stand out in these parallel cycles of myth. One is that, although neither posits an origin of baskets, in both cases they are credited with preserving the fundamental things of the kingdom without which kingship forfeits its efficacy. Amongst the Kuba this is particularly notable. The founding ruler of the Kuba, a *nyim* known as Shyaam aMbul aNgoong, is credited with having introduced the arts for which the Kuba are well known: skills in woodcarving; textile-making and -decoration; and blacksmithing. Baskets are not cited as having been invented because they were already in existence when humanity came into the world.

What is also evident is that baskets are referenced as having a dual role: they contain but they also conceal. Amongst the Luba another story of kings is pertinent and, as with the Kuba narrative above, it highlights switches in the rightful accession to kingship. This concerns a king who went off with his army to attack the neighbouring Songye peoples with whom they were in conflict. He was, however, decisively beaten in battle and when he did not return an alternative eligible male successor, Miketo, was identified and duly installed as ruler. Later, however, the missing king was found by a female relative of Miketo near the royal court and, on advice, Miketo arranged for him to be killed. This duly happened and, in accordance with practice, the head of the deposed ruler was secretly removed, prepared and put in the sacred basket. This was then placed in the care of a guardian with instructions it should never be opened, and no one should be permitted to look inside. His wife, however, disobeyed the order and, when it became known that the skull was there, it was resolved to kill Miketo in his turn and seek the investiture of a new ruler from a different lineage (Reefe *c.*1981, 116–17). Unauthorized looking inside the basket has dramatic consequences for the governance of the kingdom.

These are not isolated themes: aspects of them can be traced in the use of baskets elsewhere in the equatorial region of west central Africa, even if not so explicitly cited in myth. The most obvious examples are in Gabon where in precolonial times skulls were kept in containers often surmounted by a so-called 'guardian' figure, a sculpted wood head or full figure planted in the reliquary.[3] The skulls were those of warriors who had died at the height of their powers rather than

FIGURE 16.3 *Reliquary baskets containing skulls and surmounted by copper-plated wood images. Gabon. Engraving from Pierre Savorgnan de Brazza,* Tour du Monde, *1888, vol 2, p. 50.*

of the young or infirmed; and they might also include the relics of enemies killed in battle and sometimes reliquaries stolen from other villages. They were kept as a resource of mystical powers that might invigorate the living. Baskets were often the container of choice but, if not, they would be simply constructed from forest materials, particularly bark formed into a kind of box (Fig. 16.3). Further south, the Kongo peoples had what are known in translation as 'baskets of ancestors' which were kept suspended in a special hut above a fire kept going night and day (Van Wing 1960, 318). The contents of these baskets included the hair, finger nails and bones of chiefs, religious leaders and albinos (the later regarded as quintessentially ancestral because of their whiteness: the colour of the dead). The claws, teeth and hair of leopards killed by renowned hunters might also be incorporated with the assembled relics.

Baskets are also widely used as containers of magical and other empowered and empowering devices whose sources of agency is systematically concealed from those not professionally engaged in their use. However, evidence from the southern parts of the DRC and neighbouring areas suggests that, although the baskets used may be indistinguishable in terms of shape and materials from other baskets in daily use, they themselves undergo a particular form of what might be called initiation before they are used in divination. Among the Luvale only menopausal women may make them and it is understood that they are replicating baskets which have been made back into antiquity for divinatory purposes: they remain in existence as part of a continuous process. Indeed, when worn out, they are buried on a termite hill, unlike similarly constructed food baskets which are simply discarded. When made, they also go through a special procedure before they can be pressed into service: they are not bought but must be stolen by the diviner who is then obliged to recompense the maker for the theft (Silva, 1998). In use, the diviner sifts through the hidden divinatory materials in the special basket to determine the causes of affliction besetting a client and identifies palliative actions.

In all of these cases, then, baskets made to contain objects with an ancestral or magical agency secrete their contents within an interior space which is itself seen as having existed throughout time. Dark interiors, unseen by all but a few suitably empowered individuals, are reservoirs of fecundity, deep knowledge and efficacy. Where scientific constructions seek undeniable evidence, myth affirms hypothesis. In Kuba myth baskets are explicitly identified as *the* primordial container whose intended purpose of passing on kingly acumen is intercepted and redirected by a Pygmy, representative of the original peoples of the forests. Luba royal baskets contain royal relics passed on from one ruler to the next in a continuous chain. Baskets of ancestors are bathed in the smoke of an eternal fire while the baskets of diviners, though replaced periodically, are thought of as having a continuous existence.

Blacksmithing needs fire and associated technology to turn rock into metal tools; carving needs iron-bladed adzes and knives to turn blocks of wood into sculpture and receptacles. Of course, pottery and calabashes might provide alternative early vessels equivalent to baskets in being made from a natural source material with minimal preparation. However, as regards pottery the Kuba lack ready sources of clay and, although they use pots, these are largely imported from neighbouring areas. In myth, calabashes occur as an unreliable receptacle. They are explicitly contrasted with basketry, presented as fragile when humanity poured out into the world through cracks in a calabash which allowed its contents – people – to disperse. Baskets and basketry are, in these various guises, promoted as the original art.

The mythic logic is compelling. Baskets are much more than humble domestic objects. They provide a dependable coffer in which to preserve and conceal the most important of things. They are to that extent the model for other kinds of object. Baskets have practical use and they are also visual (and, no doubt, linguistic) metaphor. In all these features they assume a cultural priority which the archaeologist's version of the early stages of technological development otherwise sidestep. They are similarly overlooked in almost all the histories, ethnographies, and art surveys of this part of the African continent. Yet, there is an unassailable case that the fibre arts which these myths and practices from equatorial Africa highlight, served – and continue to serve – as a significant intellectual and empowering resource alongside the technological advances and materials dignified in western discourse as successive 'Ages' in prehistory.

In summary, one implication of this attribution of primacy to basketry is to associate it with ideas of authenticity. The first things of importance were those that have lasted and the source of the continuities of society and kin groups. In sub-Saharan Africa those who encountered baskets with this attributed significance were prone to give them colourful names which are still in use: 'baskets of memory', 'of the ancestors', 'of knowledge' or 'of wisdom'. Something similar may have happened amongst the Maori who also have what are commonly translated as 'baskets of wisdom'. Similarly, in Buddhist belief the term 'three baskets of wisdom' (*tripitaka*) refers to canonical texts, originally texts written on leaves and kept in baskets, *pitaka*. In west central Africa we have noted variety in their contents, but in many places where this trope occurs the baskets contain the relics of deceased rulers. And in each case, there is an emphasis on their possession, control or influence as a mark of the right of succession to authority. The baskets are, in effect, instruments that underlie both statehood and the integrity of the polity itself in terms both of governance and the intellectual and mystical attributes which support it. Baskets are the container of choice for this primordial role.

Notes

1 I have discussed aspects of these mythic foundations in relation to basketry at greater length in a contribution to an edited publication (Mack, J. (forthcoming) 'Baskets of Wisdom: An Equatorial African Complex', in *Basketry and Beyond: Constructing Culture*, ed. T. A. Heslop and H. Anderson. Leiden: Brill).

2 The one example of a royal basket I am aware of that was allowed to be acquired is a reproduction collected by Father Joseph Cornet for the National Museum in Kinshasa, DRC. It is illustrated in Cornet, 1982, 307 (Cornet, J. 1982 *Art Royal Kuba*. Milan: Edizioni Sipiel).

3 For an overview see Perrois, L. 2011 *Arts du Gabon*. Geneva: Muse Barbier-Mueller.

Bibliography

Burton, W. F. P. 1961 *Luba Religion and Magic in Custom and Belief*. Tervuren, Belgium: Musée Royal de l'Afrique Centrale.

Cornet, J. 1982 *Art Royal Kuba*. Milan: Edizioni Sipiel.

Ingold, T. 2000 'On Weaving a Basket'. In *The Perception of the Environment: Essays on Livelihood, Dwelling and Skill*. London: Routledge, pp. 339–348.

Ingold, T. 2007 *Lines: A Brief History*. London: Routledge.

Ingold, T. 2010 'The Textility of Making', *Cambridge Journal of Economics* 34 (1): 91–102.

Mack, J. 1990 *Emil Torday and the Art of the Congo, 1900–1909*. London: British Museum Publications.

Mack, J. 2019 *The Artfulness of Death in Africa*. London: Reaktion Books.

Mack, J. (forthcoming) 'Baskets of Wisdom: An Equatorial African Complex'. In *Basketry and Beyond: Constructing Culture*, ed. T. A. Heslop and H. Anderson. Leiden: Brill.

Perrois, L. 2011 *Arts du Gabon*. Geneva: Musée Barbier-Mueller.

Reefe, T. Q. *c.*1981 *The Rainbow and the Kings, A History of the Luba Empire to 1891*. Berkeley, CA: University of California Press.

Silva, S. 1998 'The Birth of a Divination Basket'. In M. Jordán (ed.), *Chokwe! Art and Initiation among the Chokwe and Related Peoples*. Munich: Prestel, pp. 141–151.

Torday, E. 1925 *On the Trail of the Bushongo*. London: Seeley, Service and Co. Ltd.

Torday, E. and Joyce, T. A. 1911 *Notes ethnographique sue les peoples communement appelés Bakuba ainsi sur les peuplades apparentées: Les Bushongo*. Brussels: Musée du Congo Belge.

Vansina, J. 1972 'Ndop: Royal Statues among the Kuba'. In Douglas Fraser and Herbert M. Cole (eds.) *African Art and Leadership*, Madison, WI: University of Wisconsin Press 45.

Vansina, J. 1978 *The Children of Woot: A History of the Kuba Peoples*. Madison, WI: University of Wisconsin Press.

Van Wing, J. 1960 *Études Bakongo, Sociologie – Religion et Magie*, Bruges: Descée de Brouwer.

17

Straw ropes and wattle walls: Aspects of the material culture of basketry in Atlantic Scotland

Hugh Cheape

This chapter gathers evidence from material culture, language and the environment to help to build a picture of rope, basketry and wattlework as essential components of everyday life and of the synergy between the raw material and long-standing skills of eye, hand and mind.

Reverend Robert Forbes, Episcopalian clergyman and Bishop of Ross and Caithness, left an impressive collection of first-hand accounts of the last Jacobite War of 1745–46 under the compelling title of 'The Lyon in Mourning'. As a piece of civil war reportage, his was an unsung initiative and a literary phenomenon in the English language. Embedded in the reportage is a sentence in Scottish Gaelic delivered by one of Bishop Forbes' informants, the celebrated poet, Alexander MacDonald (c. 1698–1770). The poet closed his account of his campaign experiences with a vivid metaphor by which the figurative rope-twister or 'thrawcrook' which had served to spin the tale was handed to another while the story-teller could go in search of more raw material for the narrative: '*Veir mi niosh a chorra himain yuit fèin, gos a faidh mi tuillad Gaoisid i.e.* I leave you the Thrawcrook till I get more hair' (Paton 1895, 332).

The word 'thrawcrook' appears in the written record of Scots in the sixteenth century and the above citation, *Corra-shìomain* (in standard orthography), is the earliest known reference in Scottish Gaelic. Such tools, in one form or another, must have long predated the literature and belong to the people's full use of the natural resources of their environment. Straw and other materials such as hay, grasses and plants, tree materials and horse and cow's hair were twisted into cords and ropes for making fastenings in processes characteristic of a self-reliant and self-sufficient economy. The poet's extended metaphor of *gaoisid*, meaning probably the hair of mane and tail, may have been chosen for its inference of the potentially finer and inherently stronger rope. 'Straw ropes and wattle walls' are proposed as aspects of the material culture of basketry that offer distinctive regional characteristics for the west coast and islands of Atlantic Scotland and a dynamic engagement with the region's past.

Straw ropes and basketry are significant if understudied components of the material culture record and have value as cultural and historical indicators of regionality. Straw was the most versatile of rope-making materials and the art was to form a rope of even thickness to ensure consistency of strength. Before the period of agricultural improvement, straw would be more valued as fodder in the Highlands and Islands and ropes were made of heather, bent grass and rushes, all of which were abundantly available. 'Bent' or 'marram' grass, growing on the Hebridean island coasts and sand dunes, was a widely used material for rope-making in the region, and the Gaelic name, *muran*, for sea-bent, could also refer to a rope of grass plaited and woven into a horse-collar (Dwelly 1920, 681). This was the genus *Ammophila arenaria* or European marram grass, but its frequent and extensive harvesting could lead to coastal erosion and the loss of precious arable and pasture land. Agricultural improvement in the Hebrides led to extensive schemes to plant marram grass and estate regulations forbidding its cutting and pulling. A detailed account of the use of marram grass in the 1820s, including the 'improving' concerns for its conservation, was recorded by William MacGillivray:

> It is made into ropes of various kinds for the accoutrement of their horses, securing their corn-stacks and thatched roofs, for chair bottoms, and mats and vessels for preparing and holding grain and meal. For the latter purpose, it is slightly twisted, and the different rounds are bound together by the long, slender and very tough roots which the plant sends into the sandbanks often to the length of twenty feet. . . . The mats are woven of small ropes in a frame, and are used in the cleaning of grain. Sacks and bags for holding grain, meal and wool are made in the same manner.
>
> WM 1831, 383

FIGURE 17.1 *Twisting marram grass into rope using a* corra-shìoman, *Bornish, South Uist, c. 1932. Photograph Margaret Fay Shaw Collection, by courtesy of the National Trust for Scotland.*

Rope-making was done by hand or with some kind of twisting device. The rope-twister – 'thrawcrook' or *corra-shìomain* – conventionally and recently used to make straw and other materials (such as horsehair) into ropes, took various forms and shapes indicating purely local manufacture (Fenton 1961, 4–15) (Fig. 17.1). Memories of these have survived; an example collected in Skye in 2012 was identified as a *corra-shùgan*, thus indicating a naming distinction in which *sùgan* means a rope of straw or hay in the Skye dialect and is the standard term in Irish Gaelic. Hay and grain stacks outside in the stackyard were tied down with straw ropes against wind and weather damage. In the Hebrides and Northern Isles, it was unfortunately not uncommon for stacks to be blown away by winter storms and roping was therefore critical. Occurrences such as this are the stuff of folk memory.

Housebuilding involved a more extensive use of ropes, joining roof timbers such as rafters to couples and purlins to rafters, forming layers of insulation and supporting roofing divots (thin slices of turf), and securing the thatch roof on the outside, for example, with heather rope (Buchanan 1997, 40). A multiplicity of uses might include a specific use such as building a granary of straw rope for the outside storage of the harvested grain where supplementary structures such as barns were limited. This technique was common in parts of south-west Ireland and has been recorded in Caithness and Orkney under the name 'corn-byke' (Fenton 1979, 144–149; Lucas 1957, 2–20).

Different types of rope were used to form containers for carrying loads. Straw, bent grass, docken stalks and rushes were the commonest materials in Atlantic Scotland for the variety of functions required. Forms of container emerged as organic solutions to particular needs such as the carrying of goods for market, peat as fuel for the fire or seaweed as manure for the fields (Fig. 17.2). The wickerwork creel has more recently been the principal mode of carrying back-loads. In 1894, Rev Duncan MacInnes noted terminology for 'Highland Panniers or *Cleibh*' in 'Notes of Technical Terms' and perceptively added that 'The following and many other technical terms being on the eve of falling into oblivion, it is desirable that they be preserved and put upon record to prevent their being lost for ever' (MacInnes 1894, 213). The cultural view today tends to be dominated by the wickerwork creel of willow, but the actuality of everyday work was more multifunctional and materially diverse.

Reverend John MacRury (1843–1907), minister of Snizort parish in Skye but drawing on his upbringing and oral tradition in Benbecula in the Outer Hebrides, was a prolific and outstanding writer of Scottish Gaelic. His writings are filled with material culture detail of unique value temporarily hidden behind a barrier of language. The barrier itself is now being lowered in the interests of lexicography and the process of assembling a new dictionary of Scottish Gaelic, *Faclair na Gàidhlig*. MacRury presented a paper in 1901 to the Gaelic Society of Inverness in which he drew on memories of half a century before and explained traditional processes of use and manufacture:

'An latha nach biodh e 'n comas do dhaoine an aghaidh a thoirt a-mach air doras, gheibheadh iad obair gu leòr anns na taighean. . . . Is minic a chunnaic mi eithrichean air an acaire agus ball làidir cheithir dual de shìoman fraoich gan cumail'.

MACRURY 1901, 385–386; see *Appendix* for verbatim translation

Although not mentioned here by MacRury, the wickerwork creel of willow must not be discounted as a major element in the material culture record since it derives from the prevalence of basketwork

625. Seic. (ill. by
MMcD.)

FIGURE 17.2 *Marram grass or reed bag of eight- or ten-pecks capacity for holding grain or meal, with the six loops* (dulan *or* dulagan) *round the mouth for closing the bag. (Image Dwelly 1967, 803).*

FIGURE 17.3 *Wicker creel, unprovenanced but possibly from Shawbost, Isle of Lewis. Photo by courtesy of National Museums Scotland.*

in this region in common with a more universal ethnological record. Many of the Lewis townships grew willow osiers in small enclosures whereas island communities in the southern Outer Hebrides acquired their osiers from those mainland districts where the evidence for creel houses is strongest. Larger items such as boats are outside the scope of this paper but merit close study; the *curach* as a form of seagoing vessel depended on wickerwork for its construction, form and strength, and has continued in use on inland waterways (Fenton 1972, 61–81; Jenkins 1974, 115) (Fig. 17.3).

The prevalence of basketry and the evidence for houses of timber and basket construction are functions of the natural history of the West Coast Highlands and Atlantic zone, with its humid climate and natural woods of oak, birch, aspen, rowan, hazel, holly and willow on indented coastline and fjord-like lochs. In general, there were old mixed deciduous forest to the west and pine forests to the east – east, that is, of the Great Glen – though there were extensive pine forests nearer the West Coast such as 'Locheil's Forest' on the shores of Loch Arcaig and in Glen Loy and pine woods round Loch Hourn and in Glen Barrisdale in Knoydart. The prevalence of timber in these areas gave rise to a proverbial expression in Scottish Gaelic which infers the same sense of absurdity in the notion of taking coals to Newcastle: 'That would be like taking wood to Lochaber' – *B'e sin a bhiodh 'toirt fiodha do Lochabar e*, or alternatively, *B'e sin a bhiodh 'toirt giuthas* (i.e. pine trees) *do Lochabar e*.

Regional techniques of vernacular building such as 'wattle walls' have been more distinctive or pronounced where there have been sharp differentials in naturally occurring raw materials, themselves a function of the Highland and Island elementals of geology climate and vegetation. Upstanding remains of buildings in rural settlements are exceptionally rare in Scotland and the limited lifespan of timber buildings is a given. Wattle walls therefore are a virtually lost aspect of the material culture of basketry in the region, but sufficient evidence remains to place them on record (Cheape 2014, 31–50). Basketry as building material attracted the attention of travellers and visitors to the region. In James Robertson's tour of the West Coast and Inner Hebrides between May and October 1768, coming to Moidart and Arisaig he described 'creel houses' in some detail:

> The houses in which they live they call basket houses. The method of building them is this: they first mark out both breadth and length of the house, then drive stakes of wood at 9 inches or a foot distance from each other, leaving 4 or 5 feet of them above ground, then wattle them up with heath and small branches of wood, upon the outside of which they pin on very thin turf, much in the same manner that slates are laid. Alongst the top of these stakes runs a beam, which supports the couples, and what they call cabers, and this either covered with turf, heath or straw.

Further north he made the distinction between respective building techniques of barns and houses:

> Their barns and houses are built in the same manner as hath been described, only the former have no turf fastened on their outer side from the ground up to the easing, so that the wind blows through all parts of the barn with freedom, and dries their corn.

MITCHELL 1898, 14; HENDERSON and DICKSON 1994, 81, 101

A significant detail to emerge from accounts of the Highlands is that, apart from the larger masonry structures such as castles, housing was undifferentiated across social spectrums. It might be a

FIGURE 17.4 *Gable end of a creel house with wattle walls and cruck couple. (Sir George Steuart Mackenzie,* A Treatise on the Diseases and Management of Sheep. *Edinburgh 1809, Plate V).*

matter of surprise, or certainly a matter of comment, that the house of the local chieftain or tacksman seemed indistinguishable from the other houses in a community. Basket or wattlework was therefore not generically of low status. At Tom-an-t-Sabhail, Inverwick, Grant of Glenmoriston lived in a house of wattle and turf, described as *tigh caoil* (willow house). The daughter of Campbell of Cawdor had eloped with Grant of Glenmoriston, being the chieftain of lower status, and this prompted her father ultimately to build *An Tùr* or 'The Tower', being a stone and lime building (MacDonald 1982, 22). Mary Mackellar, writing in 1889 on the 'Traditions of Lochaber', described 'Locheil's castle of the '45 at Achnacarry, burned by the Duke of Cumberland [following the Battle of Culloden], was all of wattle, excepting the bit of wall where the fire-places were, and which still stands' (Mackellar 1890, 267). A massive freestanding hearth and chimney have survived as possible masonry gable of a former élite 'creel house' and this 'monument' is worthy of preservation and further research.

A barn beside the present A87 road at Kirkton, Balmacara, whose repair was grant-aided from the public purse, has wattlework panels of hazel and heather in the gables and side-panels of louvred woodwork which had earlier replaced wattlework. In the textbooks, this is sometimes described as 'stake and rice', and the same term was used historically. Wattle walls as regional indicator are confirmed by Alexander Carmichael, writing in 1884 on 'Grazing and Agrestic Customs' for the Crofters' Commission Report:

In wooded districts throughout the Highlands, where materials can be found, doors, gates, partitions, fences, barns, and even dwelling houses, are made of wattle-work. In the case of dwelling houses and their partitions, the wattling is plastered over on both sides with boulder clay, and whitewashed with lime, thereby giving an air of cleanliness and comfort to the house.

CARMICHAEL 1884, 454

A small selection of evidence has drawn on a range of sources to raise the profile of straw ropes and wattle walls as cultural and historical indicators and to tease out elements of what might today be described as the 'cultural landscape'. These elements too often are allowed to fall below the scholarly and 'heritage' radar and therefore tend not to be considered as dynamic or causative. Material culture studies are a given for unlocking such elements and work in pragmatic alliance with other disciplines such as, in this case, language (Lucas 1956, 16–35). Here, the terminology of a perhaps timeless material culture still lives naturally and audibly in Gaelic song:

Bha plàid' eich agam 'na diallaid, . . .
Is srian do shìoman connlaich.
['I had a grass horse-mat as saddle . . .
And bridle of straw rope'].

SHAW 1999, 123

Sabhal Mòr Ostaig
An t-Samhain 2018.

Appendix

On the day folks could not show their face outside the door, they would get plenty work in the houses. Each man, with few exceptions, would spin ropes. There was plenty marram grass to be got; and when spread out in a dry and warm place for a week or two, it would be spun into thin, fine rope. At the time, sacks were rarely to be seen. People knew very little then about foreign meal, and that was such a good thing. Fifty years ago, few people were needing it. In the place of sacks that are now more than plentiful in every district of the Highlands, it was the rush mill-bags (*plataichean-muillinn*) that every small farmer in the country had. I saw many of them being spun, woven and sewn. After the grain had been hardened and cleaned, it would be put in the bags to be taken to the mill. They would take about ten pecks each. And round their opening there were six 'ears', as the little loops (*dulan*) would be called, with which their mouths would be closed. They were called mill-bags to distinguish them from the seaweed mats (*plataichean-feamainn*). The seaweed mats would be under the saddle and creels when people – as was common enough fifty years ago – would be manuring with seaweed or carrying peat with the creels or going to the mill with sacks of grain in bags. In many places, marram grass was not easy to get, and many a man would be making bags or mats from the straw rope he would be spinning from oat straw. It would be the small oats, or as it would be called in many a place, the 'black oats' that people usually sowed at that time. The big oats

– that is the 'white oats' – would not grow well in the Western Isles. The big oats would not swell there so well as the small oats, and they would not ripen at all so quickly. The women would be busily spinning and carding and knitting stockings when the men would be spinning marram grass, or winding straw, or winding heather. The heather would be spun not only to rope down the houses and the stacks, but also to make tethers (*teaghraichean*) for cattle and horses, and to make cables for the boats. Often, I saw boats at anchor and a strong cable of four strands of heather rope holding them.

Bibliography

Buchanan, J. L. 1997 *Travels in the Western Hebrides from 1782 to 1790*. Isle of Skye: MacLean Press, reprint of original printing London 1793.

Carmichael, A. 1884 *Grazing and Agrestic Customs of the Outer Hebrides*. Edinburgh: Neill and Company, 450–482.

Cheape, H. 2014 'Every timber in the forest for Macrae's house'. In A. Grater (ed.), *Aul'-farrant wyes o biggin. Essays in memory of Sandy Fenton*. Scottish Vernacular Buildings Working Group. *Vernacular Building* 37 (2013–2014): 31–50.

Dwelly, E. 1967 [1920] *The Illustrated Gaelic–English Dictionary*. Sixth Edition. Glasgow: Alexander MacLaren.

Fenton, A. 1961 'Ropes and rope-making in Scotland'. In *Gwerin* 3: 142–156 and 200–214.

Fenton, A. 1972 'The Curach in Scotland', *Scottish Studies* 16: 61–81.

Fenton, A. 1979 'A Note on Scottish Straw Rope Granaries'. In *Ethnografcki i Folkloristichni Izledvaniya*. Sofia: Bulgarian Academy.

Henderson, D. M. and Dickson, J. H. 1994 *A Naturalist in the Highlands. James Robertson: his life and travels in Scotland, 1767–1771*. Edinburgh: Scottish Academic Press.

Jenkins, J. G. 1974 *Nets and Coracles*. Newton Abbot: David and Charles.

Lucas, A. T. 1956 'Wattle and straw mat doors in Ireland'. In *Arctica. Studia Ethnographica Upsaliensia XI: Essays presented to Åke Campbell*. Uppsala, pp. 16–35.

Lucas, A. T. 1956 '*An Fhóir*: a Straw-rope Granary'. In *Gwerin* 1: 2–20.

MacDonald, A. 1982 *Story and Song from Loch Ness-side*. Inverness: Gaelic Society of Inverness. Reprint of 1914 edition, Inverness: Northern Counties Newspaper Company.

MacInnes, D. 1894 'Notes on Technical Terms'. In *Transactions of the Gaelic Society of Inverness* Volume 19, 1893–1894, 213–216.

Mackellar, M. 1890 'Traditions of Lochaber'. In *Transactions of the Gaelic Society of Inverness* Volume 16 (1889-1890), 267–276

Mackenzie, G. S. 1809 *A Treatise on the Diseases and Management of Sheep*. Archibald Constable & Company, Edinburgh.

MacRury, J. 1901 'O Chionn Leth Cheud Bliadhna'. In *Transactions of the Gaelic Society of Inverness* Volume 24, 184–195, 383–394.

Mitchell, A. 1898 'James Robertson's Tour through some of the Western Islands etc', *Proceedings of the Society of Antiquaries of Scotland* 32: 11–19.

Paton, H. 1895 *The Lyon in Mourning*. Volume I. Edinburgh: Scottish History Society.

Shaw, M. F. 1999 *Folksongs and Folklore of South Uist*. Second Edition. Edinburgh: Birlinn Ltd.

WM [William MacGillivray] 1831 'On the uses to which certain indigenous plants have from time immemorial been employed in the Outer Hebrides', in *Quarterly Journal of Agriculture* Volume III, 1829–1831, 377–385.

18

Woven Communities – from handwork to heritage in Scottish vernacular basketry

Stephanie Bunn

Introduction

Woven Communities was a collaborative research project between this author and the Scottish Basketmakers Circle (SBC), which began in autumn 2010 at a meeting convened by SBC Chair of the time, Liz Balfour. As with many other crafts, some basketmakers had been concerned from the SBC's beginnings, twenty-five years earlier, to learn not just how to make baskets, but also about local and regional forms and techniques. They learned from the few remaining Scottish basketry practitioners – including Lowry Copeland and Jimmy Work from Shetland, and Alasdair Davidson from Arran. Most of the traditional crofters and workshop-makers then practicing in Scotland have now passed on, but what remains is the skill and knowledge of the contemporary practitioners who worked with them.

I attended the meeting as a working anthropologist and a 'would-be' basketmaker. This seemed a project of both anthropological and social interest. Going against the long-standing anthropological discourse of 'salvage ethnography', here the practitioners and many local people were concerned, and indeed passionate about, the loss of long-held skills and all the social and cultural practices and memories that went alongside them. What the basketmakers wanted was to gather together all the information that they had learned about Scottish basketry, to find out more about aspects not yet researched, and to make this into a book. It may have seemed unlikely that we would get funding to help us, but we received an award from the Arts and Humanities Research Council *Connected Communities* programme, and so we began.

In the beginning

We began by talking to all the regional basketmakers across Scotland, gathering details of any local knowledge they had. We also worked in museum stores and began to build our website, www.wovencommunities.org. As with other crafts, basketry practitioners often know more than curators about artefacts in their collections, including about materials, basketry techniques, and also local use. We could correct misinformation, adding texture and detail about artefacts.

We had to husband our resources, so we collaborated with a limited, but comprehensive, range of Scottish museums and archives. The National Museum of Scotland held a definitive basketry collection of beautiful examples from across Scotland (see, for example, Fig 18.2), largely gathered in the 1920s by two women bird-watchers, Evelyn Baxter and Leonora Rintoul, on their travels. There was the Scottish Life Archive, created by Scottish ethnologist Sandy Fenton – a treasury of newspaper cuttings, poetry, linguistic terminology and stories which miraculously deemed 'Creels and Baskets' to be one of its eight main categories (see Fig 18.6). We visited the Highland Folk Museum, gathered by the wonderful Scottish collector of 'homely Highland things', Isobel Grant (see Fig 18.9). For coastal basketry and the fishing industry, we looked to the Scottish Fisheries Museum. And we worked with Shetland Museum (see Fig 18.1), and Museum nan Eilean and An Lanntair on Lewis, thus including both the Northern and Western Isles. We also visited many smaller collections, such as Skye Museum of Island Life, Kildonan Museum on South Uist, Dumfries Museum, Arbroath Signal Tower, Mintlaw, and the Hope MacDougall Collection in Oban. There are many highly significant collections, such as Orkney and Wick Museums, which we have still to visit. All this information was complemented by a unique online Scottish photography archive, SCRAN (see Figs 18.3 and 18.6), and the School of Scottish Studies which houses a significant film, photography and sound archive, both of which provided a visual context which was easily lost when viewing the surviving object in isolation.

We learned a great deal – from the sheer variety of regional styles and materials, to Gaelic, Scots, Shetland and Orcadian terminology, to named makers and 'basketry signatures' – comparing collections, learning about historical basketry workshops, objects' journeys and shared local skills. In return, we have shared our broader knowledge between our partner museums and makers. At the same time, two of our most committed maker-researchers, Julie Gurr and Dawn Susan, helped upload all the data onto the *Woven Communities* website, which has given thousands of people in the UK and beyond access to the project and has also helped us gain more information.

Why baskets, why basketry?

Until recently, basketry was a fundamental fabric of Scottish society, providing a quite detailed lens through which to view past social and cultural life. Weaving, twining, plaiting, coiling and knotting natural plant materials to create containers for carrying things around with us has been practiced in Scotland for literally millennia. Baskets have been woven into many aspects of Scottish social history, from carrying peat for fuel, to fishing, to harvesting tatties, to migration.

From the outset of the project, we took an increasingly broad interpretation of what basketry is. We included longline sculls made from rattan (Fig 18.2), Shetland *guisers* or *skeklers* costume[1] (Fig. 18.1), woven heather or plaited marram (*murran*) mats, Travellers' heather cleaning brushes, *murran* horse collars (Fig. 18.3) straw, marram and heather ropes or *simmens*, loom-woven grain

FIGURE 18.1 *Children from Fetlar dressed as* skeklers. *Shetland, 1909. Shetland Museum.*

baskets (see Chapter 17 by Cheape, this volume), and even willow bridles or woodies. Thus, baskets alone cannot encompass the process and practice of making and using basketry-type things. We cannot define the technique by the product any more than we can define the product by the technique. Many of these techniques and forms overlap each other, and all were practiced in Scottish basketwork.

Many of these quite mundane, everyday artefacts are now almost obsolete, following the petrochemical revolution and the introduction of plastic bags and shopping trolleys (see Tait, Chapter 31, this volume). But their very mundaneness is what makes them so interesting. They were simply a part of everyday life as it went on, woven into the background, and as a result, they have the potential to provide insights into the Scottish past and the process of social change, very much anchored and tailored to regional communities, their localities and landscapes. From coast to inland and from Northern to Western isles, each locality had need for specific kinds and forms of basketwork, each form so specific that it often had its own unique name.

East coast basketry reflected needs of local fishing and the herring industry. Line fishing required a multitude of baskets for almost every stage of the process. There were bait baskets; sma'line and gr'tline baskets (*sculls*) for line fishing, depending on how far out to sea the fishing was (Fig 18.2); baskets with handles to carry the fish ashore in; back creels for fishwives to carry fish to sell; and *murlins* to hold the gear to weigh the fish out. Creels varied in style up and down the coast. Around Edinburgh, in Musselburgh and Fisherrow, broad and sturdy back creels predominated, while further north around Moray and Aberdeenshire, back creels were slenderer and more detailed. In between, from Arbroath down to Fife, women carried finely woven

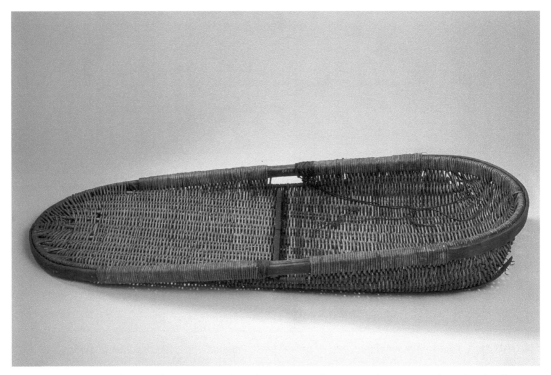

FIGURE 18.2 *Longline scull by Peter Lindsay from Arbroath. National Museum of Scotland collection.*

arm creels instead. These details of local distinctiveness were not clear until we conducted our project.

Lowland farmers gathered tatties in shallow tattie *sculls*, which were sometimes made by Travellers from spale or willow. Covent Garden sieves were used for measuring fruit, and punnets were made for picking and selling it.

Highlanders needed back creels to gather peats. Ironically, there is less material evidence of baskets and creels in the Highlands than elsewhere in Scotland, possibly due to the impact of the clearances. The majority of the Highland Folk Museum collection of I.F. Grant is from the Western Isles, but rare photographs and romantic paintings also show their presence in the Highlands in the past. There were grouse panniers, fishing creels, and curling baskets for country sports. Scottish Travellers in the Highlands also made and sold all manner of baskets, as well as mending them.

Island livelihoods, mainly a combination of fishing and crofting, required locally-made baskets in all areas of life. On the Western Isles, back and donkey creels carried seaweed for fertilising crops, brought in the peats and sometimes cleared the midden. Archival photos and museum collections also reveal woven willow screens for wind protection, marram grass horse collars (Fig. 18.3), oval willow *mudags* for holding raw fleece for spinning, and even cupboard sides made from willow.

Similar creel-type baskets, often made from a special kind of long black oat straw called *gloy,* were used on the Northern Isles, and were called *kishies* or *budies* in Shetland and in Orkney

FIGURE 18.3 *The last example from Sollas of a horse's collar made in the traditional way from marram grass. Made by John MacDonald, 3 Sollas in the early 1950s. Photograph courtesy Comann Eachdraidh, Sollas.*

FIGURE 18.4 *Corner's Basket-works in Bank Row, Wick. Johnston Collection, The Wick Society.*

caissies. There was so little wood on the Northern Isles that even chair backs were woven from straw. Here straw containers held everything from salt (in salt *cuddies*) to bait and meal.

Along with documenting the rural past, baskets also tell us about change. Indeed, the Industrial Revolution in Scotland could not have taken place without the woven skips and baskets made for carrying materials and transportation of goods. Workshops grew up across Scotland, from Leith to Wick and Skye, to supply the increased demand. These workshops also made the special herring measures, quarter crans – baskets stamped by government officials to denote their accuracy for volume of herring. There were even attempts to make baskets by machine – punnet construction was broken down into stages in local basket-works, but people were still needed for their assembly. Hospitals used baskets for surgical dressings, wicker cots and willow baby-weighing scales. They were used as clothes trunks for migration from the islands to America; and in war, for pigeon baskets, shell casings and surveillance balloons.

Materials

As elsewhere in Britain, standard Scottish basketry materials were willow and hazel. Received opinion was that most basketmakers in Scotland 'just made baskets for their own use', or for local trade, growing their own willow. We found, however, that even in the past, there had been a wide range of expertise and practices. With the Industrial Revolution and the Herring Industry, there was vastly increased need for materials, so much willow had to be bought in from England. Imported rattan later supplanted other materials to a certain extent, its strength and durability highly valued.

Scottish Travellers wove with locally available materials. Split wood for tattie sculls, willow for baskets, heather for brushes and so on. The story goes that they planted willow stems in the hedgerows as they travelled past and returned to re-harvest them every year. In certain areas, their migration routes were lined with coppiced willows.

The Scottish islands presented a challenge for growing willow because strong winds from the Atlantic inhibited the growth of trees. People had to be resourceful, working with what grew best and the variety of materials they adapted to use was impressive. In the Western Isles, however, cultural links with Ireland had made the use of willow preferable for creels and we occasionally found small willow patches, overgrown and surrounded by stone walls. One story told that two brothers would travel from Uist to Skye each year, just to gather willow from the slopes in Uig Bay.[2] Heather was also used for creels here, but for other artefacts such as ropes (known locally as *simmens* or *sughans*), or for coiled baskets, all manner of material could be used, from rush to straw, to marram grass, hair-moss and even horse hair.

Northern Islanders had closer links with Scandinavia, growing their own black oat straw or *gloy* for many baskets. But people were uniquely adaptable, using a variety of materials, according to what was available. This could change from one side of a valley to the other, from heather to *dockens* (dock), from wild rush or *floss* to marram or *bent* grass, all woven using similar techniques.

FIGURE 18.5 (a&b) *Detail of* dockens bodi *(Shetland) and* heather *cassie (Orkney), both with the same weave, but different material. Photograph: Stephanie Bunn.*

Our methods

The Woven Communities' research methods were characterized by the use of practice. From public displays, to reminiscence sessions, even to our symposia – baskets were made on every occasion. This was a method which somehow drew people in to tell us their stories and enhanced our discussions and understanding in a variety of ways.

Through making baskets in public places, people interacted with us and inevitably came and gave us their basketry stories. 'You're doing that wrong,' was one common reaction. But then they also told us about their relatives who had made and used baskets, and their different life histories. People might be reminded of family photos, tell of a carved model of a fishwife with a creel their granddad had made, or be the possessor of a child's creel from their childhood. Performing a hand-skill such as basket-weaving provided a kind of common ground, a touchstone that people were drawn to, cared about, and which evoked a form of respect.

Highlights of response to our demonstrations and public workshops included reminiscence days with the Scottish Women's Rural Institute (SWRI), retired fishermen and a group of Scottish Travellers. The SWRI had links with basketmaking from the days of Rintoul and Baxter, who themselves had set up night classes to promote basketry revival and rural crafts. They also had links with Lindburn, the centre for the Scottish War Blinded near Edinburgh and brought in baskets made there to show us.

Among the Scottish Travellers, one elder in particular told us how, in the past, Travellers had thanked the tree for providing their materials and how they had boiled willow with the bark on to dye the stems and make it easier to use. Another of the group told us about the strength woven into snares with single- and double-braiding. 'Stephanie,' she said, 'my father always told me, you

FIGURE 18.6 Murran *drying on a dais, North Uist. Scottish Life Archive, National Museum of Scotland.*

take some twine, you twist it. Then if you twist it back on itself, it's twice as strong.' This she repeated several times.

As part of our practice-led research on Lewis with An Lanntair, we followed the process from plant to basket using *murran* or marram grass. We went to Cealasay, where *murran* had formerly been harvested, to gather it using traditional sickles. Then, with a boatload of grass, we realized that we had no clue how to dry it before it rotted from the damp. Here SCRAN helped, with archival images of *murran* drying-stands. We could not make these, but while our friend was away, we laid the *murran* out over furniture around his whole house, ensuring the air got through the grass to dry it.

On Shetland, and on Uist with the *Coman Eadhraidh* (history societies), we made baskets with elders, children and local makers. Our premise was that memories are not just about the past but are a form of intergenerational knowledge that can be renewed for the future. Here, practice provided the medium. On Uist, with An Lanntair, we worked with elders with dementia in care homes, the baskets provoking 'hand-memories'. Through touching baskets and materials familiar from people's working lives, memories were inspired and people could tell us of, and even show us, old skills while telling associated stories. Children took to this form of history, and also enquired, asking their parents about what they had been making, bringing us back new stories.

Giving public talks also brought new knowledge. At a lecture in Anstruther, a couple told where their grandparents had cleaned the creels in a burn near the sea. From a talk at Taigh Cearsabaigh, North Uist, a thatcher told us it took an area of *murran* the size of a football pitch to thatch a

FIGURE 18.7 *Looking at archival photos, Sacred Heart Care Home, South Uist. Photograph: Stephanie Bunn, with permission.*

FIGURE 18.8 *Erskine Beveridge's chairs from Vallay. Courtesy the collection of Alaistair and Annie MacDonald, North Uist. Photograph: Stephanie Bunn.*

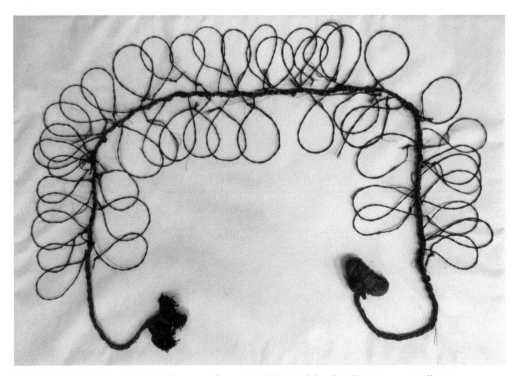

FIGURE 18.9 *Horse hair Puffin snare from St Kilda. Highland Folk Museum Collection.*

cottage, while another member of the audience showed us a pair of unique bent grass chairs made with no wood at all, bought at an auction from Erskine Beveridge's old home in Vallay.

There were also insights provided by chance encounters with museum artefacts. At the Highland Folk Museum, in a box given by the curator, saying, 'Here's a box of rope for you to look at,' we found a puffin snare from St Kilda.

Made from horse hair, it would have been highly valued and is now probably unique, the only one left. It reveals the challenges of subsistence and ingenuity required to live on St Kilda, snaring puffins for food from the cliffs. A chair with a *murran* seat from Harris at the same museum is described on the record as simply, '5 shillings, sold by a woman lone and poor', revealing the great value of a wooden armchair to a woman in the early twentieth century.

In response to museums' concerns with Intangible Cultural Heritage, we held a 'skills gathering' at the Scottish Fisheries Museum, again using practice, working in the collections with expert makers from across Scotland. This sparked the debate, 'Were we making replicas, copying or improvising, and was that a good or bad thing?' In fact, the process was rather one of renewal, a balance between 'knowing from the inside' and from the outside. New craftsman John Cowan, who had learned to make the quarter cran from Colin Manthorpe, the last known maker to have been formally apprenticed in making this form, studied the half cran – a basket, probably not made by anyone for fifty years. He said, 'It will take me five hours to make this basket.' He borrowed a damaged basket, studied it and made a new one without reference to diagrams or plans. There was a knowledge in the basket and knowledge in the maker, and here they met. One could also argue that in the old basket there was, at the same time, a kind of provocation left by the skill of the original maker, his agency, or skill, if you like, drawing in the new maker to renew it, in the same way that our makers had been drawn to study 'traditional' basketry.

Our concern with practice led us also to ask, 'Who made the baskets?' – a fact almost never recorded. This led to a concern with basketmakers' 'signatures', techniques people repeated in all their work – a characteristic weave across the back of a creel, the positioning of stakes in a frame basket, a way of fastening a handle and so on. The work of one maker, Peter Lindsay was unmistakable (see Fig 18.2). A mill worker from Arbroath, he made baskets in his evenings, using steam-bending equipment from the boat-building yard to laminate his frames. This gave his work a precise, distinctive style. His immaculate line-sculls, sometimes known as 'Gourdon sculls,' were held by museums across Scotland, though rarely identified as his. He also made arm creels and *murlins*. We found his identity from an old exhibition catalogue of the *Living Traditions* exhibition at the Royal Edinburgh Museum, 1951, and then traced his work to collections in the National Museum of Scotland, the Scottish Fisheries Museum, and Arbroath Signal Tower. While each basket is slightly different, we can identify his baskets in any collection.

Making into memories, mind and recovery

We did not begin the project thinking how important it was to work with practitioners. The basketmakers simply wanted to learn about the skills and their histories, and their love of this, and the possibility of this learning and knowledge being 'lost' inspired us to collaborate. But we found that making was at the core of our research on multiple levels.

Makers had a knowledge of artefacts that no other expert had, and people, from curators to school children, respected this and cared about it. Witnessing basketry skills also inspired people to tell us their stories, the act of skillful making becoming a kind of inspiration to communicate. We also learned how, for elders with dementia, once having practiced a skill, that skill was embedded in bodily memory, and could still be repeated effectively, and also evoke stories from the time when it was learned and practiced. We found that children both loved working with skilled practitioners and continually problem-solved, played with and tested what they had made, spatially and for strength.

Furthermore, when inspired by our basketmaking partners, we held symposia where making took place alongside lectures and discussion, we found that making helped debate. It brought an enhanced quality of discussion, new ideas seemed to flow, and there was a kind of synthesis to our debate rather than analysis. So, we concluded, along with inspiring memory, making helps our minds, it helps us make sense of things, and to communicate.

Since then, the Woven Communities project has developed further research into the value of practice for learning and healing. We have worked with mathematicians to explore how basket-weaving can enhance geometric understanding and explored the value of basketwork for memory loss, rehabilitation and war injury. We have worked in schools, care homes and in a stroke recovery unit.

Learning skills such as basketry embeds a kind of understanding and knowledge in and of the basket, held in memory by both makers and users. Alongside memories, the very act of skill embedded in the basket is a kind of provocation, to learn the skill anew, to learn about the basket, its history, to tell its story. It provoked us to begin this book. Engagement with materials and technique encourages basketmakers to think about the world in a constructive way, to make connections, see patterns, solve problems, experience forces, connect with their environment and keep learning. And so as long as people practice and care about these skills, this is a story without an ending.

Acknowledgements

Thanks to all basketmakers from the Scottish Basketmakers' Circle and beyond, to all our museum curators and their assistants, and our funders AHRC, the *Knowing from the Inside Project*, University of Aberdeen, University of St Andrews Knowledge Exchange and Impact Fund, Royal Society of Edinburgh, and our friends and supporters, without whom this project could not have happened.

Notes

1   http://www.documentscotland.com/skeklers-skekling-shetland-scottish-photography/
2   Personal communication from Caroline Dear.

19

Making baskets, making exhibitions:

Indigenous Australian baskets at the British Museum

Lissant Bolton

In 2011 I curated a small exhibition at the British Museum called *Baskets and Belonging: Indigenous Australian Histories.* The exhibition surveyed the diversity of basket traditions across Indigenous Australia, including traditional, historical and contemporary forms, and used the baskets to discuss aspects of Indigenous Australian histories. In a sense the exhibition was contradictory: Indigenous Australian thought places a priority on place, on what is known in Australian English as 'country' – one's place of belonging and identity – rather than on the notion of linear time that underlies the concept of history or memory. For Indigenous Australians – meaning both Aboriginal Australians and Torres Strait Islanders – baskets evoke country rather than memory in several different senses, and country is the source for baskets. As the Tjanpi Desert weavers say 'The land inspires us to make things'.[1] This chapter discusses both the exhibition and the traditions it displayed, focusing on the way baskets can be an opening into understanding something about people's lives.

Australia has been inhabited for more than 60,000 years. It was settled initially by waves of migrants who from the late Pleistocene entered the continent from the northwest, travelling across the water from what is now eastern Indonesia. There is no specific evidence for this, but those first immigrants must have used fibre technologies to enable that journey, perhaps in some kind of sailing canoe. If so, the sails may well have been made with plaited leaf fibres, like the sails used millennia later when the rest of the Pacific was settled. It is certainly probable that they brought with them some kind of container, perhaps fibre baskets or bags. As Ronald Berndt recorded in the 1940s, in the epic histories of the Yolngu people of northeastern Arnhem Land, baskets and mats were included as 'the original sacred objects of the creation period, carried by the first ancestors on their journeys' (cited in Conroy 2009, 32). There is some evidence for ancient baskets in rock art in Arnhem Land in northern Australia. Although the dating of such images is difficult, the 'dynamic figures' style of rock art, which has been suggested dates to some 20,000 years ago, depicts both men and women with baskets and string bags (Chaloupka and Giuliani 2005, 10).[2]

People settled what is now Australia comparatively quickly, creating a continent of diverse but linked societies speaking somewhere around 700 languages. The societies were, and are, distinct groups, related rather as European peoples are, with many similarities in knowledge and practice, but nevertheless separate from each other. Goods and ceremonies were traded and shared widely between groups. Generally speaking however, people stayed within their group territory, moving regularly around it, often on a seasonal basis. They often used established camping sites within those territories, and sometimes left possessions in them. In southeastern Australia, for example, large wooden water containers were left at camping grounds.

One of the shared characteristics of the diverse Indigenous Australian societies is recognition of the ancestral beings who created the landscape. However, although people speak about things that ancestral beings did, that concept doesn't involve a sense of the past. Rather ancestral beings and ancestral activity is present in the landscape, just in another layer, so that in Indigenous thought ancestral power, action and event are right here and right now. As in Yolngu stories, ancestral beings are in the landscape, with the baskets and bags that feature in the accounts of their actions.

If there were and are shared characteristics between different Indigenous groups, there also were and are significant differences, some of which reflect the diversity of Australian environments. Australia has many different climates supporting a wide range of different plants, and that is reflected in the range of resources people used to make bags and baskets. Using cane, grass, spinifex, sedges, rushes, reeds, flax, vines, leaves and bark, and also animal fur, human hair and feathers, people spun threads, twined cords and ropes, split cane, and treated leaves, vines, rushes and reeds in specific ways to extract and use the fibres from them. They looped, knotted, coiled, twined and plaited fibres, using different techniques for different fibres and for making different sorts of objects. Different techniques and materials were used in different areas of the continent: for example, before the European incursion, coiling was a technique used only in southeastern Australia.

Early Europeans observers thought that Indigenous Australians made and used only a limited range of objects, but in fact people made (and make) a great variety of things. Fibre objects included hunting and fishing nets, fishing lines, fish and eel traps, ropes, sails, bags, baskets, mats, sandals, clothing and ornaments.[3] In the centre and west of Australia the range of fibre objects people made did not include many – or even in some places any – baskets. For example, in the far south west, around what is now Albany, as Harley Coyne reports (pers comm 2016), Menang people made temporary rush baskets while fishing, but otherwise did not make fibre containers. I am not aware of any Menang fibre containers in any museum collection.

People also made, and make, a diversity of different basket types, even within one area. In the rainforests of eastern Queensland, for example, people made small baskets, known in Girramay language as *mindi*, as well as bicornual baskets or *jawun* (Girrimay). Bicornual baskets, strong two-cornered forms, twined from lawyer cane, were made in a series of different sizes, some painted and some not. Painted bicornual baskets were used by men to carry their personal possessions. Unpainted baskets were used to collect and process food, for example some were set as fish traps in rivers. Larger bicornual baskets were used to carry babies and small children. Across Australia there were sometimes specific rules about who could or should make baskets: in the rainforest, it was men who made bicornual baskets, a tradition maintained today by the Girramay artist Abe Muriata. For Abe, making *jawun* means being a master craftsman, involving not only an understanding of materials but also skilled engineering in their manipulation (quoted in Bolton 2011, 34).

For contemporary makers, one of the critical aspects of basketmaking remains accessing the raw materials from the landscape, from country. The term 'country' refers to a territory or place, but also invokes a deep sense of connection and ideas of family, law and responsibility: it refers not just to the landscape, but to the layered present of ancestral activity. Just about every time that I have visited an Indigenous community across Australia to talk about objects, people have responded by showing me their country. In some cases, this is land they now hold as a result of a native title claim, in others it is more a case of accessing a known landscape that is legally owned by others (including the National Parks Service), but which is nevertheless their country. Today, harvesting the materials to make objects is part of the affirmation of connection to country. It provides a direct connection to place (Conroy 2009, 30), an expression of an enduring belonging to everything that is present there. Indeed, basketmakers are often not comfortable harvesting materials from places that are not part of their own country. As Roy McIvor from Cape York Peninsula says, 'We can only take grass that belongs to us, here in our own country' (Callaghan 2006, 46).

Indigenous Australians had widely varying experiences of the European invasion. In the south-east, where British settlement of Australia started, people lost their land and their autonomy very early, as their lands were invaded. In the north, north-west and centre of Australia, where settlement arrived much later, people continued to live untroubled by Europeans for another century or more. In the south-east, the knowledge and skills that enable people to make their specific basket types were altered by European settler action. There, the forms of some baskets also changed quite early as people modified them to sell to settlers for European uses, adding different handles, for example. Perhaps for this reason, the earliest collected Tasmanian baskets (between the 1830s and 1850s) have, as Julie Gough observes, a 'teardrop' form with a curved base, while she argues that those collected from the 1860s have a low, flat-based shape (2009, 21; 35, n.58). Whereas the earlier baskets would almost always be kept suspended, the later form may have been designed to rest on a table or other flat surface.

Today people continue to innovate in basketmaking. In central Australia where baskets were not made traditionally, basketmaking techniques (such as the technique of coiling), were introduced to a number of central Australian communities in the mid-1990s. This technique reached Martu women in north-western regions near Newman in Western Australia around 1999. Leading Martu fibre arts practitioner Nola Taylor says that basket-weaving became so popular amongst Martu women that it 'spread across the desert like a *waru* (fire)'. Martu women make baskets mostly from *minarri* grass (*Amphipogon caricinus*). The fine bundles of grass are wrapped in brightly-coloured wool, coiled and stitched. Martu women collect *minarri* grass when they travel across their homelands to visit family, attend ceremonies, look after country and gather bush foods. Thus, making baskets is a way to connect to country even in regions where it is a new innovation. And collecting grass for baskets is also always about moving through country.

Making an exhibition about baskets invites a play on words, for just as one makes a basket, so one makes an exhibition. Stephanie Bunn, talking about working with willow in making basketry comments that the strength of the made artefact 'is an outcome of the *resistance* produced between maker and material'. She remarks further that 'working with willow can be a battle at times. . . . the willow worker has to find a kind of attunement with the material' (2014, 266). In the same way, making exhibitions is about working with materials, a whole range of materials including not just the objects, but the cases, the room, the lighting. In fact an exhibition is always the outcome of the resistance between constraining material conditions and the exhibition's objectives.

FIGURE 19.1 *Wool and* minarri *grass basket by Janice Nixon (Yuwali) 2010, Parnngurr, Western Australia W: 28cm.*

The architectural space in which the exhibition is created is very important: the characteristics of the room or rooms in which it is mounted have a very specific impact on an exhibition. Exhibition makers have to come to an attunement with that space. The location of walls and doors, the ceiling height, the siting of lighting tracks and power points and of any fixed furniture such as cases, all provide a framework with which the designer and curator have to wrestle together. There needs to be reconciliation between the exhibition's ambitions and what the space will allow.

In every exhibition the combination of the intellectual content, the objects displayed, the room itself, and the cases, graphics and lighting, create a three-dimensional experience. Objects, by their adjacencies, provide perspectives on each other. The collaboration between curator and the designers is a form of skilled work, and in many senses, this is an embodied skill, like making baskets. As much as the designer, a curator needs to know how to structure an exhibition so that it uses the space: to know how to set the rhythm of the ideas and the objects, balancing the different elements so that there is a sense of coherence overall. The biggest ideas may not be attached to the most important objects. An exhibition team bring what Ingold and Hallam describe as 'the improvisational creativity of skilled practice' (2007, 14) to bear on those materials and *make* an exhibition.

The British Museum is privileged to care for a significant collection of Australian baskets from across the continent, from very early collections to very recent acquisitions. The exhibition *Baskets and Belonging* was developed for a specific gallery space at the British Museum. In this room, two walls of the gallery (north and south) each have a fixed, wall-long, floor to ceiling case. The other two walls contain openings – one at the eastern side into the space, while at the western end a wide door leads into a further small room. In the centre of the gallery there are four smaller freestanding cases, and there is an introductory foyer. The exhibition had to have a logic that those cases would facilitate, in this case the wall cases focused on different basket traditions across Australia, while the central cases balanced that emphasis by exhibiting some of the other kinds of containers made in Australia, specifically those made to carry or hold water. These included a large wooden water container of the kind left in camping grounds in eastern Australia.

If an exhibition is made as a three-dimensional artefact, its success is nevertheless always dependent on the ideas it communicates. The diversity of Indigenous basketmaking across the continent was one story easily told, but the opportunity the exhibition offered was to introduce aspects of Indigenous history, both before and especially after the European invasion. Through the places the baskets come from, the histories in which they were collected, the transformations in basket form and the new styles of basket made in more recent periods, baskets enabled a perspective both on the diversity of Indigenous experience and on the flexibility and tenacity of indigenous knowledge and practice. I was able to make a collection of baskets of some of the more recent innovative traditions for the exhibition, bringing some of the recent history of Indigenous Australia into focus. The specific baskets chosen for exhibition were selected on the basis of which baskets were available and could tell good stories, and which baskets could be included from design and conservation viewpoints.

On the southern wall, for example, one section focused on bags made to contain *pituri* (*Duboisia hopwoodii*), a native tobacco used only by senior men. *Pituri* was traded over at least a quarter of a million square kilometres of inland Australia in distinctive looped bags. Traditionally the string for these bags was made from native flax or possum fur, and sometimes, human hair. The *pituri* bags in the exhibition, however, were partly made from re-spun wool sourced from colonial-government-issued blankets. Blankets, given even as land was being taken and thus symbolising cultural destruction, were repurposed to make beautiful striped bags. The creativity and elegance of the bags overlies a painful history of rejection and denial.

The northern wall included a number of sections devoted to new forms of basket – including, for example, central Australian coiled basketwork that developed in Ngaanyatjarra Pitjantjatjara Yankunytjatjara (NPY) lands in Central Australia. Coiled basketry techniques were introduced to the NPY Women's Council in a workshop in May 1995. Using the existing practice of making *manguri*, hair rings, from bound grass, women began 'trying different plant materials, drawing on a long history of working with fibres to fashion objects for ceremonial and daily use . . . bridging the gap between *manguri* and basket, between historical and contemporary practice' (Foster 2012, 151). In 1996 Kanytjupayi Benson, who became a leading figure of this movement, added a handle to the side of a basket and made a grass mug. She went on to make a set of camp crockery and a frying pan (Foster 2012, 155). From this a wide array of sculptural forms developed, not least the famous *Tjanpi Toyota*, a life-size coiled grass Toyota four-wheel drive truck, which won the prestigious Telstra National Indigenous Art Award in 2005.

We could not possibly have borrowed the *Tjanpi Toyota* from the museum where it is now displayed for a small exhibition in Room 91, but we were able to acquire and display a coiled raffia jug made by Tjunkiya Tapaya. Focusing on the humour and vibrancy of this tradition was also a way to draw attention to the strength of contemporary central Australian women. As Thisbe Purich, who introduced coiling in that 1995 NPY workshop, remarked of Kanytupayi Benson 'At the end of

FIGURE 19.2 *Pituri bag, wool and other fibre. Maker unknown. North-western Queensland. Acquired 1897. W: 38cm. British Museum.*

FIGURE 19.3 *Coiled jug, raffia by Tjunkiya Tapaya (c.2011), Ernabella, South Australia. H: 15 cm. British Museum.*

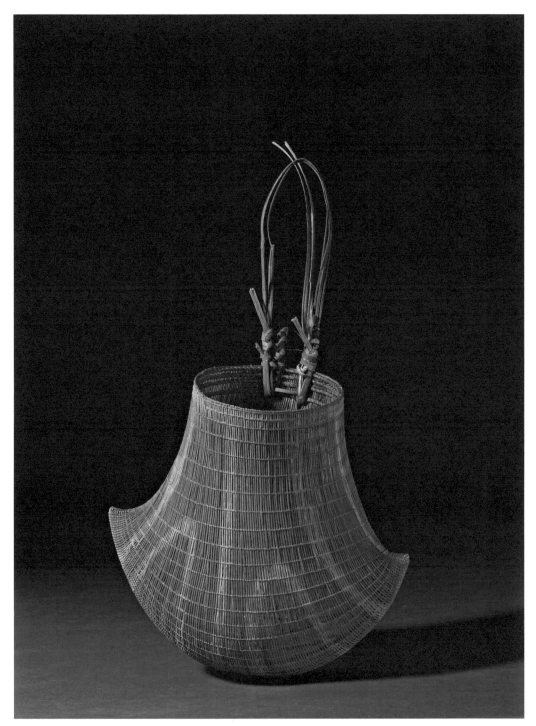

FIGURE 19.4 *Painted Bicornual basket, lawyer cane and ochre, maker unknown. Mulgrave River, Queensland collected c.1900. W: 33cm. This was the lead object for the* Baskets and Belonging *exhibition. British Museum.*

FIGURE 19.5 *Abe Muriata with the catalogue for* Baskets and Belonging *and a bicornual basket he had just made. Cardwell, October 2012. Photograph: L Bolton.*

the day it was always difficult to separate Kanytupayi from her great stories, her vibrant personality, her Country and the creations that sprung forth from her hands.' (Purich 2012, 161).

Some exhibitions have a life that extends beyond the few months that they are open to the public. Catalogues extend that life and we were very fortunate that because *Baskets and Belonging* was part of a wider Australian season, it was possible to produce one.[4] The exhibition arose from a collaborative research project on our Indigenous Australian collections implemented with colleagues in Australia, and was followed by a major Indigenous Australian exhibition in 2015, curated by Gaye Sculthorpe.[5] The baskets exhibition influenced the later show in several different ways, not least in having stimulated the acquisition of further contemporary baskets.

The lead object for *Baskets and Belonging* was a historic painted bicornual basket of great beauty and elegance. The final object in the *Indigenous Australia* exhibition was a new painted bicornual basket made by Abe Muriata. In the context of that exhibition it seemed to provide a conclusion brimming with possibilities for the future. If displaying baskets can enable understanding of Indigenous Australian histories, and represent the ongoing connection of people to country, then the value of the exhibition was also the way it pointed to the energy that baskets contain now, present, in the landscape.

Notes

1 Quoted at https://www.mca.com.au/artists-works/works/2013.63A-G/ accessed 15 July 2019. The Tjanpi desert weavers say: 'We like working with the grasses that grow on our land. The land inspires us to make things.'

2 Rock art dating is the subject of ongoing research and analysis. Chaloupka's proposed dating of this style may be overtaken by more recent research (see Johnston, I. G., Goldhahn, J. and May, S. K. 2017.

3 See West 2006 (West, A. L. 2006) for more detailed lists of fibre uses.

4 *Baskets and Belonging* was part of a wider 'Australian Season' at the British Museum, sponsored by Rio Tinto. The season also included an Australian Landscape garden in the museum's forecourt, part of a series of such interventions: Kew at the British Museum. The catalogue (Bolton, L. 2011) was made possible by the Rio Tinto funding.

5 This exhibition was Indigenous Australia: Enduring Civilisation. See Sculthorpe, G. et al. 2011.

Bibliography

Bolton, L. 2011 *Baskets and Belonging: Indigenous Australian Histories.* London: British Museum Press.

Bunn, S. 2014 'Making plants and growing baskets'. In E. Hallam and T. Ingold (eds), *Making and Growing: Anthropological studies of organisms and artefacts.* Farnham, Surrey: Ashgate.

Callaghan, M. (ed.) 2006 *Mangal-Bungal Clever with hands: Baskets and Stories woven by some of the women Hopevale, Cape York Peninsula.* Hopevale, Queensland: Hopeville Community Learning Centre Aboriginal Corporation.

Chaloupka, G. and Giuliani, P. 2005 'Strands of time'. In L. Hamby (ed), *Twined Together: Kunmadj Njalehnjaleken Gunbalanya (Oenpelli).* Northern Territory: Injalak Arts and Crafts.

Conroy, D. W. 2009 'Touching the past: hunting the future'. In *Floating Life: Contemporary Aboriginal Fibre Art.* Brisbane: Queensland Art Gallery pp 29–37.

Foster, J. 2012 '*Winneringu!* Tjanpi desert weavers'. In T. Acker and J. Carty (eds), *Ngaanyatjarra: Art of the lands.* Crawley, Western Australia: UWA Publishing, pp.149–157.

Gough, J. 2009 *Tayenebe: Tasmanian aboriginal women's fibrework.* Hobart: Tasmanian Museum and Art Gallery.

Ingold, T. and Hallam. E. 2007 'Creativity and cultural improvisation: an introduction'. In E. Hallam and T. Ingold (eds), *Creativity and Cultural Improvisation.* Oxford: Berg: pp.1–24.

Johnston, I. G., Goldhahn, J. and May, S. K. 2017 'Dynamic figures of Mirarr Country: Chaloupka's four-phase theory and the question of variability within a rock art style 109'. In D. Bruno, P. S. C. Taçon, J.-J. Delannoy, J.-M. Geneste (eds), *The Archaeology of Rock Art in Western Arnhem Land, Australia Terra Australis*; no. 47. ANU Press: Canberra.

Purich, T. 2012 'Kanytjupayi's attraction'. In T. Acker and J. Carty (eds), *Ngaanyatjarra: Art of the lands.* Crawley, Western Australia: UWA Publishing, p.161.

Sculthorpe, G. et al. 2011 *Indigenous Australia: Enduring Civilisation.* London: The British Museum.

West, A. L. 2006 *Aboriginal String Bags, Nets and Cordage.* Victoria: Melbourne Museum.

PART FOUR

Basketry: Healing and recovery

Introduction
Stephanie Bunn

Basketry's role in occupational therapy and healing has been well documented from the start of the twentieth century. Even before this, in the nineteenth century, basketry was a standard occupation taught by regional Blind Schools and 'Asylums'. The question of why basketry is so valuable for recovery is explored in this section with reference to three key areas of work: for people living with dementia, for people with psychological problems and for people recovering from brain injury or stroke.

This role of basketwork may seem to be the opposite of its role as a facilitator for developing mathematical understanding (discussed in Part 2), where the hand-skills of basketwork enhance the kinds of complex understandings required for design, engineering and architecture. Pause for reflection reveals that the same technical basketry movements are carried out in all cases and that these spatial, fluid, rhythmic, patterning skills of basketry are also an invaluable basis for memory work, psychological recovery and re-establishment of neural pathways.

Occupational therapist Florence Cannavacciuolo gives a valuable overview of the key reasons why basketry is so helpful in this regard across many areas of disability, from the requirements of hand-to-eye coordination and alternating left and right attention for brain development, to its rhythmic, meditative bodily practice, its collective and community involvement, and the sense of achievement embodied in the final artefact.

One might imagine that it would be difficult for people living with dementia to learn new skills such as basketwork, but the movements and social relationships are invaluable. Equally important are the deep bodily memories of past skills such as basketry and net-mending, incorporated in the hands through years of practice, as discussed by Paula Brown. These 'hand-memories', practiced again, can also trigger memories of life experiences which took place while skills were practiced in the past. Jon Macleod reinforces just how important such skillful and social memories are for people who grew up in primarily oral communities, such as on Gaelic speaking Uist and Lewis, where memories of making are embodied in proverbs, poems and sayings.

Uist was also home for 'Weaver of Grass', Angus MacPhee, who responded to the traumatic psychological impact of leaving home for war by working with the skills and materials of his childhood, creating clothing by twining and weaving grass while he was in psychiatric hospital for many years, as discussed by Joyce Laing and Joanne B. Kaar. The overlap of war trauma and injury is addressed by Hilary Burns, who shows how the development of shell-shock cures using basketry developed in tandem with other forms of occupational therapy in the early twentieth century. This is developed further by Catherine Paterson, who discusses the history of how occupational therapy's use of craft such as basketry for brain and physical injury links to the capacity of craft to be broken down into stages, its use of simple materials and its role in attention development. Finally, Tim Palmer provides a physiological explanation for why basketry is so valuable in re-establishing neural pathways for stroke patients, giving an enlightening account of the different kinds of basketry techniques and stages that can help different kinds of brain injury and trauma.

20

Basketry as a therapeutic activity

Florence Cannavacciuolo

Florence Cannavacciuolo is an occupational therapist who reveals her experience of basketry therapy through several concrete examples. She suggests reflection on the many potential benefits of basketry as therapy.

Introduction

Basketry, or the art of intertwining vegetable fibres, has existed for over 10,000 years. People from all around the world weave baskets and can learn it at any age. It is a universally applicable activity. The potential of basketry as a form of therapy became acknowledged at the start of the twentieth century, and basket-weaving soon became recognised as a new form of treatment. In fact, basketry is an extremely valuable therapeutic tool and has applications in a number of domains: in psychiatry, geriatrics, neurology, rheumatology, paediatrics, for sensory problems, for people in socially marginalised situations, etc.

Breaking down the activity into its elements, which is one feature of occupational therapy, makes it possible to identify several major potentials of basketry as a therapeutic activity for: sensory-motor skills, cognitive abilities, behavioural skills, time-management and psycho-affective and social skills. This diversity of the potential of basket-weaving can provide interesting results in clinical contexts too, such as with coordination difficulties, dyspraxia (developmental coordination disorder), attention difficulties, memory problems, neurological problems and neuro-visual problems amongst others . . . In my work as an occupational therapist, I use basketry in one-on-one sessions; or I may follow individuals within a group; or I may work with whole groups, according to the need, the nature of participants and the environment.

Basketry activities have many therapeutic uses that can be adapted according to the person, their age and the difficulties which they are encountering. In what follows, I present just a sample of the therapeutic effects that can be gained.

Basketry as a sensory-motor activity

Basketry requires movement from the whole upper body. It is an essentially bi-manual activity, with one hand helping and collaborating with the other at every step. As occupational therapy, basketry is therefore an interesting activity for people suffering from neurological problems or trauma affecting their upper body.

Basketry, and the complexity of movement that it requires, according to the materials, develops prehension, strength, sensibility, and coordination. Prehension – holding and grasping – is vital to basketry and is mostly done through the 'tridigital grip', using the thumb, index finger and middle finger. Basket-weaving and plaiting also develops manual dexterity, because it requires careful use of the fingers and awareness of movement and coordination when picking up, placing, stitching, twisting and bending willow rods into shape. A basket maker needs to adjust the size of their wrist, elbow and shoulder movements according to the length of the stick they are handling.

Basketry is an excellent strength developing activity. Strength is needed for the frequent use of secateurs and for splitting willow rods of different diameter, for example. Many patients are not able to control the force with which they manipulate willow, which affects the shape of the finished object. The development of motor-sensory control which comes with growing awareness of the pressure required to exerted on the material is very important. Flexibility and tonal variation contribute to the quality of braiding or assembly. Many children with writing problems have difficulty regulating the pressure they use when handwriting. Through weaving and manipulating willow, children learn to regulate, at their own rate, the pressure exerted on materials. Thus, in developing the motor control necessary for weaving, children can apply this in other aspects of their daily lives, which includes handwriting.

Packing down willow rods also helps to significantly reduce rheumatological problems with the hands, including malformed fingers, such as so-called 'swan-neck' deformities of the fingers. Using both hands with an upright stake between each finger, the pressure felt on the underneath of the fingers both significantly helps in the care of these conditions and in the reduction of pain.

Finally, basketry necessitates a fine-tuning of the senses. Through touch, a person can become sensitive to all the qualities of the material; its moisture content, warmth, roughness, suppleness, elasticity, resistance, variations in thickness, capacity to work with it in combination with other materials.

Basketry as visual-spatial activity

Currently, my occupational therapy work is centred around children who have additional support needs that are connected to difficulties in making sense of their visual and spatial surroundings. Their therapy involves discovering and experimenting with basketry activities to help the children to develop all essential abilities and capacities for themselves. Notably, the following capabilities are worked on:

- Exploration and visual discrimination – when seeing anomalies and controlling the quality of willow sticks, their shape and curvature.

- Hand-to-eye coordination for control of work – 'a basket maker weaves without looking: he or she has eyes at the end of his fingers and uses sight as a vital form of control'.

- Spatial awareness – to differentiate between shapes, lengths and widths of willow sticks.

- Spatial positioning – to control the placement of the willow in the right spot.

- Directional sense – to be aware of and follow the movement of willow sticks.

- Abstraction and creation of mental models – to form a mental image of the object while it is in the process of being made and anticipate its form.

Basketry can therefore have an important role in treating difficulties with visual and spatial comprehension.

Basketry as cognitive activity

Children with dyspraxia also respond positively to regular basket-weaving activities. These bring about positive changes in the children's abilities to concentrate, plan, remember and anticipate change, as well as development in their logical and mathematical abilities. Indeed, through playful and pleasant basketry activities:

- Their planning and sequential ordering are solicited from the intermediary steps between preparing materials and obtaining a finished object.

- Their logical and mathematical skills are stimulated through counting rods, organising rods by length and thickness, comparing their dimensions, calculating circumference, volume and much more, which helps visualisation and even intuitive appreciation of the plaited object.

- Their memory skills are developed when naming basketry construction techniques and remembering the sequence of activities, when remembering specific key points on the basket, or when remembering the order of steps in the production of a basket.

Basketry as structuring and constructive activity

Having completed their first woven object people often exclaim, 'Nobody will ever believe that it was me who made this!' But basketry can have an important role in developing self-confidence and self-esteem. According to Gaëlle Riou, an occupational therapist specialised in psychiatry, the development of self-esteem through such activity is in part due to the amount of time needed to finish the given project (2015). The necessary perseverance to continue, despite encountering problems, is key. This deep engagement, which is recognisable in the eyes of others through basketry, has important therapeutic effects.

At the same time, the patient has created a new object and can form a relationship with it. The quality of this relationship is another important aspect of their recovery. The attachment to such objects is, in fact, a characteristic shared by us all. For example, at the start of a treatment, a

FIGURE 20.1 *Collective, contemplative nest by Florence Cannavacciuolo. Photo Julien Humbert.*

patient will be surprised if asked, 'Who is the object for?' and they will not be sure how to respond. 'It's for no one!' they say, and they do not want to take it home with them, or show it to people, or give it to anyone. The following week, they won't remember what they had done. However, as the treatment progresses, patients become more and more attached to the objects they are making. The patient begins by deciding that they will keep the object when it is finished, then later they decide to give it to someone special. 'I already know who I will give this to!' they say. The plaited object effectively becomes an emotionally-loaded message.

Basketry also allows a person to establish an idea of limits, a clear sense of rules and thus, it helps them to become more adaptable. It is not about immediate returns: the end product is not reached for some time. This allows patients to imagine their future selves. 'I'll be able to use this in the garden, or for shopping.' However, the relationship between basketry and time is complicated for patients with certain problems. Here, basketry can also help patients rediscover their present through integrating that which qualifies for an expression of frustration with that which is simply going to take time. In this information technology age, we are often swallowed up by the immediacy of everything. Basketry can help suspend time.

There's the time to wait for the right season to harvest materials. There's the time to dry and soak materials. There's the time to prepare and sort sticks according to their length and thickness. There's the time we don't see passing as we dive into a succession of simple gestures that can be accomplished without conscious thought. According to Dr Herbert Benson, repeated sounds or movements trigger a 'relaxation response' that slows the heartbeat, releases muscular tension and slows the breathing rate. He compares this reaction to the body's reaction during meditation (1993, 222).

In this way, basketry is therefore an interactive activity as it enables not only relations with oneself, but with others, too.

Basketry as socialising activity

Firstly, basketry requires attention to basic rules in order to complete a woven form. Secondly, basketry, if displayed publicly in an exhibition, will be seen and judged by others. This can cause strong emotions within groups. Thirdly, basketmakers working within a group will, from time to time, be confronted with the creative difficulties that arise from the technique, and these people will be able to work together to overcome their problems. These periods of discussion will become a time of meeting and a space of elaboration, where members can talk about anything and everything, from the important things, to the banal. This reflective process helps people to mend.

Young people in social or judicial care have often not had the opportunities that would have enabled them to develop positive relationships with others from childhood, to calmly gain a foothold in the world and be socialized and develop into a well-rounded person. For these young people, for whom new things may be viewed with apprehension, if not suspicion, practising basketry gives them a symbolic way to create structure. It also creates a space and an atmosphere

FIGURE 20.2 *Plaiting in the Quartier Les Beaudottes, Sevran, Paris. Photo Florence Cannavacciuolo.*

where worries and concerns can be shared. Thus basketry, with its rules and regulations and the necessary confrontation with materials, engages these children who are struggling in school or are refusing all teaching, and allows them to develop self-confidence.

Basketry provides the opportunity to work on one's basic competencies, to write oneself into the history of the world, and to become the kind of person who tries to understand that world. Basketry thus enables young people to enter into processes of socialization and personal development.

The collective character of basketry is one of the aspects that helps patients, especially those suffering from similar problems, to discover a better acceptance of technology, a comparison and exchange of meaning in their actions, without value judgements. Basketry also renders communicable to others features which express a person's personality, such as aesthetic choices of materials and colours. It valorises intention as much as results, and in doing so, valorises people, especially those who are suffering.

Conclusion

The many benefits of basketry have wide-reaching effects: relational, mental, cognitive, physical and so on. When considering basketry as part of the process of a course of treatment, we can say that basketry is therapeutic. The practice of basketry can help people with disabilities and teaches them how to solve their specific problems.

Basketry is therefore a manual, spatial, constructive, structuring, interactive and socializing activity. These are just a few of the multiple ways that basketry can help therapy. The field is vast, the possibilities are almost endless.

Bibliography

Benson, H. 1993 *The Relaxation Response*. London: Crown Publications.
Riou, G. 2015 'Le tricot en psychiatrie: le renouveau d'un médiateur oublié', *Revue Santé Mentale* 202 (November): 64.

21

The hand-memory work of An Lanntair in the Outer Hebrides[*]

Jon Macleod

When undertaking research for the *Woven Communities* project and for our broader memory project at An Lanntair, working with people living with dementia, we were reminded of the nature of language and culture here in the islands. Knowledge is often disseminated as part of an oral tradition, face-to-face, so if you need to find anything out you need to speak with people. Books are sometimes refered to here as the 'memory of the white paper'. Local knowledge is often solely in peoples heads, research takes time.

A good memory and face-to-face communication have always been highly valued in Gaelic society, as it is in any oral culture that, by its very nature, does not rely on the written word to remember or record. This oral tradition has been essential in keeping island culture and the Gaelic language alive. It provides a sense of continuity, a generational bridge and a way of learning about local and family history in a truly interactive way, marking time and logging experiences. It expresses the basic human need for humour, gossip, conversation and song, as well as for genealogy, storytelling, poetry and words for naming and mapping.

Ways of remembering work slightly differently here. Pre-plastic, ear cuts denoted sheep ownership, as expressed in the codified combination of marks shown in the *West-Side Telephone Directory,* linking croft number to a person's official name, village name, address, ear mark and telephone number. For example: 'Donald John MacPhail – Fionn – 38 South Bragar – Barr Tasgeal agus Toll, Dha Beum Bho'n a'chluais Deas'.

An ear-mark combination has a poetic cadence when recited and lovers would sometimes compare the ear marks from each other's croft to see whether, if their flocks merged, the resulting ear mark would sound right. One islander had committed to memory every ear-mark combination for every croft on the island and had made his living by going to sheep round-ups (*fanks*) and repatriating lost sheep to their owners.

[*] This chapter by Jon Macleod is complementary to Chapter 22 by Paula Brown. Both of them worked on the same dementia-friendly community project for An Lanntair on Lewis and Uist, dealing with memory and hand-work.

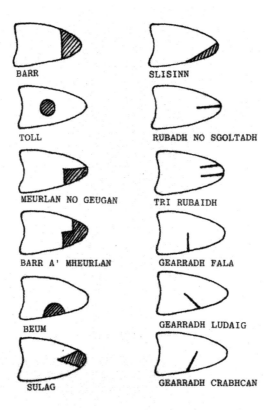

FIGURE 21.1 *Extract from the* West-side sheep ear-mark telephone directory. Comunn Eachdraidh an Taobh Siar/*Westside Historical Society'*.

In similar vein, in the past ocean knowledge would often have been passed on through mnemonics, a string of names lining up places on land until the boat was on the right spot for good fishing. These fishing marks also have a poetry to them.

Memory and baskets – some examples

In regard to baskets, in our work with Gaelic proverbs this one using a creel (*cliabh*) reference seemed appropriate. Its literal meaning is 'Good quality peats (*caoran*) don't fall from empty baskets'. We asked lots of people what this might mean or refer to. We got many different possibilities, all of them rather vague or off the mark. So I asked my neighbour – 'It's obvious . . . pearls of wisdom don't fall from empty minds.'

Another aspect of our recent work has been to look at 'hand memory' and haptic stimulation when working with people living with dementia. At what remains in the 'memory of the hands' from a lifetime of use, once the memory of the mind may have become less reliable.

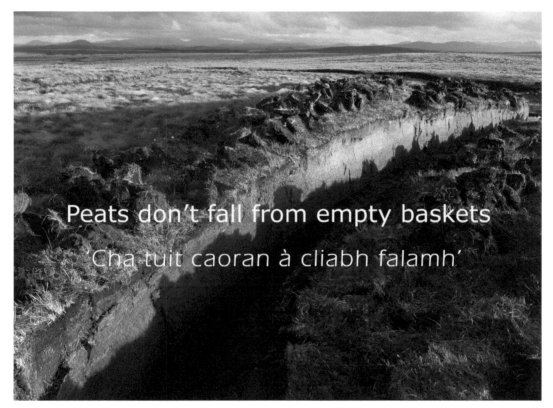

FIGURE 21.2 *Jon Macleod – peat cutting on the Barvas moor.*

We held sessions that recall common local work tasks from the past such as net-mending, basketwork and twining (a skill used in making marram horse collars), creel carrying, spinning, weaving and preparing local delicacies such as herring, gutted with a thumb in seconds. It was incredible to see service-users who hadn't spoken or moved much in months, come to life once their hands and brains were engaged with something familiar.

Later on, in our research with the *Woven Communities* project, we also focused on the use of marram grass weaving and basketry in Uist. The island is known as *'Tìr A'Mhurian* – Land of the marram grass' in Gaelic and has a great tradition for use of marram, or bent grass, for making horse collars, grain sacks and grain meal baskets (*ciosan*). Using imagery from the School of Scottish Studies, we held informal village knowledge sessions that filled in the missing gaps in conventional archive information and put names and stories to the faces in the photos.

Amongst other things we learned from local elders in Kildonan that Duncan Macdonald, the man in our marram weaving archival images, was known for his great skill and industry and that himself and his wife in one day sheared all their sheep, processed and dyed the wool and started weaving a tweed from that wool. A huge undertaking.

Bringing flowers into the care home during this work inspired memories too. 'The Yellow flag is in bloom – the Herring is here', a saying that recalls the time of year that herring would come into

FIGURE 21.3 *Duncan Macdonald – Peninerine, South Uist, weaving a marram grass horse mat – or* plàt-eich. *This* plaide *or 'blanket' was used across the horse's back and stopped the creels hurting its flanks. The extra section in the weave made a pad for the saddle to rest on. This was a small wooden crook-saddle – the* srathair – *from which the pair of creels was hung on each side in balance. Photograph by Werner Kissling, courtesy School of Scottish Studies archive.*

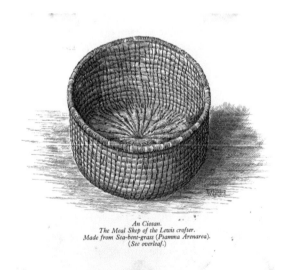

An Ciosan.
The Meal Skep of the Lewis crofter.
Made from Sea-bent-grass (Psamma Arenarea).
(See overleaf.)

FIGURE 21.4 Ciosan *(grain meal basket)*, The Basketmakers of Newstead and Ness, *William Thompson 1926.*

local waters. Perhaps simply seeing a picture of a flower is not enough, the sensual, experiential and shared is what makes life worth living.

A fourth basketry illustration can be learned from, Dr Finlay in Shawbost, whose great-grandfather, Iain Buidhe, from Ness made the marram grass grain meal *ciosan*, pictured in Figure 21.4, as a wedding present for his daughter, and from whom we collected the following anecdote:

> Also known in my family was the use of the *ciosan* as a measure of time: by New Year that the day will have lengthened by enough time to allow you to mill an extra full *ciosan* of meal. That's the length that had come on the day. I still refer to that each year.

22

Hand memories in basketwork and net-making among people with dementia in Uist and Lewis, told through life-moment stories and associated images[*]

Paula Brown

Conversations with Paula Brown, ARORA Project, An Lanntair, Lewis

The memory work we have been doing through our An Lanntair project always focuses on who we are and what we have. Our common ground, our knowledge. Each person is valued on an equal level. So often dementia is seen as a loss, as a deficit of something we once had. Through these sessions, we welcome the lived experience and knowledge of the people participating, aiming to pass this on to the community, to share that knowledge, given so generously, which we would be losing without this gift of sharing.

The clarity with which memories are recalled of childhood and young adulthood events and landscapes has been a powerful opportunity to glimpse back through the lens of dementia to past skills and techniques. A lot of the joy in this work is in recognizing when people shine and connect. It is often a tiny moment that is barely noticeable, but something shifts when a person contributes in some way to a shared task. It does feel good to be able to share some knowledge or a skill where it is valued and welcomed.

---

[*] This chapter by Paula Brown is complementary to Chapter 21 by Jon Macleod. Both of them worked on the same dementia-friendly community project for An Lanntair on Lewis and Uist, dealing with memory and hand-work.

Hand-memory work

When we practiced skills that people had done during their youths or working lives, we found that witnessing these skills could sometimes prompt the ability and associated memories for participants.

Example 1. Marram rope and *ciosan* making. Intergenerational session at Sacred Heart Care Home, South Uist, with students from Iochdar School 23rd November 2016

Part of our work with *Woven Communities* was about sharing community knowledge and physically remaking almost-out-of-living-memory objects. We decided to take a *ciosan* (meal measure basket) along to Sacred Heart Care Home to see if anybody remembered it and what the binding material might have been, a concern of our local basketmaker Dawn Susan.

    We had been working with the children at Iochdar School making marram grass and bailer twine rope prior to this session, which offered the opportunity for the children to show off their rope-making skills and discuss the intricacies of this new-found skill with potential experts in the community.

- 'That's very good rope, strong, it takes skill to make it strong. We made baskets in Shetland, we called them *kishies*'. Jessie, an elder from the home.

- 'I think I remember this lady when she was a neighbour. And this lady over here is an aunt of my mother.' (Boy from Iochdar School, enthusing about the joy of the conversations).

FIGURE 22.1 *Making rope with children and elders at Sacred Heart Care Home, South Uist, 2016. Photograph: Paula Brown.*

I noticed the community cohesion in the children's framing of the elders within the community at this session. The shared Gaelic language was a wonderful connection between the generations, and the community connections were quickly established.

- A particularly wonderful moment was noticeable recognition from the children of the concept of living history in connecting historical evidence of local weaver of grass, Angus MacPhee, from school books, projects and films, with lived experience of his neighbours. As one girl explained, 'She was telling me about how she lived nearby and often saw Angus in the street and how he was a gentle, quiet soul. I can't believe she knew him. I've been learning about him.'

- And Mary Godden, from Cille Amhlaidh (Kilaulay in English), South Uist, aged 101 at the time, born in 1915 and the only child in the village after the others emigrated,[1] was able to solve a mystery that we hoped to uncover during the remaking of marram grass horse collars with a simple phrase, 'You cover the wire. . .'. I can still picture the moment of connection in Dawn Susan's face as she realized and said afterwards, 'Of course you cover a wire! How else would we strengthen it? I'd never have known that without that first-hand knowledge.'

Example 2. Net-mending session at Blar Buidhe Care Centre, Stornoway 22nd September 2015

As part of the *Eilean* exhibition at An Lanntair, 2015, there was a performance piece entitled *Net Mending & Yarning*, where Ian Stephen told local stories while Coy, a retired fisherman from

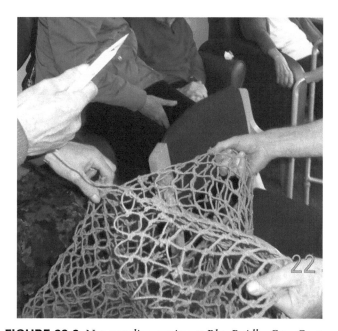

FIGURE 22.2 *Net-mending session at Blar Buidhe Care Centre.*

Stornoway, demonstrated net-mending. I knew of a retired fishing captain, J, living in a local care home, and thought this could be a wonderful session to share with him and his friends. I had spent many sessions reading the local newspapers with J, picking out stories of seafaring and rescue missions, which he particularly enjoyed.

Recently, J had become withdrawn and had not had a conversation for some months, only using facial expressions, nods and eye contact to indicate requests and needs. During the course of the net-mending session, his face gradually became more engaged with what was happening in the room, following Ian around the space with his eyes as he told local stories in his animated, engaging fashion. He took the nets on to his lap and held them, until eventually, I heard a familiar voice say, 'Twenty years'.

I hadn't heard J speak in such a long time that I had to glance around the room to be sure it actually was him speaking to me, before I saw him looking up at me with his striking blue eyes. I sat next to him and we shared a wonderful conversation, which started in single words and ended with whole sentences about the images of his boats in his room. All the while, he was eagerly sharing his skill, demonstrating the movements for me to watch and follow, as is often the Hebridean way with teaching hand-skills.

J's words:

J – Twenty years, since.
P – Since you last mended a net?
J – Aye, since the nets. A long time.
Good knots. Strong.
The nets always break, you can't help it.

It's a net-mending needle. No fancy word, no.
Hold it further back, no, not like that, like this, see? Watch me. Aye, that's it. Now over and over. Yes, I did this. Every day.
I know him, Coy, aye. I know him well. It's been a long time.
We were the best.
We were good, we had to be.
No room for mistakes, slow, lazy, no.
Very brave.
A hard life. All weathers. Every day. No choice.
But the seals would follow my boat, most days, and the birds. I liked that.
I read about the lifeboats. I'm glad when they get back ok.
Pictures of my boats. Two of them, photos and art. In my room.

Through these moments, we find ourselves inextricably woven into each other's lives and stories.

PAULA BROWN OCTOBER 2018

Since Paula wrote this piece, she has documented birds-nests and rope-making workshops with basketmaker Dawn Susan, children and elders on Lewis. See https://dfclanntair.wordpress.com/img_7293/

She has also been taught to knit socks in Hebridean fashion by Mary Kate, from the Leverburgh Care Home. Paula recounts:

The phrase 'while knitting a sock' is so often heard, when talking about the harsh labour of crofting life. I took the plunge and had a go while carrying my peats back from Shawbost this summer. I felt I had to, quite literally, walk a mile in these incredible women's shoes. Dawn made me a wonderful creel and strap and I set about knitting as I went because I was informed, 'You can't carry a creel without knitting a sock!' Everyone had a small piece of knitting tucked about them. Industriousness was highly valued here and still is. 'The devil makes work for idle hands,' I'm told.

Notes

1 This information was accessed from an interview by Gaelic interpreter Maggie Smith with Mary, shortly afterwards, see at dfclanntair.wordpress.com.

23

Meeting Angus MacPhee, the Weaver of Grass

Joyce Laing OBE and Stephanie Bunn

Interview with Joyce Laing, 2016

The case of Angus MacPhee is well known in Scotland as an example of a person who, through making art, tried to relieve their own inner challenges. In Angus' case, having been hospitalised in Inverness in the 1940s with psychiatric problems, he began to make familiar items, such as clothes from woven grass at the hospital farm. The rope and weaving techniques he used were ones he would probably have learned as a child living on South Uist; the materials would have been familiar to him from his home environment. This chapter provides a short account by Joyce Laing, the art therapist who first recognized Angus' work. The next, Chapter 24, provides an account by Joanne B. Kaar, an artist who explored the techniques and materials that were so familiar to Angus for a later project by travelling theatre group, *Horse and Bamboo.*

Joyce Laing was one of the first art therapists in Scotland. She was originally employed by the Scottish Office prison department. From 1973 onwards, she worked at the Special Unit in Barlinnie prison with men, including Jimmy Boyle, who had staged the (in)famous protests there on the prison roofs. 'Any art material you want, you can have, as long as it keeps them quiet,' she was told, and so her career in art therapy began, working in several hospitals across Scotland and staging exhibitions of prisoners' work.

Through this work she developed a growing interest in what she calls 'Art Extraordinaire', sometimes known as 'Outsider Art'. For Joyce, such creative work formed a kind of 'raw', untutored art, reflecting the personal world of the makers who, in many of the cases Joy encountered, were people with psychiatric disorders. Joyce's first meeting with Angus MacPhee in the early 1990s came about through this interest.

Angus MacPhee grew up on a croft in South Uist, a uniquely beautiful island on the Outer Hebrides. In 1940, during the Second World War, he was sent to the Faeroes as one of the Lovat Scouts. He was fine at first, but soon developed the symptoms of what later became known as schizophrenia. The doctor realised he was not well, and he was transferred to the army hospital. He seemed to get better and went back to Uist to recover. But he started to neglect himself, and

FIGURE 23.1 *Angus MacPhee. Photograph: Joyce Laing and Timothy Neat.*

was sent to Craig Dunain Psychiatric Hospital, Inverness. He was many years in this hospital before Joyce first met him. In the 1940s, medicine for such illnesses was in its infancy, and farm work was one common activity for people with mental illness. And so it was, that Angus was set to work in the hospital farm-ward, working in the vegetable garden, perhaps reflecting his early life working on a croft.

It was almost by chance that Joyce met him, advised by a local taxi driver taking her to the hospital to meet 'the old man who made things from grass'. Once directed to the hospital farm, she said,

> Jim and I began to rummage about under the bushes. 'Look!' I cried excitedly, 'It's a boot.' Seconds later, Jimmy emerged from the undergrowth, triumphant with another boot. We placed them on the grass – they were a pair. Then like kids at a party, we ran in and out of the bushes, bringing out all manner of garments, a coat, trousers, a peat creel and on it went. The charge nurse watching us from the ward window, decided to join us to find out what we were up to. He could see by our glowing expressions of amazement and delight that we were overwhelmed by the discovery of Angus's grass work.
>
> LAING 2000, 47–8

Angus soon appeared, a 'fine, handsome man, over 6 feet tall' (ibid.). Aside from grey hospital garb, he was also wearing a hand-woven grass cap, a sheep's wool muffler, and a sheep's wool handkerchief tucked into his jacket pocket, all that he had made himself. Apparently, he wore these clothes he made from grass, beech leaves and fleece outside, but not in the house, though

FIGURE 23.2 *Grass coat and trousers by Angus MacPhee at* Art Extraordinaire. *Photograph: Joyce Laing.*

he was allowed to bring in the wool to spin, which he did with his fingers while sitting at his bedside.

A Gaelic speaker, Angus was an elective mute, and at the time that Joyce first met him, she said that he looked straight through her. Twice a year, as part of their pruning and tidying, the hospital groundsmen burned the grass artefacts that he had made, and Joyce said that he would sometimes go and watch, apparently undisturbed by the destruction of his work. A tragedy, she said, that so much of his work will never be seen.

Following this serendipitous meeting, through Joyce's initiative, Angus's work was shown at the *Art Extraordinaire* exhibition at Glasgow Print Studio, and later, elsewhere in Scotland. In 1996 he returned to Uist, dying there in 1997, aged 81.

Angus alternated from gathering grass to collecting sheep's wool from local fences adjoining the hospital grounds. The techniques that Angus used all involved him twisting or twining the material into long yarn or ropes, and then, (employing no tools except two lengths of broken fence wire), using a mixture of looping, netting and stitching to make clothing and containers. These were all skills he could have learned in his early crofting life. For Joyce, these techniques, and Angus's use of grass, beech leaves and wool, reveal something both timeless and fundamentally human about the methods he used, reminiscent of archaeological artefacts, and also reflecting the love of materials and 'social sculpture' of the twentieth century work of German artist Joseph Beuys, and the ways that contemporary UK artists Andy Goldsworthy and Chris Drury never lose

FIGURE 23.3 *Grass boots by Angus MacPhee. Photograph: Joyce Laing.*

the intrinsic qualities of their materials in their work. In this, his work reflects approaches 'manifest through the endless generations of mankind' (ibid. 71).

Artefacts known to have been made by Angus MacPhee include:

A jacket made of grass; full-length trousers with woven pockets; grass ankle-boots; a peat creel; a pony harness; several pouches interwoven with wild-flowers; grass waders; grass ropes; a sheep's wool vest; a sheep's wool muffler; a handkerchief; sandals; and hats (ibid. 80).

Bibliography

Laing, J. 2000 *Angus McPhee: Weaver of Grass*. Loch Maddy: Taigh Chearsabhagh Art Centre and Museum.

24

Making grass replicas inspired by the work of Angus MacPhee

Joanne B. Kaar

For Joe, a quiet, unassuming and extremely talented man. You were my world.

My name is Joanne B. Kaar. I live in Dunnet village, on Dunnet Head in Caithness, with views to the village of Brough, where I grew up. The Pentland Firth and the Orkney Island of Hoy are in the distance. In 2011, Bob Frith, the artistic director of *Horse and Bamboo* Theatre in Lancashire, contacted me as they were planning to develop a show about Angus MacPhee, a man who had lived on South Uist on the Hebrides. They needed costumes and props and wondered if I could help with this. Angus was known as the 'Weaver of Grass'.

I had seen Angus' incredible work while it was on display in Stornoway many years ago. Angus was a crofter. He lived in South Uist but had spent almost 50 years in Craig Dunain Psychiatric Hospital in Inverness. He chose not to speak, instead he made garments from grass and leaves growing in the hospital grounds, twisting the plants into ropes or *simmans*, a traditional technique he would have learned at home in Uist. When he'd finished making, Angus just discarded each artefact and started another one. It was fortunate that Joyce Laing OBE, an art therapist and supporter of Outsider Art, discovered Angus and saved some of his work. I made plans to start research and visit Joyce in Pittenweem, Fife, to take a closer look at the grass garments made by Angus. Exactly how Angus made his garments was a mystery Joyce wanted to solve and I've plenty of grass in my field to experiment with!

The grass 'weavings' made by Angus are now old and fragile. With the help of my husband Joe, who made a sketch of the construction by looking at a patch of more open weave, and with the information from Joyce's first had experience of seeing Angus work, I took measurements and made notes in my sketchbook. Next, with a ball of cotton string, I made a few test pieces. The construction techniques Angus used were not traditional to the UK. In his isolation, with grass, hands and time, Angus 'invented' and perfected his methods.

Back home, I drew out a full-size paper template to work from. Starting at the waistline, I made a grass rope to fit the width, then, by opening up the rope at regular intervals, I made a series of loops, threading the grass rope in and out of the gaps. I used dried grass as this helped hold the twist in the rope. Using a looping technique, I worked upwards towards the neck of the garment,

FIGURE 24.1 *Joanne B. Kaar making replica Angus MacPhee garment. Oct 2011. Photograph: Joanne B Kaar.*

the same direction as in the original. The loops were small and pulled tight at the waistline, getting larger towards the chest. I used my fingers as a gauge and pulled the rope to the size I wanted. While keeping the same number of loops in each row, the garment widened at the chest, because each individual loop was bigger. This made a flat section for the front of the garment. The arms were to be added later.

Working with a short length was easier, as I didn't have to pull so much rope through the loops. When I ran out of rope, I simply made it longer by twisting in more grass. The cuffs of the sleeves and base of Angus's garment were deliberately frilly. The loops on these parts were too matted and confusing to understand how they were made. So, I decided to use the same looping technique for everything as this was the only one I was sure he had used. Working from the original waist band, I made two large loops into every one in the row before – this instantly made it wider and uneven. Working from the waistline down, I followed the paper template and adjusted the loop-size to complete the front side.

Making the back of the garment was easier. I started with a waistband as before, but at the end of each row, I looped through the sides of the front piece, connecting the two halves together as

FIGURE 24.2 Swallowtail coat *from grass made for* Horse and Bamboo *Theatre. Photograph: Joanne B Kaar.*

FIGURE 24.3 Grass boot replicas *by Joanne B. Kaar, April 2012. Photograph: Joanne B. Kaar.*

I worked back and forth, leaving gaps for the sleeves and neck. The construction technique was easier to see on these larger loops. The garment was getting quite heavy, so I made the sleeves separately. Again, starting with a rope, I made a series of loops, but this time I tied it into a circle, the same diameter as the sleeve, working in the round, not two flat pieces. This was stitched with a grass rope to the main body section. It's difficult to see on the original garment if the sections were made in the round or sewn together later. I used a combination of both. The sleeves attached and only the neck to do. I worked this in the round, picking up loops from the back and front of the garment until it was finished.

The looping techniques Angus used are found in many other cultures, including those used by indigenous people of Australia. Socks made more than 800 years ago, using the same looping technique have been discovered in a cave in Arizona, made from combed yucca plant, with fragments of feathers to make them more comfortable.

I went on to make grass garments for the *Horse and Bamboo* Theatre, which toured to rave reviews and sell out shows in 2012 and 2013. I have also made full-size replica garments, including the iconic grass jumper, trousers with pockets and belt, and many, many shoes. My replicas are now held in collections with Glasgow Museums as part of the *Art Extraordinary* collection, along with Angus's originals; at Whitworth Art Gallery, Manchester in their *Outsider Art* collection as part of arts and health; at Northampton shoe museum; and at *Craftspace*, Birmingham's outsider craft collection.

I continued to develop and research related techniques which have been found in the UK – using nalbinding (knotless netting), a technique once used by Norse cultures, using wool to make a dense fabric for garments including socks, hats and shoes. This predates knitting and is a more complicated series of loops, with many different variations. I combined local plants with nalbinding to make contemporary artwork.

I have notebooks with diagrams and photos detailing many of Angus's grass garments, waiting to be made.

25

The legacy of the First World War for basketmaking

Hilary Burns

Basketwork provokes a variety of contradictory responses. Despite the time and effort it takes to become a proficient maker – a three to five-year apprenticeship in the past – basketry has often been perceived as lower status compared to other crafts. There is also a commonly held understanding that basketwork is therapeutic, yet at the same time, confusingly, one might be called a 'basket-case' for practicing it, hardly a compliment. Through the *Basketry Then and Now* project at the University of Hertfordshire, we have had the opportunity to examine the impact of the First World War on the craft and its materials, how views of basketry have changed, and how the association with therapy arose.[1]

Today, basketmaking is practiced by relatively few professional makers, but at the end of the 1800s, it was a commonplace occupation and it was hard work. Many baskets, often large, were made in a day, and the working week was long. The beginnings of industrialization in Britain demanded enormous numbers of containers. Baskets were everywhere and essential, on a scale now hard to imagine. Basketmaking then was a viable trade. It was done by men, working as individuals, or in large workshops 'on the plank', side by side, and an efficient apprenticeship system had developed. From at least 1850 lists of wages, sizes and prices were printed in order to standardize output. These included hundreds of basket types for agriculture and government departments, such as the Post Office and War Office, from whom large contracts were sought.

Making on this scale demanded a consistent source of high-quality material. Willow, light enough to be easily handled and transported, strong enough to produce robust work, was the natural choice. Before 1918 the largest, most productive growing area in England had developed in the East Midlands. The alluvial flood plains of the valleys were ideally suited to growing the best willows and the industry was huge. Growers maintained the willow beds on a thirty-year rota. Associated trades such as rod merchants involved vast numbers of workers. Women and children peeled the rods to produce white willow by hand in the spring.

During and just after the war years, many willow beds fell into decline owing to the loss of manpower required for the intensive work of maintaining them. Regenerating a bed neglected for more than a year was not cost effective. Food shortages meant that other crops were planted. Imports that had started to fill the gap before and during the war were now cheaper than could be produced at home and there was, over time, a total collapse of the industry in this area. Today the Somerset Levels, less suitable for growing other crops, is the only remaining area of willow production on any scale in the UK.

Willow was always important to the War Office. Reviewing the situation after the war in order to secure supply, it appointed a National Willow Officer. A living collection of basketry willows was established at Long Ashton (now held at Rothamsted Research Centre, Hertfordshire). Today, as well as providing cuttings to encourage basketmakers to plant their own willow beds, and developing varieties for biomass planting, the rich chemistry of willow is providing scientists with the potential to create new medicines to treat diseases.

During the First World War, basketmaking was a reserved occupation. There was an ever-increasing demand for baskets for transporting food and goods on the railways. Uses included for woven airplane seats, for over 22,000 carrier pigeons, for observational balloon baskets, medical supply panniers, gun mats, and for artillery shell baskets that held the shell cases transported to the front line. Wounded men flooded the hospitals and many needed invalid chairs and spinal carriages, many of them woven from willow. These men were the so-called 'basket-cases'.[2]

The history of the Dryad Cane Furniture Works in Leicester, later Dryad Handicrafts, highlights the rapid changes that took place at this time. Harry Peach set up Dryad Cane Furniture Works in 1907 and by 1914 his factory was producing a range of furniture, using imported cane (rattan), from Indonesia. Dryad Handicrafts grew out of the company's strength in basketmaking and its use of 'pulp' or centre cane, the pith of the rattan. Compared with willow, it was a rather lifeless material, but much easier to soak and handle. The cane basketry that those who did school craftwork in the 1950s may be familiar with, took over from willow in the public consciousness. A social reformer, Peach thought that that weaving and pottery were the most important crafts, and that industrialization had caused a degradation of work. Dryad's motto was 'Quality First'. By 1923 the Dryad Press was established. It was Charles Crampton, a local master basketmaker, who provided the know-how and brought Peach's ideas to life. His book *Canework*, running to many editions, was first printed in 1924.

When war began the workshops held a pool of trained basketmakers, and there was an established route for importing materials. All efforts now were diverted to weaving many thousands of artillery shell baskets, using split cane. Mary Crabb (see Chapter 10), speaking about one of these shell cases in her work on remembrance says, 'It was a curious object, with a slightly sinister cyclic quality about it. Woven to offer protection to objects of death and destruction – those injured by the shells it protected were then taught to weave baskets as a means of therapy and rehabilitation'.

The First World War saw unprecedented one to two million wounded men returning home. The War Office had both an urgent need to get men back to the front to maintain the army's fighting strength, and to ensure productive living by finding employment for them, while minimizing pensioning men off. Long before the First World War, there were already established 'Blind Asylums' where basketmaking had been taught to the blind as a useful occupation. Workshops for the otherwise disabled were not so common but at this time, although basketry was slowly declining as a viable trade, it was still promoted as a viable way of earning a living. Reasons for this were the small start-up cost, few tools required and the fact that simple baskets were not difficult to learn to make.

What made basketry a suitable occupation for the less able? It was incremental in the making, built up row-by-row – you can feel your way round a basket. Texture, pattern and three-dimensional awareness combine to make something that can be 'read' with eyes closed. It can be easier to grade willow in this way, and blind basketmakers were said to be able to 'hear' mistakes when weaving.[3]

'St Dunstan's' (now 'Blind Veterans UK'), set up by Sir Arthur Pearson, helped men 'learn to be blind and make a success of it'. It was the institution where all English war blinded were sent. Willow work was done in the traditional way, but those who could not bend to work 'on the plank' learned canework sitting at a table. Training for six to eight months was frequently done in conjunction with occupations such as poultry farming. When men returned to life outside, St Dunstan's supplied materials at cost and distributed orders for work.

Institution such as the 'Royal Star and Garter Homes' and 'Orsett Works' in Essex were set up for otherwise wounded men. At 'Chailey Heritage Craft Schools' men learned to deal with loss of limbs alongside disabled children in basketmaking workshops. Basketmaking also provided work for prisoners of war. Scottish institutions included the 'Royal Northern Counties Institute for the Blind' in Inverness, the 'Scottish War Blinded Centre' at Linburn, near Edinburgh, and 'Oldmill Curative Workshop' in Aberdeen. Newspaper images, calls for financial support, as well as sales of baskets by these institutions, created an association between basketry, disablement and healing in the public mind.

In the second half of 1916 following the Somme, almost forty percent of the five-fold increase in casualties were suffering from a new, barely understood disorder, 'shell shock'. Men showed no obvious physical damage but displayed a baffling range of symptoms. Shell shock shares some features with what today is known as post-traumatic stress disorder (PTSD). Before 1914, mental illness was generally thought of in terms of heredity and degeneration. Many felt that the men

FIGURE 25.1 *Basketmaking, Seale Hayne Military Hospital, Devon, Feb 1919, silver gelatin photograph. 8.5 x 13.5 cm. Margaret Preston archive, Art Gallery of New South Wales Archive. Gift of William Preston 1963 © Margaret Rose Preston Estate. Licensed by Copyright Agency Image: AGNSW ARC100.8.19.*

were malingering, feeble-minded, or suffering from hysteria – 'a women's disease', and treatment was often unsuitable and brutal.

In response to the increasing need for beds, Seale-Hayne in rural Devon, built as an agricultural college, was offered to the War Office as a satellite to Netley military hospital in 1918. A charismatic doctor, Arthur Hurst, took up the offer, relocating to Seale-Hayne with many severe or incurable cases of non-organic, hysterical, functional nervous disorders, 300 of whom were from hospitals all over Britain. He had studied in Paris, between 1907 and 1908, under the French pioneers of neurology.

Hurst abandoned hypnotherapy and electric shock treatment, and promoted holistic treatment and humane methods, including simple psychotherapy, 'explanation, persuasion and re-education', encouraging the men to take an active part in effecting their own cure (Hurst, 1943, 299). He used physical manipulation, moving one limb manually while the patients looked from the working to the non-working one repeatedly. Perhaps he was practicing an early form of EMDR (eye movement desensitization) and reprocessing therapy, used to treat PTSD in recent years. The time it took to cure his patients decreased significantly as he practiced. Following the making of a very early Pathé film to accompany his lectures and the press branding his treatment 'the 10-minute miracle cure', there was much scepticism, and some branded him a charlatan.

Treatment after patients had recovered the use of their limbs included farm work and handicrafts in conjunction with good food and peaceful surroundings. A planned and funded feature of Hurst's proposal for the hospital was the provision and fitting out of craft workshops. Hurst too, thought basketry and pottery were the best crafts because they involved the use of both hands and he felt that this would aid recovery of his patients' normal muscular function by 'necessitating them to exercise careful and precise control of their affected hysterical limbs' (Hurst 1941).

His most celebrated patient, Percy Meek, from a basketmaking family in Snettisham, Norfolk, taught in the basketry workshop. In 1916, aged 23, Meek had had to be forcibly prevented from going over the parapet to attack German mortars firing at his trench. He became completely paralyzed, mute and regressed to early childhood. None of the treatments he had undergone had been successful until he came under Hurst's care. The Pathé film shows Percy before and after treatment, with the class, and the men berry picking with their baskets.

Artists Margaret McPherson and Glady Reynell ran the craft workshops. Later, discussing her work there, Margaret said:

Perhaps the most valuable of them all was basket-making. This simple craft has the greatest right of all the handicrafts to the name, as it is about the only one that cannot be carried on by machinery. The great help that basketmaking gives to twisted hands and stiff arms is now acknowledged by doctors who have worked in war hospitals. Pulling of the canes and holding and separating the rods used muscles and fingers that had become stiff and hard. Another thing that helped was the simplicity of the craft. It did not worry tired brains and took very little concentration to obtain a good result. These facts place basket-making well on the way to being one of the most useful of the handicrafts for war-time work . . .

Basketmakers will recognise the challenge of working with fresh hedgerow material:

The materials are inexpensive and substitutes can be easily procured. When cane gave out at the hospital, young rose shoots, raffia, and Paddy's lucerne were used. . . . sold to the local housewives of Newton Abbott (the nearest town), some of the women complained that the baskets 'started to shoot' . . . . but it was pointed out to them that these were really 'war baskets', so no money had to be given back.

PRESTON 1939, 27

There can be no certainty that Hurst's claims that his 'cures' were 'permanent' were correct, as there was no known follow-up. Research by Seale-Haynians; alumni and volunteers, traces the descendant families of the patients treated at Seale-Hayne. Percy Meek appears to have made a good recovery, returned to Norfolk, married and worked in the family business.

On both sides of the Atlantic there was a huge impetus to help heal the wounded. The use of crafts in recovery became known as 'Rehabilitation', and later, 'Occupational Therapy'. The early curative workshops offered in hospitals included 'bedside occupations' designed to give them something to do, help their injuries and, importantly, have a beneficial psychological effect. These generally included cane basketry. The craft occupations were delivered by educated women who now entered the professions following the war years. Basketmaking therefore became the flagship craft for Occupational Therapy, which itself gathered pace with the Second World War. By the late 1950s, however, with the growth of medical science, and development of vaccines, shorter

FIGURE 25.2 *Percy Meek in later life, courtesy of David Drewery, Snettisham.*

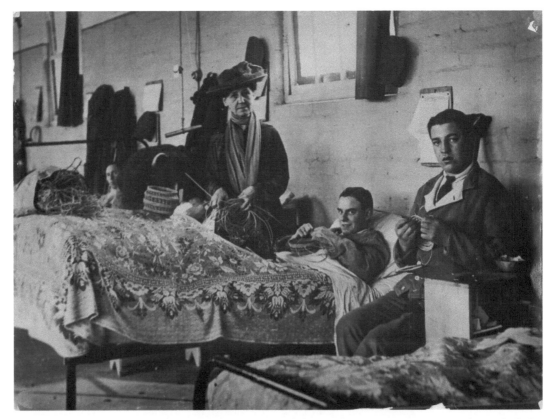

FIGURE 25.3 *Patients at the 5th Northern General Hospital, Leicester, 1920. Dryad supplied this hospital with cane off-cuts from the chair making business. © Record Office for Leicestershire, Leicester and Rutland, DE3736/1127.*

periods in hospital were needed. Patients moved from hospitals to community care. Basketry as part of Occupational Therapy became, by the 1960s, an embarrassment, a 'useless' craft, with no scientific value, a view that has to some extent coloured the perception of the craft.

Basketry's association with the war wounded, with Occupational Therapy and healing has left its mark. The protective role, the essential function of containment and holding, contributes to how we experience it. We are, after all, nurtured in baskets, from cradle to grave, literally from crib to coffin. There has been a resurgence in using and growing willow, a material grounded in nature, relying on the cycle of the seasons. The recent proliferation of books about making, and why it is good for you are changing our understanding of creative manual activities. Being 'in the zone' or experiencing 'flow' are talked about. Basketry, particularly, requires that you pay attention and focus on the often repetitive, almost meditative, strokes of the weaving. Ensuring that you are in the here and now allows the 'other' to be put aside for a while, and recent research shows that creative sensory activity promotes neural plasticity in the brain. Making may be our 'well' state. Today 'mindfulness' is something to aim for, but it's nothing new, as you will know if you've ever made a basket.

Notes

1 www.everydaylivesinwar.herts.ac.uk *Basketry Then and Now* project

2 It is likely that this American slang phrase means not that these men made baskets as a therapeutic aid, but that they were placed in baskets during recovery and often for life, see discussion in next chapter by Catherine Paterson.

3 Personal communication, Liz Balfour

Bibliography

Collier, D. 1918 *Cassels 'work' handbook on basketmaking.* London: Cassell and Company Ltd.

Dryad Works Committee Minutes 1911–1917 via Alan Beavon, director of Specialist Crafts, inheritor of Dryad Handicrafts.

Dunn, M. 2009 Hysterical War Neuroses: A study of Seale-Hayne Neurological Military Hospital, Newton Abbot 1918–1919. Unpublished University of Exeter degree dissertation.

Fitzrandolph H. E. and Doriel, H. M. 1926 *The Rural industries of England and Wales II. Osier-growing and basketry and some rural factories.* Oxford: Oxford University Press.

Hurst, A. F. 1941 'Hysterical contractures following injuries in war', Occupational Therapy & Rehabilitation 20 (4): 271–272.

Hurst, A. F. 1943 'War neuroses', *British Medical Journal* 1 (4289): 299.

Jones, E. 2014 'Battle for the mind: World War 1 and the birth of military psychiatry', *The Lancet. Legacy of the 1914–18 War* V 384 (9955): 1708–1714, November 08.

Kirkham. P. 1986 *Harry Peach, Dryad and the DIA.* London: Design Council.

Pearson. A. 1919 *Victory over Blindness.* New York: George H. Doran.

Preston, M. 1939 'Crafts That Aid'. In *Art in Australia*, November 15, Third Series, No 77. Published by John Fairfax and Sons Pty. Ltd, Sydney, 1939.

Twinstitute BBC 2 2019 Programme about creative sensory activities' effects on the brain.

26

Extracts from an interview with Dr Catherine Paterson, MBE, from a collaborative film made with the University of Hertfordshire and *Woven Communities*

Catherine Paterson

Dr Catherine Paterson (CP) (also known as Irene), was founder of the Grampian School of Occupational Therapy, later, the Department of Occupational Therapy at Robert Gordon University, Aberdeen. Along with Catherine, also present at the interview were Dr Tim Palmer (TP), former consultant pathologist from Raigmore Hospital, who is also a practicing basketmaker (see Chapter 27) and Dr Stephanie Bunn (SB), coordinator of the *Woven Communities Project*. The following extracts examine the rise and fall of basketry as a therapeutic and rehabilitative activity and the recent renewed interest in basketry as a therapeutic tool.

SB Well Catherine. . . with all your experience in occupational therapy, I wonder if we could start the whole discussion by you telling us what is meant by the term 'occupational therapy'.

CP The very first definition was coined in 1922, by a physician in the USA called H.A. Pattison – the same definition I learned in 1960, the first week I was an occupational therapy student in Edinburgh. And the definition is: 'Occupational therapy is any activity, whether mental or physical, definitely prescribed with the distinct purpose of hastening recovery from disease or injury.' Of course, there are many modern definitions reflecting modern practice.

SB What are the origins of occupational therapy and when did it develop?

CP If we talk about the origins of *occupation* being used *therapeutically*, it goes back a very long way in history. But specifically, if we look at moral treatment in psychiatry in the nineteenth century, as practiced by Philippe Pinel in Paris, by Samuel Tuke at the York Retreat, and by W.A.F. Brown in Scotland, they all saw *occupation* as central to the treatment of people who were in asylums, as a way of normalizing life within the institutions.

A second way of looking at the origins of the therapeutic use of occupation was in sanatoria. Tuberculosis was, of course, a huge problem [before inoculation], and the only way of treating it was in good surroundings with good food, and, in the initial stages – the febrile stages – with bed-rest. The rehabilitation of the patient started with light activities in bed, and basketry would be one of the activities, which could be graded from undemanding over a short period of time and increasingly made more complex and involving the patient in more exertion.

Another important influence on the development of occupational therapy was the establishment of curative workshops during the First World War by Sir Robert Jones, for the rehabilitation of the war wounded using purposeful, creative occupations to improve morale and physical function.

SB So, what impact did the First World War have on the development of occupational therapy?

CP The important development was in North America. They, of course, had their own injured servicemen who went back home to Canada and the USA and they took the concept of the curative workshops with them. Of course, the UK hospitals where the curative workshops were developed, were mainly staffed by American orthopaedic surgeons. So, the first [educational] course in occupational therapy (followed by twenty-seven others) in the USA, was set up in order to rehabilitate the soldiers returning from the War.

So, first of all they were 'reconstruction therapists'. 'Reconstruction' was the word used for rehabilitation in the First World War, and all these [initial] short courses, set up as emergencies to treat these returning soldiers, were all developed after the War into full occupational therapy courses. The first British occupational therapists trained in the USA.

SB Could you tell me a little about how the theory behind occupational therapy developed?

CP I have already said something about the use of meaningful occupations to normalize life within asylums, and the grading of activities, which was very prevalent within sanatoria, and also in the First World War with patients with physical disabilities, where the aims of treatment were in relation to improving muscle strength, dexterity, coordination, stamina etc.

But in the early days, when I trained, the theory was very much more implicit rather than explicit. We sort of learned it by doing and by observation. We didn't really have the vocabulary to express what we were doing. We did know some of the theory from e.g. psychology, so we knew about 'operant conditioning', and the importance of 'positive reinforcement'. We knew something about 'projective techniques' that came from Freud's work with people with neurosis.

But nowadays, of course, with evidence-based practice, occupational therapists are having to develop their own theories, and have developed e.g. frames of references, approaches and models of practice, so that modern therapists have a much better ability to articulate the theory behind their work. We also now have a worldwide movement of occupational science which is looking to develop the evidence and theory base of the profession.

SB   I was very struck, in your book, when you talk of going right back to the early twentieth century, about the influence of philosophers and educationalists. People like William James and John Dewey, and how you felt that their ideas were being played out, in the way that occupational therapy developed.

CP   Absolutely! Learning through doing, Dewey's famous motif, I think, is just as relevant today as it has ever been. And this is how we all learn, through doing. And the use of your bodies in learning is complimentary to learning intellectually.

TP   And learning through doing requires repetition; it requires doing frequently; and doing the same thing and building on that. Just like the graded exercises you talked of earlier. And again, that's something that occupational therapy doesn't have the luxury of [today]. . . .

But I wanted to come back, Irene, to the influence of psychoanalysis, Freud and psychology, because one of the things about shell shock, and the sort of thing that Sir Arthur Hurst was quite keen on, was that these people were physically healthy [but often unable to speak or move their limbs] and that there was something in their brain that was inhibiting them . . . And that is echoed in what is now a diagnosis of 'functional neurological disorder', where you can find no structural or organic basis for a person's symptoms, which are very real. And you have to use physiotherapy and exercises, and in effect persuade them that everything is still possible.

SB   How does the practice of craft work in these kinds of cases then, what does it do?

TP, CP in unison   It depends on the condition!

TP   If you have a physical condition, then you can tailor your tasks to the disability that they've got, or the sequela of the stroke or the head injury. So, if they've got a weak hand, or can't see to one side, you can tailor the activity to take that into account. But also, to encourage them to use the side that is weak.

If they have got what is technically known as 'cognitive impairment,' which means they can't think very straight or they can't problem-solve, then your activities can be tailored in a different way – you can encourage them to see patterns through repetition, to learn what to do.

CP   There are these physical aspects to it, the physical movement. But there's also the psychological aspects to it. Patients who have these difficulties, they're in a distressed state. They are dealing with loss. And you have to cope with the psychological and social aspects as well, because the losses are not just personal, they can be within the family and society. And it's very important that you, in some way, help them to see a road ahead that is positive. And a piece of craft work that they have produced is very positive and something that they can show people that they can do. It is a symbol of hope that not all is lost with the terrible things that has happened to them.

SB   We are talking about one thing, basketry, and yet it seems to achieve a lot of different things. On the one hand it achieves *hope*. And on the other hand, it achieves *physiological changes* at the same time. That is really interesting.

CP   Absolutely . . . it has the social aspect, because you can give things you have made as a gift to someone. 'Here, I've made this for you!' And that connects them with their family again.

SB   And it matters, as well.

CP   Yes it matters, it is important.

TP   In the work I've done with the patients at Raigmore. You start by placing sticks across, and weaving over and under alternatively from opposite sides. So, you're alternating right and left. You're having to use right-hand/left-hands. You're having to look at the pattern that you're creating, you're working with attention. So, it is using the separated-ness of the two halves of the brain and making them connect.

CP   And the practice of doing those things [craft in occupational therapy] is often best done with skills that are not familiar, because then there can be no comparison with what you were able to do before your injury and afterwards.

SB   What made basketry such a popular craft to use in occupational therapy?

CP   Well it has got a lot of attributes that we require in therapy. It has the ability to grade. The fact that it is a bilateral activity. It uses the brain. The fact that it produces useful articles, and it can produce an article quickly. Within a session or two, you've got something that is the finished project. For the complexity of it, it can go from very simple to incredibly complex.

TP   If you think about where basketry started, as rehabilitation, it really started as a means of giving people who have disabilities a job . . . In areas of the world where baskets are still in use, they still use it. One of the consultants at Raigmore came from India, where they still used basketmaking until very recently.

SB   One of the factors that some of the Scottish War Blinded cite as a good reason for people learning basketry is that it actually increases sensitivity in their fingers so that they become more dexterous and were better able to sense the world . . . .

SB   How about when basketry fell out of use [in Occupational Therapy]?

CP   Again, there were multiple causes. Firstly, there was a lack of time. With advances in medicine, patients spend less and less time in hospital. Secondly, the occupational therapists wished to get rid of the 'fluffy bunnies and basketry' image. It is costly in time to do craft work with patients. It needs the time of the therapist, not only with the patient but to prepare the work. It needs resources, it needs facilities.

SB   Do you think that the fact that basketry has become less relevant, and indeed almost a pointless occupation has had anything to with the rise with the use of the term 'basket-case?'

CP I had always assumed that this name was to do with psychiatric patients making baskets in psychiatric hospitals. That it was a derogatory term to do with someone being mentally ill, in some way. But, in fact, the internet tells us that it comes from America. It was American slang from the First World War, when patients came back, some having lost the use of limbs through injury, or through amputation. These people were seen as people in baskets [needing to be transported in basketry chairs], therefore the name 'basket-case' came about . . . .

SB My last question is, given the need for meaningful work in occupational therapy, is there any way you can see craft becoming relevant again?

CP Well, the use of a meaningful activity depends on culture and depends a lot on fashion. I am aware that young people are knitting again. There's a proliferation of craft shops throughout the UK. And there are programmes on television now about craft, about making clothes, about baking. So, these things become relevant again to the population. But also, there are residents in long-term care, and activity organizers will use craft in care homes, and with long-term patients with mental health problems.

But then we have to remember that occupational therapy is no longer confined to the West, it's a worldwide profession now. There are something like seventy-two different countries who belong to the World Federation of Occupational Therapists and in different cultures craft will be a big activity. And occupational therapists will therefore use basketry.

Dr Catherine Paterson is author of *Opportunities not Prescriptions: the Development of Occupational Therapy in Scotland 1900–1960*, 2010, Aberdeen: Langstane Press.

27

Basketmaking as an activity to enhance brain injury neurorehabilitation

Tim Palmer

Introduction

There has been empirical evidence of the usefulness of basketmaking in the rehabilitation of brain injury since the end of the nineteenth century. Basketmaking was not the only activity used for these purposes, but it offered considerable advantages over, for example, carpentry or textile weaving. Basketmaking requires very few tools, and little infrastructure in the workplace. The materials are readily available, cheap and renewable and require little preparation. It is also tolerant of a wide spectrum of disability, including blindness and amputation.

Despite falling out of use as an integral element of rehabilitation from the late 1960s,[1] there was growing appreciation in some quarters that physical activity could play a positive role in re-establishing function following brain injuries. Better knowledge about the potential for recovery following brain injury has led to a better understanding of the mechanisms by which recovery can be encouraged. The concept of 'plasticity' in the brain has developed. 'Plasticity' is the ability of the brain to open up new connections following damage, thus allowing return of function. Plasticity is relevant to both incoming signals — sensory pathways — and outgoing signals — motor pathways — as well as to connections within the brain itself. The discovery that the connections between nerve cells — synapses — are dynamic and are both encouraged by activity and lost following disuse is crucial to the concept of plasticity and the ability to open up new pathways to by-pass damage.

Basketmaking is an activity particularly rich in sensory and motor signals and requires considerable cooperation between various parts of the brain. It also poses challenges to comprehension and decision-making abilities. For these reasons, it is ideally suited to rehabilitation that attempts to exploit this plastic potential of the brain. In collaboration with the Stroke and Recovery Unit at Raigmore hospital, Inverness, and the *Woven Communities Project*, along with basketmaker and occupational therapist Monique Bervoets, I have been trialling how different techniques of basketmaking can be useful in helping neuroplasticity develop.

Organization of the brain

The brain is organised into two fundamental components — 'grey' and 'white' matter. The grey matter comprises the regions where the nerve cells are found, and broadly corresponds to the areas where incoming signals are processed and outgoing signals are generated. The white matter consists of the connecting pathways between the cells in the grey matter. The connecting pathways are made up of extensions of the nerve cells that connect to other nerve cells some distance away. This may be on the other side of the brain, or the other end of the body. Damage to the extensions of nerve cells can be repaired or circumvented, but if the cells in the grey matter are damaged and die, they mostly cannot be replaced, although remaining cells may adapt to compensate.

In addition to division into grey and white matter, the brain shows distinct spatial organization, with different areas doing different things. There is the oldest part of the brain — consisting of the hind – (cerebellum, pons and medulla) and mid-brains — which controls important processes like breathing, heart rate, balance, and cooperation between muscle groups. The newer part of the brain — the forebrain (cerebrum) — is responsible for complex movements and sensory abilities, for our ability to think, and our sense of who we are (self). The older parts of the brain are generally less often damaged than the forebrain.

The right side of the forebrain receives signals from and controls the left side of the body, and vice versa. The hind-brain and mid-brain control the functions on the same side. In addition, the left side of the forebrain is concerned with linear activities that involve a sense of time, of logic and organization. By contrast, the right side of the forebrain is non-linear and responds in an associative way, that is, is empathetic and emotional, conceptual and imaginative. Both sides are in constant communication with each other, and damage to one may lead to a disproportionate influence of the other.

Types of brain injury

In general terms, injuries to the brain can be considered within a framework of cause, distribution of damage, and effect on brain function (see Table 1)

1. Physical deficit
The physical effects of brain injury can be divided into two broad categories. First, sensory/receptive effects (the brain isn't receiving messages so doesn't know what to do) and secondly, motor/expressive (the brain cannot create the messages to do something, or cannot get messages to the muscles) Physical defects may be a manifestation of a local injury, but may also be the result of more widespread damage to the grey matter, as in a traumatic or toxic/hypoxic injury, or to dysfunction of a particular region of pathway as in functional neurological disorder.

Table 27.1 Brain injury causes and effects

Cause	Distribution of damage	Effect

Vascular
    Blockage of a blood vessel
    Rupture of a blood vessel
	Focal/local
	    Localized to area supplied by
	    affected vessel
		Physical
		    Ability to feel and do
		Cognitive
		    Ability to understand
		Sense of self
		    Psychological damage

Traumatic	*Diffuse*
	    Widespread damage to
	    nerve cells and pathways	

Toxic/Hypoxic
    Alcohol/drugs
    Lack of oxygen		

Functional
    No physical damage to
    explain the symptoms.
    Psychological factors
    operating that are associated
    with physical symptoms.
	Biochemical
	    Disruption of connections
	    between nerve cells/
	    pathways	

2. Cognitive deficit

A cognitive deficit is one that compromises the ability to concentrate, think and plan. This may include inability to plan a movement or recognize it is necessary even if the physical body is unaffected. This encompasses several components, starting with understanding what to do; then deciding how to do it, starting and finishing the task; how to recognize mistakes and how to analyze and respond to the mistakes. Just as physical ability is crucial to daily life, so is cognitive ability. It is difficult at times to distinguish between a cognitive problem and a sensory/receptive physical problem, and both may lead to an apparent motor/expressive physical disability.

3. Sense of self

Suffering a brain injury necessarily means a portion of the pre-injury life will not be the same again. This may be obvious to the patient and cause considerable psychological distress. However, this is not always the case if the patient does not have the insight to recognize and analyze their changed circumstances. The change from capability to incapacity, from being useful to being useless and a burden, from being independent to becoming dependent or interdependent, causes distress, sadness or grief because of the change in self-image, comparable with bereavement. Regaining function after brain injury requires building a new self, itself dependent upon a degree of insight. Here, the difference between the right and left sides in terms of how they perceive the world can influence the perception of disability and response to it.

What basketmaking has to offer

1. Physical disability

Basketmaking provides excellent graded physical therapy for the upper limbs and torso. Because both hands are involved, the dexterity and strength in the non-affected side may improve, and this may also stimulate the affected side. The repetitive nature of the stimulus may encourage the opening up of new pathways. The similarity in movements required from each limb also encourages new pathways in a manner similar to mirror-work. Fine motor skills are encouraged and developed, and coordination between the two upper limbs that is necessary for basketmaking is also important for carrying out many day-to-day tasks safely. When both hands are involved in a task, the muscles of the torso have to support and stabilize the shoulder girdle and chest. Patients with hemiplegia (weakness or paralysis of one side of the body) may have difficulties in maintaining posture when sitting or walking, and this is helped by basketmaking.

As all sensory modalities are used in basketmaking, there is the opportunity to train the senses to compensate for a sensory deficit. This is particularly relevant in visual impairment, where touch, proprioception and temperature all contribute to building up a mental pattern and, together with hearing, help to assess the state of the material being used.

Examples of basketwork undertaken by patients in the Stroke and Recovery unit in Inverness for physical disabilities include tension trays and square work. Platters or 'tension trays' are very useful exercises as they are simple enough for most patients to understand and can be completed within a 90 minute — 2-hour session. The repetitive nature of inserting and weaving the rods means that the same action is performed fifteen to twenty times by each arm and hand, or up to forty times if only one arm can be used. This is excellent physiotherapy and is good for manual dexterity. The development of new pathways is encouraged. Improved finger and arm movement has been observed during a course of treatment. The work can be braced against the abdomen, and the affected hand used as a dead weight if necessary.

FIGURE 27.1 *Tension trays (platters) showing variation in pattern and use of different willows.*

FIGURE 27.2 *Square work basket for gathering flowers/vegetables, with integral handle.*

Patients with a dense weakness of one arm find tension trays difficult, and square work or round cane baskets on a wooden base can be used as the workpiece does not need to be supported by the patient. The need to control the weave and maintain posture, however, does encourage use of the affected limb and the trunk. For example, the fingers of the affected hand can be splayed and laid onto the weave between the stakes, being lifted and moved as necessary. A variety of useful objects can be made using a square base as a starting point.

Cane is easier to manipulate than willow, but the length of the weavers has to be considered in relation to the patient's dexterity. It also has the advantage of requiring less preparation and is more readily available if patients wish to work on their own.

It is possible to make jigs and aids to get around motor problems. These range from a standard screw block when making square work to platforms and turntables that allow round or oval baskets to be supported, stabilized with the affected limb, and the weaving done with the non-affected limb. Other jigs can be devised to help make shaped articles, for example boat shapes, and in making round woven bases. Tasks can be chosen that enable the torso to be used to support and stabilize the work.

2. Cognitive deficit
Basketmaking presents a considerable challenge to cognitive function, even in healthy individuals. Making a basket requires understanding of the many components of the structure, how they are formed, their physical and temporal relationship with other components, and an appreciation of the expected outcome of the activity. Comparison with the actual output is then possible, and from this develops the ability to recognize mistakes — departures from the expected — and then to rectify them. Making a basket requires the patient to make decisions all the time. For example, starting a new weaver is making a decision. All these activities are important in daily life and are compromised to varying degrees in patients with a cognitive deficit and are summarized in Table 2.

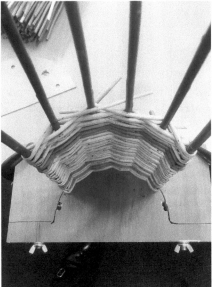

FIGURE 27.3 *Use of jigs and aids for motor problems. Clockwise from top left: a) screw block for square work; b) variation for making curved pieces; c) turntable for a round plywood base for cane or willow work. The hole for the spindle can be plugged with a contrasting piece of wood.*

Table 27.2 The cognitive components of basketmaking

Understanding the task	Pattern recognition Sequence of activities Recognition of left and right Cooperation between left and right
Recognising mistakes	Departure from the pattern/expected outcome
Sorting out mistakes	What went wrong What to do to get it right Not repeating the mistake
Making decisions	Starting a new weaver Taking down and redoing incorrect weaving

The below examples demonstrate improvement in cognitive function of a patient with a toxic/hypoxic brain injury. Initially, making a fish, Figure 27.4a, was a considerable challenge, and square work, Figure 27.4b, required instruction for every movement. After a couple of sessions, the tension tray, Figure 27.4c, was possible and the amount of intervention required reduced over subsequent sessions. In the final session before discharge, the patient instructed the tutor. The intention had been to make a tray with alternating buff and white weavers but the initial instructions by the patient were such that pairs of weavers, i.e. a paired weave, were created, see Figure 27.4d. This pattern was entirely new to the patient. The patient understood the different pattern and proceeded to complete the tray by themselves with little intervention. It was apparent that considerable learning had taken place over the course of the sessions. (Handle and weave round the edge put on by tutor.)

A similar improvement was encountered in a patient with a vascular lesion. The improvement was initially in terms of work-rate, with the first basket taking twice as long to make as a second, larger basket. Later work extended the improvement to enhanced complexity, where the complexity of a circular cane basket with five different weaves was considerably greater than the earlier willow baskets. No significant problems were encountered in understanding the weave, and the ability to see, analyze and correct mistakes was greatly improved from earlier work. This patient was the only one who has managed to do the challenging weave around the edge of a tray (see Figure 27.5), a task with which many able-bodied people struggle.

Additional features include pattern recognition, which is of major importance in basketmaking. Colour can be used to help make the pattern more obvious. The use of alternating white and brown willow when making a tension tray provides a visual cue for which side to insert the next weaver. With a weave using either two or three elements, different-coloured willows or cane emphasize the weave. All basketmakers have 'mantras' that they use to remind them of the pattern of a weave ('in front of two, behind one'; 'no overtaking'; 'take the one on the left') and these prove very useful for patients. They could often be heard saying the relevant mantra softly to themselves.

FIGURE 27.4 (a-d) *Improving cognitive function through basketwork.*

3. Sense of self

The damage brain injury does to a person's sense of identity is profound. Basketmaking, along with other craft activities and with the physical rehabilitation provided by physiotherapists and occupational therapists, all play a part in helping the patient discover who they now are. A return to the life before the brain injury is rarely possible and the patient has to discover what they can do and not do; what they enjoy and no longer enjoy; what they can understand and now have difficulty comprehending. They have to learn again how to live their life. Basketmaking provides a means of exploring these issues and providing some answers or help in arriving at answers.

FIGURE 27.5 *The challenging edge of a tension tray.*

FIGURE 27.6 *Pattern work: cane basket stained with cochineal, logwood and iron.*

One patient was eloquent about being 'useless'. He made several tension trays that were given away as presents. Another won first prize in the local show with a cane basket. The benefit of being able to make gifts was immense, as was the external validation of the first prize.

Another patient realized, through basketmaking and the difficulty of correcting mistakes when willow had been already kinked, that their previous *modus operandi* was no longer appropriate. Previously, they would have got on with a task and sorted out mistakes later; they could no longer do this and learned that it was now better to go about something more slowly and get it right first time. The old proverb 'Softly, softly, catchee monkey' was the relevant mantra in this case.

Basketmaking with patients with brain injury is an intense activity for both the patient and the tutor. The patient has usually never done anything like it before; they have to be willing to try and probably have difficulty, possibly may not be able to manage, They are therefore vulnerable. A relationship develops between the patients attending the sessions and between patients and tutor that indicates that they, the patient, has value. They also learn about themselves, their capacity for concentration, their physical abilities and their ability to understand tasks. All these are valuable in arriving at a sense of the new self. There are two patients per session, and the patients come at the same time each week, generally until discharged. They forge friendships and also help each other. Having been previously independent, they now learn the value of interdependence.

Conclusion

Craft has long been recognized as helpful in recovery from injury, both physical and neurological. Changes in the practice of medicine in the recent past has led to a situation where craft activities are no longer included in formal rehabilitation nor provided in rehabilitation units. Experience at Raigmore and elsewhere suggests that basketmaking has particular benefit in the rehabilitation of brain injury. This is attributable to the complex nature of the activity, with a multitude of sensory, motor and cognitive components; the ability of basketmaking to produce tangible results in a time span achievable by most patients; and our better understanding of the organization and function of the brain. Better understanding allows a more focused use of basketmaking to build on the progress achieved by physiotherapy, occupational therapy, and time.

Basketmaking, like other rehabilitation activities, is time and labour-intensive and requires particular skills. It is possible, however, to learn enough relatively quickly to be able to help deliver basketmaking as therapy to brain-injured patients. As an activity, it requires space and materials, both at a premium in the NHS. As improvement following brain injury continues for many months and years, continued provision of basketmaking following discharge from hospital would be beneficial. These are the challenges.

Acknowledgements

All photographs except figures 4a and 4b (courtesy of Monique Bervoets) by TJP.

Rhona Palmer, for preparing the images for publication

Dr Ashish Macaden Consultant in Rehabilitation Medicine, Raigmore Hospital, Inverness, for encouragement, advice and enthusiasm for the role of basketmaking in neuro-rehabilitation.

Monique Bervoets, Basketmaker and trained occupational therapist, for her companionship, willingness to travel long distances to work with the patients, and the valued perspective she brought to our discussions.

Note

1 See reasons outlined in Catherine 'Irene' Paterson interview.

PART FIVE

Renewal and realignment: The embodied knowledge of basketry

Introduction
Victoria Mitchell

What remains the same and what is new? What particular aspects of basketry today will be passed on, sustained, renewed or reconfigured? Or is realignment a more apposite term, conveying as it does an opening up of basketry to the critical field of inter-disciplinarity, envisaged as fundamental to questions of embodiment, new materialism or artificial intelligence, for example. In the context of an increasingly urbanized socio-economic fabric, basketry that once sustained rural economies has been transformed, not only in the way in which it functions but also in consideration of how it is perceived as a materially grounded, cultural phenomenon. Arguably, the domain within which basketry can be re-envisioned does not reflect a narrowing-down of skills and functions but is, rather, open to expansion, renewal and realignment.

In many respects the work undertaken by Felicity Irons in her studio-barn in Bedfordshire demonstrates how little has changed in terms of material resources and techniques. The rush is still harvested annually by hand and while the braiding of the rush that forms traditional-type mats also serves to create the odd high-heeled shoe or designer chair, the technical know-how needed has been generated by what has gone before. One thing grows out of another, but in one respect there is a significant difference. Whereas traditionally such work would have been local in resources, making *and* consumption, now the market for such goods is more likely to be globally determined and realigned in the context of digital technology. Basketry bridges the work of one set of digits (from the Latin *digitus*, finger or toe) to another, the algorithmic digital.

For Ian Tait, this is a challenge, indicative of an alignment that does not always work in favour of basketry traditions that, in the Shetlands, have been eclipsed by imported materials, mass-production, hobby crafts and the proliferation of easy-on-the-eye, globally transportable 'Fair-Isle' knitting. As Curator of Shetland Museum and Archives, Tait can nevertheless explore this shift as history and can engage new audiences, including those for whom traditional making forms an aspect of living memory. His poignant photographs demonstrate that the ways in which basketry is represented constitute a significant aspect of the renewal and realignment that history confers on the present.

Living memory and 'passing-on' are vividly recounted by Des Pawson, whose recreation of a bow pudding fender demonstrates how the very particular skills of some kinds of knot-making can be sustained and learned through example, whether from illustrations, word of mouth, extant artefacts, or (and this is crucial) the knowledge and enthusiasm of one who knows how it can be done. We learn from each other. In Paulina Adamska's account of the success of Serfenta, a basketry organization in Poland that is included on UNESCO's list of intangible cultural heritage, the passing on and realignment of traditional basketry skills is effected not only through recorded visits and workshops but also through informative videos and liaisons with contemporary designers. Serfenta has drawn inspiration from basketry collectives in other parts of the world, where traditional skills are being adapted to new markets, enabling livelihoods to be sustained, skills to be protected and social communities strengthened.

While the basketry skills of the past have become increasingly specialized they can also be recognized in fields and disciplines that are comparable or in the early stages of development, as in the case of robot science, explored here through Cathrine Hasse and Pat Treusch's fascinating research collaboration with basketmakers and knitting in developing the experience of embodiment necessary to enhance the function and 'sensitivity' of robots. Embodiment and the rhythmic actions of movement also inform Victoria Mitchell's critical reading of braid and braiding. Material practice and concept are 'opened up' to one another through an alignment between braiding and dancing, together forming and informing the social fabric through embodied experience.

The renewal and realignment of basketry both affects and reflects the myriad ways in which basketry-related makers and thinkers are finding their voice, not only through workshops, artefacts and collaborations but also through writing, as in this volume.

28

Rush to design

Felicity Irons

All my work starts in the memory of my fingers. A standard piece of work will involve the setting out of stakes and weaver rushes in patterns that I have repeated thousands of times. While the fingers do their work, a look at the rushes - their colour from shades of dark blue-green through to honeyed tones – will show me the weather for a few days in July, when they dried, and remind me of special places and time spent on the river during the last year's harvest (Fig. 28.1).

FIGURE 28.1 *Rush bolts at Rush Matters, Bedfordshire. Photograph: Felicity Irons.*

My hands know all the techniques used in each process, from knowing if a rush will suit the work from its conformation and place in the bolt to pulling it out tip first to stop tangles. My body position, whether standing at the bench or sitting on a stool by a chair to reseat, applies tension to the rush. This embodied knowing-through-tension is common to all the plaiting, coiling and weaving that goes into my work and combines with rhythm to transform rush stems from a river into a tight and strong, single piece of work. There are also times when the rush is transformed through experiment into forms I have invented or imagined, such as *High Rush* (Fig. 28.2).

For a while and perhaps for its lifetime the work retains memory and blemishes of its time in the water. Peat clings to the outer skin and gravel minerals stain the white butts, red and purple. Slowly, use and sunlight will bleach and even the colours to a characteristic shade of straw yellow that all but denies its origins, yet even at that point a piece stored away in a cupboard will fill that space with the unmistakable scent of rush, spice and hay, and I like to think a hint of ozone from the weir.

All of this and much more about my working life I try to explain to those interested by it, whether through teaching workshops, discussing the characteristics of the harvest as a rush wholesaler, or increasingly and most excitingly in talking to designers interested in incorporating the techniques into different places and formats. For this work my hands and fingers are in altogether new territory, such as where to start on a piece that arrives on the computer screen as

FIGURE 28.2 *Felicity Irons, High Rush, 2010. Photograph: Felicity Irons.*

FIGURE 28.3 *Felicity Irons, Rush Chair, 2017. Photograph: Michael Franke.*

FIGURE 28.4 *Harvesting rush on the Great Ouse. Photograph: Felicity Irons.*

a projection in a pdf file that is a precursor to telephone conversations with the designer Christopher Jenner about a weave to form the main body of a chair that will be supported by an oak frame cut by laser to produce the complex curves required by the design (Fig. 28.3). To realise the shape a large polystyrene forma, like a giant shoe last, arrives. Two hundred hours ensures the work is done within the fine tolerances needed.

Such work has also introduced me to designer Faye Toogood and the chance to contribute to the realization of her design for a Mulberry™ store in Regent Street. It is thrilling to see the beautiful sale goods exhibited on display totems and customers resting on benches covered in woven rush.

It is March now and it is my head that tells me that the dwindling store of rush in the barn must last another four months before the cycle is over and the harvesting team can reassemble, the rush knives taken down and sharpened and the boats made ready again to see if the river and weather will give up another two and half thousand bolts of rush (Fig. 28.4).

29

Nearly lost:

Learning knots, knowing knots, loving knots and 'passing it on'

Des Pawson MBE

My passion for knots and ropework goes back to the time when, aged 7, I was given a book with some knots in it. At that early stage I learned to read the pictures, understand the diagrams and follow them to make the knot. I have always found it difficult to learn from others by the 'show and follow me' way by which so many people learn. Somehow, I remember the illustration and understand the process and technique but have a problem in recalling something that has been demonstrated to me. Much practicing on my own, even at the back of the classroom tying Turk's Heads and Monkey's Fists, developed my natural aptitude.

Of course, this is not the only way to acquire knot-making skills. This chapter addresses some of the many ways in which knot-making knowledge can travel through time, survive or be lost, including a specific case study of a Royal National Lifeboat Institute (RNLI) bow pudding fender, for which an extant example served as a kind of illustration and expert know-how enabled the passing on of knowledge, both to me and to a knot-maker in the making.

Not all have aptitude for ropework. Teaching has shown me that some people are bemused by drawings or cannot follow when shown. I have also found that, however hard someone wants to learn, without aptitude there is little progress. I had a particular student, an Italian sea captain, who was desperate to make fancy knots, but however hard he tried, he could not master them. His wife, a reluctant student with him, progressed and manged to achieve what he was unable to do. Some students just need to be shown something once.

Given that the easiest way for me to learn has been from the illustrations in books, I can usually understand the drawings in Swedish or Japanese books, as the illustrations are a language I understand, or at least can learn to understand. I have collected many hundreds of books on knots, ropework, rigging and such over the years and have realized that most are based on earlier works, resulting in strange inclusions and exclusions. Thus, the Sheepshank, an almost useless but strangely named knot or hitch, is mentioned by Sir Henry Mainwaring in the first seamanship work in English (Mainwaring and Perrin 1920), yet more useful knots, such as the Sheet Bend (9,000 years old), Clove Hitch or Bowline, for example, are missed out. The Sheepshank still appears in almost every knot book today (Pawson 2016b).

In the earliest publications, illustrations were generally drawn from the artist's point of view but not from the view of the person needing to tie the knots. Sometimes difficult methods have evolved to complement difficult, uninformed illustrations, while simpler principles of tying are often lost. Sometimes illustrations are drawn incorrectly or given the wrong number, so that illustration and description are mixed up, giving rise to confusion down the years.[1]

For thousands of years the art of tying and using knots passed from person to person, kept alive by constant repetition. Special knots and ropework techniques could be developed to perform a special function, then someone's new idea could find its way into the wider community. This was especially true for sailors, who developed many knots and techniques not found elsewhere, some with practical applications, others with a more decorative function. In the case of some decorative knots a sailor may have needed to wait several years until he sailed with the person who could show him how to tie a particular knot (Ashley 1944, 3). Crews could be multi-national, which enabled transfer of knowledge from one maritime culture to another. It was not until the late eighteenth and early nineteenth centuries that seamanship publications appeared that showed how to tie knots, make splices and explain some of the rope working techniques needed on a boat or ship (Steel 1794, Lever 1819). These were aimed at officers rather than the men who would normally be carrying out the work. The passing of skills from hand to hand was still the normal route, thus 'to learn this you will find it best to get the Boatswain to teach you, you are then more likely to remember them, and also to learn the best way to make them, than if you try and learn them from the illustrations in your seamanship books' (Dreyer 1900, 69). It was not until the late nineteenth century that books dedicated to tying knots began to appear, often aimed at a general public, some more successfully than others and rarely, if at all, explaining the actual making of rope items such as the fenders, mats and chaffing gear needed on board ship. It is from these early seamanship and knot books that today's publications have developed, sometimes keeping alive curious survivors from an earlier era (Pawson 2016) or perpetuating errors from an earlier work.

A craftsman who has worked all his life in a trade will develop skill, understanding and knowledge that will have been assimilated, often in an unconscious way, from the family if it is a family trade or from the master if an apprentice. This kind of knowledge can never be captured in a book (as considered and analyzed in Sturt, 1923) Experience over a long period builds on inherent aptitude. There is a great difference between an amateur and someone working for a living, perhaps making the same thing many hundreds of times. One professional fender maker can make a top-quality product, yet another can be skilled at producing a cheaper product.

Sadly, in most trades the days of apprentices are gone, and many hand-craft businesses are very economically marginal, with little room for supporting an apprentice. If an apprentice is taken on, even in an informal manner, there is no certainty that the skills will carry on, as often better paid work in another field attracts the apprentice and the transfer of skill is lost. My solution to keeping the knowledge alive is to write books and I hope that what I have put in print will be around for many generations to come. An example of the way that the knowledge of the making of an item *can* survive, and how easily it could become extinct, can be shown by my experience with the RNLI bow pudding.

RNLI lifeboats have, until very recently, sported a particular style of fender, which they have always called a bow pudding, a style of fender (Fig. 29.1) which is exactly the same as that illustrated in D'Arcy Lever's *Young Sea Officers Sheet Anchor*, first published in 1808 (Lever 1819) (Fig. 29.2).

In 2005 I was asked by the Small Craft Maintenance Depot of the RNLI in East Cowes to make a fender for their RIB (rigid inflatable boat) tender that serviced the Spurn Point Lifeboat. I asked if they wanted the RNLI style of bow pudding and was answered, 'ideally, yes'. I asked why they did not go to their workshops at Head Office in Poole for the fender and was told that there was nobody there that could make them anymore. I agreed to make the bow pudding for them. I asked

FIGURE 29.1 *Bow pudding fender on* Lucy Lavers, *Stiffkey, Norfolk, 2015. (Copyright John Worrall, with permission).*

FIGURE 29.2 *Bow pudding, illustrated in D'Arcy Lever's* Young Sea Officers Sheet Anchor, *1808.*

what was going to happen to the old one and they said it would to go in the rubbish skip. I protested and suggested they send it to me as a pattern, so I now have what is probably the last pudding made in their workshops. While I knew what the fender looked like, indeed had a number of photographs of men making them over the years and was sure I could replicate the look of the fender, I did not know the 'trade secrets' to making a true bow pudding, knowledge that would have been passed down through many generations of RNLI craftsmen (Fig. 29.3). While books and their illustrations had been my main source of knowledge there are times when the passing on of know-how from an expert is essential, especially for the subtle twist of the wrist or special hidden tuck so often overlooked in a book.

Luckily, two years before this, I had had a brief correspondence with one of the men, Frank 'Winkle' Ide, who had worked in the RNLI workshops at Poole. He was still alive and I was able to find his phone number. A conversation with him set me right and with that stroke of fortune 'special secrets' have been preserved. The fender consists of a core of old rope around a rope or wire backbone with a thimble each end as a hard eye. The cover is woven using an even number of what they call 'nettles' running the length of the fender as 'warps', with a lighter line being wrapped round the body as a 'weft'. It is the tightening of the weft that is the very special secret that 'Winkle' Ide was able to explain to me over the phone, as well as explaining how to deal with the finishing of the nettles at each end of the fender (Fig. 29.4).

FIGURE 29.3 *A rigger crafting an RNLI bow pudding, 1942. Getty Images.*

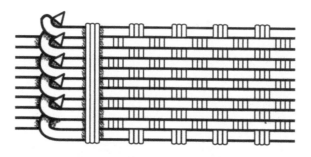

Finishing with the double tuck binding and the top layer crowned

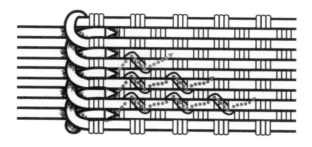

Tuck the crowned ends back 3 times to finish

FIGURE 29.4 *Des Pawson, double tuck binding and finishing for RNLI-style bow pudding. Illustrated in Pawson 2016b: p.63.*

I have since made two more fenders for the RNLI and a number for restored lifeboats. The task of making them is made easier if there is a second pair of hands and for the most recent request, for the ex RNLI and Dunkirk Little Ship, *Lucy Lavers* (Fig. 29.1), I remembered Tom Curtis, aged about 14, the son of a boat builder who had shown interest in my ropework. I had heard that he was making knotted objects to get a little pocket money. On contacting his family, there was an enthusiastic response to the suggestion that he should come and help and learn. He did, and it was a joy that he really had the aptitude, understanding and willingness to learn, while making my job easier. He had learned something and was proud to show what he had helped to make to his family (Fig. 29.5). The charity that commissioned the bow pudding, Rescue Wooden Boats, came and made a short film of us working together.[2] Photographs I took while making this fender enabled me to include its full construction in a book (Pawson 2016b, 59–63). So, the knowledge that was almost lost has been saved, both in the mind of young Tom Curtis as well as in the book and film, all of which I hope will keep alive the tricks of the trade for future generations.

FIGURE 29.5 *Des Pawson and Tom Curtis with finished fender for* Lucy Lavers. *Photograph: Liz Pawson.*

Notes

1 When D'Arcy Lever's *Young Sea Officers Sheet Anchor* was published in 1808, as well as showing the Sheepshank, it contained instructions for making both the Flemish Eye and the Artificial Eye, together with illustrations. From contemporary corrections in an original in my possession, I suspect that the titles of the illustrations were reversed. This in turn may explain the change of name identified in Richard Henry Dana 1841 *The Seaman's Friend*. Boston: Charles C. Little & James Brown, and James Loring & Co. C. W. Ashley also writes of the confusion in *The Ashley Book of Knots* (1944). Thus, at the time the oral tradition was at odds with the written word. Mistake or no mistake, today the original named and illustrated method is certainly known as the Flemish Eye.

2 http://www.rescuewoodenboats.com/films/lucy-lavers-films-restoration-other (visited 09.12.18)

Bibliography

Ashley, C. W. 1944 *The Ashley Book of Knots*. Garden City. NY: Doubleday and Co.
Dreyer, Lieut. F. C. 1900 *How to Get a First Class in Seamanship*. Portsmouth: Griffin & Co.
Lever, D. 1819 *The Young Sea Officer's Sheet Anchor*. First published Leeds 1808. London: John Richardson.

Manwaring G. E. and Perrin, W. G. (eds.) 1920 *The Life and Works of Sir Henry Mainwaring, Vol. II* (including *The Sea-man's Dictionary*, first circulated 1620–23). London: Navy Records Society.

Pawson, D. 2016a 'Why people know of The Sheepshank', in *Knotting Matters*, No.130, March 2016.

Pawson, D. 2016b *Des Pawson's Knot Craft and Rope Mats*. London: Adlard Coles Nautical.

Steel, D. 1794 *The Elements and Practice of Rigging and Seamanship*. London: David Steel.

Sturt, G. 1923 *The Wheelwright's Shop*. Cambridge, Cambridge University Press.

30

Renewing a 'dying craft':
The Serfenta Association of Poland

Paulina Adamska

The Serfenta Association began research on basketry in Poland in 2009 with the following remit:

> The Serfenta Association exists so that basketry could live. We travel across thousands of kilometres to learn everything about basket making. We work to preserve the tradition and knowledge passed on from generation to generation. We teach this fading skill to young people. We help master basket makers get into the market. We show this beautiful craft to the whole world.[1]

The first meetings with basketmakers took place close to the river Vistula and were followed by others in Podlasie, Kaszuby, Wielkopolska, Podkarpacie and other regions of Poland. In 2011, researchers from Serfenta, including myself, began travelling abroad, meeting basketmakers in Ukraine, Czech Republic, Germany, Norway, Iceland and Japan, confirming that basketry is still a living craft and that there are hundreds of artisans who daily use their hands for weaving baskets or other products such as hats, shoes, bags, decorative objects and fish traps as well as architectural elements such as fences and walls. The weaving materials vary but willow, straw, cattail (reed mace), calamus (sweet flag), roots of pine and spruce and the bark and wood of trees such as oak, hazel or aspen, are all still used in Poland (Figs. 30.1–30.2)

However, the average age of a basketry craftsman in Poland is seventy and basketmaking is one of the professions termed 'dying crafts'. Serfenta aims to change this situation, carrying out a number of projects, such as the 'Master of Tradition', an annual support program for leading basketmakers who are required to teach young makers from their local community for a year, for which they are paid through grants from public resources. The basketmakers have generously shared their knowledge and skills and in response we have produced books as well as ethnographic and how-to-do-it films.[2] In addition the basketry skills acquired have been used in workshops with adults and children, touring exhibitions have been staged and international events in Poland and abroad have been attended, such as 'Fira Internacional del Cistell' in Salt (Spain 2013), 'Korbmarkt'

FIGURE 30.1 *Józef Gawlik and grandson Marcin, basketmakers in oak splint, Łoniowa, 2014. Photographed by Paulina Adamska, copyright Serfenta.*

FIGURE 30.2 *Bronisława and Jan Madejscy, Lucimia village, 2009. Photographed by Paulina Adamska, copyright Serfenta.*

basketmaking festival in Lichtenfels (Germany 2016) and design festivals in Poland (Gdynia Design Days, 2017; Łódź Design Festival, 2018).

After ten years of experience it is clear that direct support for the artisans is the most effective aid and that sustaining good relations with them is indispensable. Serfenta organizes the sales process and connects makers and clients from around the world through an online shop, guaranteeing manual craft production, based on Polish traditional design and acting in the spirit of fair trade. The basketmakers spend hours acquiring and preparing the materials and finally weaving. The Serfenta team appreciate their efforts and want to reward them with dignity, enabling them to become partners in accomplishing Serfenta's goals. The experiences of The New Basket Workshop (South Africa) and Lupane Women's Centre (Zimbabwe), which sell African products combining tradition with design have served as guiding models, and cooperation with 'Slow Art handmade from Poland',[3] founded by Izumi Fujita, has enabled engagement with Japanese culture and their craft market.

In the longer term it s essential to develop innovative solutions for traditional woven products, such as new designs and adaptions of older forms. A series of design workshops in cooperation with the Faculty of Industrial Forms of the Academy of Fine Arts in Kraków has taken place and classes have been prepared for the Academy of Fine Arts in Łódź. Young designers have followed a workshop of traditional weaving (as in the 'Źdźbło design' project, 2017), helping to create new designs which are viable for the marketplace, such as a *szyszak* (bottle basket), designed by Aleksandra Polek's *szyszak* and woven by Grzegorz Gordat, among others.

As well as developing new markets Serfenta is also building an ethnographic identity, enhancing the value of woven baskets through accreditation, such as for the skills of weaving the *kablącok*,[4] a traditional willow basket with an unusual half-round shape on a frame known as *kabląk*, made in Lucimia, a basketry village in central Poland, and which was included on UNESCO's list of intangible cultural heritage in 2017. The following year Serfenta itself gained the UNESCO accreditation as a Polish non-governmental organization. We weave, connect and act to share a passion for the handmade.

Notes

1 www.serfenta.pl (last accessed 18.06. 2019). The Serfenta Association is funded from public resources and from the economic activity generated through selling products, organizing workshops or exhibitions.
2 For example, https://www.youtube.com/watch?v=_OQ4-9PNqsk (last accessed 18.06.2019)
3 https://www.slow-art.pl (last accessed 23.01.19)
4 For a film of *kablącok* basket weaving: http://serfenta.pl/en/products/kablacok-ze-wsi-lucimia/ (visited 23.01.19)

31

The cultural wastepaper basket

Ian Tait

It would be trite to say Europe was once woven of many cultures, just as a basket is; it's just too compelling an analogy. It implies an interwoven matrix, meaningless unless viewed as a whole. A better comparison is that of a patchwork quilt whose dye has run; there were areas of this or that culture, which had contact points with others, and a degree of cultural influence has leached out through the dye, into places to varying intensity. From disparate pasts, European cultures through two-and-a-half centuries have become part of a wider global society in which regional difference is lost to generic ideas and artefacts. To examine the reasons for this shift, and whether we can counteract convergence to save native basketry, I shall focus on my native islands of Shetland. Shetland is fairly remote and life was peripheral to the outside world for most of history; traditions lingered for a long time and trading little affected the everyday life of the commoners until the nineteenth century. The story of our basketry is an example of what fate holds for basketry as a whole.

The little picture

Societies begin with subsistence – a condition where populations depend on local resources to answer their needs to feed, shelter, and clothe themselves. Isolated from industrialised Britain, Shetland maintained self-sufficient status, with a minimum of imported goods, into the early nineteenth century. (Fig. 31.1).

This was of necessity, for smallholders had no economic means for improvement. In terms of material culture, agriculture, fisheries, and domestic life were sustained with labour-intensive methods that had changed little over centuries. Equipment was low-technology, made from local resources, within a pattern of work governed by seasonal cycles that balanced the needs of land and sea, home and farm. However, the workforce was plentiful and activities were shared, be it cutting rushes or herding sheep. Just as each family grew its own crops and had shared rights to wild plants, so it was with access to fauna. Each family kept their own livestock and had access to wild species on a common basis. Shetland had plentiful resources that supported life in return for unending hard work. There were birds for their flesh and eggs; seals for skin and oil;

FIGURE 31.1 *Willie and Violet Jamieson at the Westing, Unst, c.1930. Shetlanders who made this straw pack saddle mat are likely to have also tanned leather, twisted hair fishing lines and knitted socks. Photograph courtesy of Shetland Museum & Archives.*

whales, fish and shellfish. Most of these activities involved rope and baskets, all of which were handmade.

In an economy of self-sufficiency, the yearly cycle of tasks meant that making equipment, be it of wood, straw, or hide, largely took place in winter, when weather was poor and daylight short. The intensive use of basketry and thatch was a special characteristic of Shetland life, differentiating it from the Norwegian motherland, where wooden containers and grass-roofing were commonplace. In Shetland, driftwood and imported timber were scarce, so many basketry receptacles were perfected and rope and thatching were abundant. Marram, dock, reed-grass, rushes and other species were used in various techniques to make a multitude of items, some practical, some for fun. Such productions were used intensively and had a short life.

So long as local subsistence prevailed, the way of life remained stable. The land's resources remained the same, as did native livestock breeds and crops, and islanders had no financial capacity to import goods. Whatever the political changes, life went on. The imposition of Scottish feudalism hampered development, further favouring continuity. Increments of change advanced while the underlying pattern of activities remained the same. Long after cash economics took over, artefactual elements from bygone centuries survived, even into the 1960s, as access to outside ideas was tempered by individuals' lack of capacity to pay for imports and localized preferences to retain indigenous customs (Fig. 31.2).

FIGURE 31.2 *The clothing of Jimmy Halcrow sowing a field at Stove, Sandwick, reveals this to be the 1950s, but in many respects the scene could have been the 1750s or 1550s. The grain is held in an oat-straw* kessi. *Photograph courtesy of Shetland Museum & Archives.*

Add to basket

Imported goods are an important indicator of economic change for a host culture. They reveal how conditions have altered in order to transform self-sufficiency into a multi-faceted economy, where folk have started to use the same objects as people elsewhere and stopped making them themselves. In the nineteenth century Shetland's economy took a definitive tilt, caused by external forces that had huge implications on society and its material goods. Britain's pre-eminent manufacturing and trading benefited the populace. Men obtained work as seamen and women as domestic servants. From the 1880s came a herring boom, with boats and tools all being imported. Herring baskets appeared by the thousand. Whitefish were now shifted in willow baskets, and these, like the equally standardized ones for herring, became ubiquitous on Shetland farms, albeit they had nothing to do with indigenous tradition (Fig. 31.3).

The move to the cash economy was fed by the UK's industrialisation that produced myriad goods for sale. This was the golden age of British shop-keeping, and Shetland had a couple of hundred firms, all locally owned and catering to local families whose little cash bought goods they couldn't make themselves. The growth of the mercantile sector was brisk, moving from limited retail in the early nineteenth century, to larger-scale shop-keeping and also manufacturing by the mid-century. Some production was for the local market, such as baking that became practicable

FIGURE 31.3 *Gremista, Lerwick, c.1909. From the late nineteenth century herring was landed in willow baskets made to government specification in workshops throughout Britain; for Shetland, Aberdeenshire was the main source. Photograph courtesy of Shetland Museum & Archives.*

because of the growth of an urban centre at Lerwick, and some manufacturing was even for export, as in the case of woven fabric. Baskets were far from niche, and businesses imported them along with crates and barrels by the hundred and, in the case of the aforementioned sectors, Shetlanders now encountered the bread delivery basket and the tweed storage basket. A middle class came into being, with time and money to pursue pastimes, and eventually lower classes too could enjoy hobbies. We find leisure baskets in this changing social structure, giving us the sewing basket and the angling basket.

In the later nineteenth century we see radical change in Shetland basketry because, although people continued to use medieval basket forms and terminology, islanders now started employing imported cordage. This wasn't simply because imported twine was more durable, for now the cost of buying it was low enough to afford. Manila and cotton were used in coiled baskets and coir and hemp were common in twined ones to make bindings and carrying-bands. So pervasive was the influence of the nation at large by 1900 that some imported objects themselves came to be copied within the local tradition, seemingly turning development on its head. Just as some islanders copied wooden door-latches from mass-produced steel ones, a few replicated the familiar oval willow shopping basket in local black oats, demonstrating that so long as prosperity wasn't general, local manufactures continued. In actuality the effort of producing such things was hardly worthwhile

FIGURE 31.4 *Robbie, Maggie, and Meena Henry delving at the Bridge of Walls, Sandsting, in 1937, using a* kessi *made of cane. As alien materials supplanted local materials, were they still Shetland baskets at all? Photograph courtesy of Shetland Museum & Archives.*

because the cost of the import was attractively low, so Shetland's straw shopping basket was more of a virtuoso novelty.

The most remarkable transition of all was the genesis of the cane (rattan) basket. This was predicated on the availability of cane imported from the East Indies into Britain because of the hobby-craft basketry sector. Such baskets, ubiquitous in Shetland, would never have come about were it not for this external force. The fascinating thing is that this wasn't an imported basket; for the first time a raw material, not just cordage, was employed. Enterprising shopkeepers took cane into stock, and farmers copied the basic form of Shetland's *kessi* and *bøddi*, for land and sea respectively. They were used for traditional chores, but were the antithesis of local styles, being recent-comers to the islands that came about because of Shetlanders' rejection of tradition, rather than adherence to it. This whole phenomenon occurred very rapidly during the 1930s; by 1950 a straw basket was a most uncommon sight (Fig. 31.4).

Second-hand imported baskets were pressed into service in many ways, such as the ingenious overhead wire apparatus employed in some districts to flit baskets of peat fuel from hilltop to home. The whole set-up took advantage of the herring baskets found all over the islands in the 1930s. However, the system can't be said to be indigenous, for the baskets were imported, as were the wires, stays, and pulleys. To reiterate, imported baskets – for all that they were made by hand elsewhere in Britain – were still that, imported, and a stage in the extinction of Shetland basketry.

Transport changes also affected basketry. Moving overland with horses bearing a pack saddle was the method used for centuries if cargo was shifted other than by sea, for there were no roads in the islands until 1850. Roads simply meant travel with horses was easier, and this didn't affect pack equipment, which comprised a thick straw mat under the wooden saddle which, in turn, supported a *kessi* (basket) supported by a *messi* (mesh) on each side. However, the shop goods people sought did affect the set-up, because as the range grew, and the ability to afford them increased, thus piece-by-piece the indigenous paraphernalia of the pack disappeared; the cotton flour bag replaced the straw *kessi* and coir rope replaced the rush *messi*. More critical to the abandonment of pack equipment than imported components were the roads themselves. Wheeled traffic hugely increased, as it was possible to shift heavier loads further. This transition saw the packhorse being replaced by horse and cart by around 1900, with motor traffic taking over by the 1920s.

As people moved to paid employment and buying their garments, food, furniture, and services, so Shetlanders eventually left the land. Most today have no substantive link to it, and 100% of the populace is dependent on mass-produced imports. The effect on basketry can be illustrated with one example. Everyone used peat fuel in the nineteenth century, and all those peats were transported in baskets, whether it was from hill to home, or tipped into a boat, sledge, or cart. Today, homes are heated by electricity or paraffin, and those who do burn peats take them home in plastic fertilizer bags in a trailer.

Substance dependency and guaranteed supply

Now to the second-half of our tale, and an examination of the bigger picture, for Shetland's story is similar to that in other regions, whether they experienced such change contemporaneously, or earlier. Today we're in a world economy dominated by goods on the move, yet for all this colossal scale it is strangely unseen. Ships have smaller crews and container ports are few, but vast, far from residential areas. Goods are hidden in huge containers that go from haulage depot to ship and to massive retail distribution parks. Today, most of what we buy is imported in some way, from vehicles to clothes, and furniture to baskets.

Consumers can be said to benefit by ever-expanding choice, but the corollary is that nations are no longer able to maximize their own resources and instead depend on similar materials traded over huge distance, powered by global corporations and international trade agreements. The lusty economy of scale means we now import raw materials that exist abundantly in Britain – slates from Spain, coal from Poland, lime from France. This becomes clear when considered from a longer historical standpoint. Thus, international trade doubled in three centuries, from 1500 to 1800; from 1800 to 1900 it increased threefold, which is astonishing, but nothing compared with 1800 to 2000 when trade increased twelvefold. Three notable factors feed this transformation and impact the material culture of basketry: consumers, producers and suppliers.

Once, people bought hemp rope or sacks of flour from pure necessity but today we're leisured enough to buy knick-knacks for home, garden, person or pet. One-upmanship and perceived notions that things are out of date feed customers the fallacy of the necessity to keep buying. Even more critical are producers. Although the market is bigger than it ever was, through company takeovers many firms are powerful enough to get their manufacturing done economically by poor people elsewhere, such as the Far East, for wages and conditions Europeans wouldn't countenance.

Thankfully, machinery can't make baskets, but big businesses can get impoverished people elsewhere to make them cheaply, ensuring that the buying public have little or no appreciation of basketry's skill or worth. For other customers the feel-good factor plays on how baskets are made by hand and thus a traditional craft, steeped in the past. But that is far from the case in crafts that have become monetized, because producers – rather like those Shetlanders of long ago – have harnessed whichever modern means they can to make life easier. However, there's a crucial difference, in that Shetland baskets were made by the people themselves, for their own use. What feeds production e.g. in Vietnam, is that the crop is harvested for commerce, not for home consumption. Because multinationals seal supply contracts, the producer can't muck around on the sidelines.

Products are often tailored to consumer tastes rather than reflecting makers' cultures. For example, we can buy satchels from Vietnam or shopping bags from Indonesia, fabricated from plastic strapping industrial detritus. Consumers are happy to pay less as a result of the marked difference in the economic contexts of those who make and those who purchase. And where the materials used are branded with the feel-good factor of 'recycled', there is little or no awareness of the fact that they may well have originated in their own country as waste. I'm certainly not decrying the craftsmanship of basketry made in this way, far from it. What is lamentable is that supply is governed by globalised trade that demands supply in large number, with predictable regularity and homogenization, and accompanying loss of local distinctiveness, so that products can be catalogued and advertised in the same way as they could had they been made of moulded plastic.

Basketry traditions of any culture have regional characteristics. Today, some cultures have maximised their traditions to earn income on the global pitch and that's laudable. However, the economy of scale that favours gigantic production can affect basketry because producers are still the powerless players in the producer/trader relationship. Consider the gorgeous multicoloured baskets beautifully made by people in South Africa from telephone cable insulation. They're made by hand from industrial waste – somewhat like the strapping shopping bag from Indonesia. But for all the promotion of recycling, makers can't make the output of numbers required by large companies who want guaranteed big number supplies. Occasional numbers, of differing shape and design, aren't convenient to the predictable retail offerings that typify high streets and the internet.

Woolly mindedness

To preserve and promote our vernacular traditions, someone needs to care about them. Shetlanders were generalists, and they had many of what we'd now term 'crafts', in wood, iron, straw, wool, leather or stone, none of which were any more or less crucial than others. So how is the history of these crafts appreciated? Aside from industrial mass-production, the other mechanism for their continuation is the 'hobby'. The best way to see how they are faring in this arena is to look at the published corpus, and the best collection of books and articles is in the Shetland Archives. Here there are fewer than ten craft books on anything other than textiles, with none exclusive to Shetland, whereas most of the 227 books on textiles are Shetland-specific. The internet is also a fair gauge of current interest. There, my recent search yielded hits that are flabbergasting, with citations of 'Shetland knitting' having 386,000 hits against nine citations for other crafts; 'Shetland basketry' might have returned no results were it not for an exhibition that had appeared in the Shetland Museum.

How can we explain this? Aside from knitting, most Shetland crafts – especially basketry – are unlikely to be taken up as hobbies because the materials can't be readily acquired. Whereas basketry was once one of all the equally crucial crafts, straw items (for example) weren't durable, thus never became known outwith Shetland, unlike the Fair Isle scarf. Monetization enables popular crafts to make geographical jumps over the world as hobby markets. Mechanised processing of wool is geared to quantity, so you can buy whatever you want, and knitting is tidy and needs little space. The case of straw-back chairs is a salutary one, in how a brand identity can be created but be impossible for others to muscle-in on later. These chairs, with backs made in a coiled straw technique borrowed from basketry, were traditionally made for home use in Orkney and Shetland. When an Orcadian firm started making them for sale, in proto mass-production, the success was such that others in Orkney produced them too, and today the straw-backed chairs are unthinkingly called Orkney chairs.

Once the products of the outside world became affordable to Shetlanders, indigenous basketry changed rapidly, with imported cordage leading to ultimate oblivion. The consequences of this shifting pattern are not confined to the experience of Shetland nor to basketry. Whereas the subsistence economy was circular, planet earth is increasingly driven by the 'buy-to-dump' imperative of a linear economy, wasteful of resources, but benefiting producers. Politically driven recycling (as opposed to local initiatives), facilitated by container ships full of metal or glass bound for the opposite side of the globe to be re-made into things that come back to be bought by us again, have little to do with waste reduction. In the face of massive forces, there's little individuals can do, but posterity will thank us for recording information, collecting artefacts, passing on skills and being inspired to create innovative art. Our British-made wastepaper basket may have been eliminated by the plastic or wire one, but the real foe for us is the globalized natural-fibre basket that comes from thousands of miles away. Let's not toss our traditions into it once it gets here.

32

Braiding and dancing:
Rhythmic interlacing and patterns of interaction

Victoria Mitchell

This chapter considers how braiding with materials, as in basketry, engages interactive rhythms, patterns, processes and structures which are understood not only to resonate within the body of the maker and the formation of braid but also, extended through its function as metaphor, across and between a range of practices and contexts. The example of dancing is used here, as a parallel but intersecting practice, with particular attention to dancing which incorporates actions akin to braiding. The patterns and movements of braiding and the sequential braid-like formations of such dancing can be aligned not just as an idea but as a kinesthetically generative archetype of cognition, whereby embodied actions are understood to shape the mind and engage connectivity within and between bodies.

The patterns of dancing as a formation of braided manoeuvres between couples or within groups activate an 'underlying structural form' of social bonding (Spencer 1986, 35–6). Country dances, in which we might enjoy 'a group of dancers kaleidoscopically advancing and retreating, swinging each other about, crossing from one side to the other, moving up or down inside the lines or outside, weaving in and out, passing under an arch of hands . . .' (Baskerville 1929, 371 – paraphrasing John Playford in *The Dancing Master*, 1651), can inspire such bonds. Although only a few centuries old as we know them today, country dances are deeply embedded, intergenerational and symbolically coded in dynamic relation with times of the year and special occasions. They are social customs within which relationships are articulated and can be fostered. There is friendliness and perhaps suggestive touching, but the dance patterns and musical accompaniment keep everything in order. When we dance, we twirl and twine, perhaps as a prelude to entwining, or later to 'tying the knot'. Such dancing-as-braiding also lightens the burden of hard lives. Whereas dances of the court could be elaborate in sequences of patterning or complexity of steps, traditional country dancing tended towards greater simplicity in rhythm and pattern, further encouraging social coherence.

Dancing and braiding share elements of rhythm which are figured as pattern. Although it is often perceived from the perspective of the decorative or mathematical, pattern is a fundamental trait of biological processes, embodied through symmetry, repetition or cyclical rhythms as well as encoded scientifically through such phenomena as RNA and DNA. The patterned minutiae of organic life unfold as active agency within the orderly expansion of galactic space and time, attesting to processes which are everywhere active, emergent, materially self-replicating and self-organizing (Mitchell 2020). In this context the patterns of our actions can be perceived as intra-actively and materially embedded and as possessing agency. My argument is that patterning and rhythm, as active in dancing or braiding, are intrinsic to the (bio)morphology of connectivity as it infiltrates tissues of knowing. It will partly draw on the currency of 'new materialism' to qualify the notion of intra-active matter as central to the intimacy and intricacy of exchange between materials, mind and body, but it will also suggest that the actions, patterns and perceptions of braiding and of dancing are such as to shape relational experience more broadly, socially, culturally and through language.

Characterized by the interlinking, intertwining and interconnecting of 'active' strands into an orderly geometric form, braiding neatly avoids the potential chaos of entanglement. Perhaps, in this braiding-which-begins-within-the-body, long or unruly hair might serve as a precursor of braiding with bundled strands of fine grass. The distinctive, typically symmetrical, repeated and textured pattern that is formed is characteristic of the dance-like movements experienced in the making process, thus interlacing, 'under and over' crossing or precisely numbered, sequential 'steps' form processional movement through iteration of actions. From the knowing action of the hands as they work the material(s) an inherently aesthetic length of braid gradually emerges, as if giving shape to the measured actions. In theory at least a satisfying operational rhythm effects the formation of an equally satisfying visual rhythm in the pattern that results. In extending and facilitating the formation and movements of the body, the actions effect a para-prosthesis, an 'advancing line' which 'begets the illusion of growth' (Langer 1953, 65).

Stimulated by the pattern-rich agency of matter, it is as if the symmetry and pattern inherent in the evolutionary physiology of the body (Fig. 32.1) are articulated and externalized in the object form of a braid. Such physiology is as if braided in itself, not only in the interconnectivity of muscles, tendons, joints and nervous system but also through the agency of bilateral symmetry and bipedal evolution. Within this physiological para-braiding, the senses, notably in the kinesthetic relationship between haptic and optic, are especially and acutely active in the coming-into-being of braided form. In return, the formation of the braid activates the coming-into-being of its maker and also, through affordance, of its beholder. Inspired by Edmund Husserl's idea of 'intertwining' (*Verflectung*), Maurice Merleau-Ponty draws attention to the optic chiasma or *chiasmus*, the crossing point or intertwining (*entrelacs*) whereby, as if between the flesh of the body and the reflections of the mind, '[t]here is double and crossed situating of the visible in the tangible and of the tangible in the visible' (Merleau-Ponty 1968, 134). The partial crossing of nerve fibres at the optic chiasma enables the left cerebral hemisphere to process right hemispheric vision and vice versa, effecting a crucial balance between the two sides of the body as well as between the senses and other cerebral processes.

The active agencies of matter are also formative of the emerging braid, such that it is as if we are interactively both embodied and embraided in and through the patterning of the material strands. Making a braid necessitates intimate and precise interaction between maker and material and it's worth remembering that the roots of the English word 'skill' (from the Old Norse *skil* and *skilja*, in turn cognate with the Proto-Germanic **skaljo-*) carry notions of discernment and

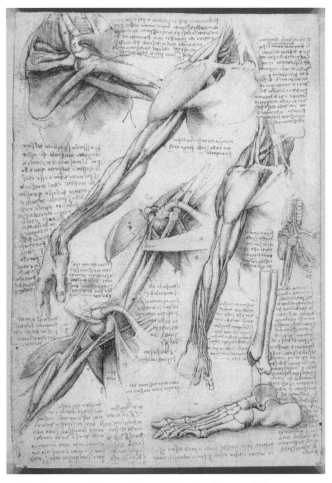

FIGURE 32.1 *Leonardo da Vinci, The muscles of the shoulder and the arm, c.1510–11. Pen and ink. Royal Collection Trust/© Her Majesty Queen Elizabeth II 2019.*

distinction, separation and reasoning. For Gregory Bateson, making which is performative – interlocking, going around, touching, directional, ever-changing, active, social and patterned – is related to an 'almost universal linkage in aesthetics between skill and pattern' (Bateson 1971, 148) and to a conceptual system which is '*both* itself internally patterned *and* itself a part of a larger patterned universe' (ibid. 132, Bateson's emphasis). As increasingly confirmed by investigations of the brain's 'mirror neurons', pattern recognition can be transferred between domains of experience, thus even though it is now a critical commonplace that knowing from within, by enactment, is necessary for knowledge to be understood as embodied, the distinctive actions and patterns of braiding can also be envisaged as endlessly 'distributed'.

As one who is not a practitioner, I have benefited hugely from basketry courses and braiding workshops at which beginners are welcome, above all in understanding how even the making of a simple braid can entail skillful decision-making at every haptic-optic twist and turn. A well-made braid (or braided object), for example, depends on artful manipulation, with fingers and hands, separately and together, holding down, lifting, hooking up, tensioning, drawing together, teasing apart or disentangling, twisting, folding, smoothing and ensuring even density, all the while adding more fibre, of the appropriate dampness, density, pliability or colour. Once preparatory tasks are in place, a skillful braider quickly establishes a rhythm (a form of timing) through a succession of synchronized 'moves' or units of action, many of which call for precision and all of which in combination generate a force, sometimes meditative but also having the potential to evoke a sense of being mesmerized or rhythmically lulled, as if flowing. Etymologically, rhythm combines notions of measure and flow, of which flow may have the deepest (i.e. Proto-European) roots. Of course, the industrial and economic exploitation of the body's ability to braid mechanistically cannot be idealized in this way, but that is another story.

In alternation and combination, measure and flow encapsulate the actions of braiding and dancing at many levels. When a group of rush workers are braiding side by side it is not uncommon for the rhythm of their actions to work in concert, as if collective muscle memory or entrainment is activated.[1] When Willeke Wendrich examined basketry techniques, including plaiting, in two Egyptian villages where she visited makers in their homes she noted that 'all skilled basket makers distinguished themselves by a very steady working rhythm, intense concentration and a very regular appearance of the product' and that not only does each technique operate different rhythms, but each individual maker too (Wendrich 1999, 391, also in this volume, Chapter 3). She likens the detailed making of the baskets to a kind of choreography for which the dance is the basket as a whole, thus 'the body as instrument' engages many parts of the body and not just the hands, in 'a kind of choreography', for which the basket, 'in its material aspects such as the shape, fabric and decoration' and its 'immaterial aspects of function, meaning and social signaling', is not so much the choreography but the dance itself (ibid. 391). 'It is not until watching the dance as a whole', she notes, 'that the meaning [of the basket] can be sensed' (ibid. 389, Wendrich's italics).

Embedding the actions of braiding into this broad perspective exemplifies and effects a critical interlacing between materials, making, metaphor and meaning. By this measure, braiding 'matters', not only in its physical manifestation but also in the way we talk about it and the manner in which it functions within language, thus although it is as embodied action-metaphor that braiding can be 'materially' articulated, it also functions as a familiar, yet complex, verbal metaphor. Even the verb 'to braid' demonstrates continuous exchanging and interweaving of linguistic strands, as if braiding not only functions as representation but also as active and performative in the connective evolution and tissue of language (Barthes, S/Z, 160). The very notion of metaphor in signifying the drawing together or transference between different concepts can be envisaged as braid, connecting disparate strands into a single concept while enabling them still to be distinguished from one another.

Translation, itself a criss-crossing from one side to another, also complicates the braiding of meaning, as does the passage of meaning from one braid-related word to another. In her *Manual of Braiding*, Noémi Speiser notes that the German word *flechten* (generally translated as 'to plait, to braid, to wreathe') is considerably broader in reference than the English terms 'plaiting' and 'braiding' (Speiser 2018, 9). Whereas *flechten* and plait both descend from the Greek πλέκω, (*plecto*) or πλέκειν, (*plectere*), which denote techniques such as winding or intertwining strands, cognate with the Proto-Indo-European (PIE) *plek-*, to plait, the origins of the English word 'braid' have less to do with intertwining than with rapid, jerky but rhythmic, zig-zag movements from side to side, suggesting swords being brandished or a weaver's shuttle; the movements also function like sewing needles in action – hence em*broid*ery – or knitting needles. In simple braiding, each continuous directional strand is turned at an angle (typically of ninety degrees) at the edges of the braid, zig-zagging through the braided structure. Through the strong sense of rhythm and zig-zag movement there is a suggestion of dance, and dexterity and virtuosity are also pertinent to both. Thus, the complex Old English and Old Saxon *bregdan* (from which *breiden*, then braid, evolved) indicated movements so nimble as to be associated with a cunning sleight of hand as well as referring to shaking, swinging and joining together.

Braiding and dancing are, of course, primarily experiential, kinesthetic, proprioceptive activities which facilitate communication without resort to words. The archaeologist Nicole Boivin suggests that such non-verbal communication can be regarded as metaphorical in itself, thus '[w]ith material metaphors, there is no necessary conversion of an experiential metaphor into a verbal one' (Boivin 2010, 55). This is significant, especially when, in a society often dominated by representations, it often seems as if words, as Karen Barad says, 'are untethered from the material world' (Barad 2007:132). Barad instead points to performative, intra-active, 'material-discursive practices' as far more intrinsically instrumental, than words or abstractions, in advancing knowledge (ibid. 132, 183–4). She would therefore argue that it is only from within the discursive potential of material practice that the relational attributes of braiding and dancing can be intra-actively figured. Although etymological evidence demonstrates that language constitutes one of the many interlaced strands that make up and enrich the knowing that arises through engagement with matter, Barad's focus on material-discursive practices is prescient if such 'untethered' accounts of linguistically derived meaning are to be challenged. Crucially, the 'matter' of discursivity, as positioned by new materialists such as Barad, refers not only to materials (such as a maker might use) but also to the human-animal body of the maker (or dancer), both of which have agency and are 'intra-active' in their coming-into-being; 'matter's dynamism', says Barad, 'is inexhaustible, exuberant and prolific' (ibid. 170).

'Matter's dynamism' is activated when, in responding to materials, the hands of a braider differentiate meanings and patterns that not only originate within the body but also within the material that is worked. Materials stimulate a response, and although they have invariably been processed to some extent, they nevertheless carry a form of memory of their having come-into-being (Trewavas, 2014: 222, 229) and can be considered as co-respondents in the making process. We interact with them and they interact with us. For animal or plant materials or their derivatives, traces of their organization as living, adaptive systems remain; they have structure and perform in certain ways, enabled by the actions we tease out of or impose on them. For Donna Haraway, 'the tissues of one's knowings' extend beyond the human and engage common biological ground, such as in plants, which she describes as 'consummate communicators . . . . . making and exchanging meanings among and between an astonishing galaxy of associates across the taxa of living beings'. Haraway cites weaving, string figures and interlacing (to which we might add braiding) as especially potent manifestations of the 'relational action' between human and nonhuman fibres and as formations through which kinship and behaviour are sustained (Harraway 2016, 91–93).

For the architect and writer Lars Spuybroeck the connective interlacing characteristics of braid constitutes a significant conceptual framework which is as embedded within materials as it is within consciousness (2016, 116). Infinitesimal detail structures pattern and materiality such as to take on the quality of thought (ibid. 96). Inspired by Gottfried Semper and John Ruskin he describes technology as a 'acting on the inside of matter' and pattern as an effect of the 'self-crafting of matter' (ibid. 102). This is exemplified in Ruskin's *The Ethics of the Dust* (1904, 76–77) where fine crystalline structures are likened to fibrous threads, thus creating 'white webs of quartz more delicate than your finest lace' and establishing a correspondence between matter and geometric pattern. In this fictional but instructional tract Ruskin even organizes a group of girls to hold hands and perform the topographical organization of the crystal, as if in preparation of a dance. For both Ruskin and Spuybroeck, threads are lines of force, whether found in crystals, braided in baskets, painted in the carpet pages of Irish manuscripts or patterned through Maypole dancing, for example.

In the Maypole dance, or related seasonal dances such as the Tamil traditional Pinnal Kolattam, braiding and dancing are irrevocably combined in expression or re-enactment of cultural memory. For Ruskin, the combination of dancing and braiding around the Maypole was especially significant. *The Ethics of the Dust* was written for Whitelands College, a teachers' training college for girls in Roehampton where, in 1881, he organized a May festival, with garlanded May Queen, dancing and revelry. This festival and its annual iteration have been cited as influential in the late nineteenth-century revival of Maypole dancing in the United Kingdom (Buckland 2013, 47), albeit the 'revival' of Maypole or Ribbon Dances formed an aspect of spectacle from at least 1846, when a 'garlanded tent formed by . . . glittering streamers of different colours' was a central feature of a popular play staged in a London theatre (Judge 1983, 3). Such festivities, often celebrating the arrival of spring or commemorative well dressing, bring braiding and dancing together around a pole that would once have been growing as a branch or tree trunk. As the (often young and female) dancers braid the ribbons, social patterns and ecological symbolism are also braided, enacting a patterned articulation that is botanically and culturally synchronized.

Dances often convey occupational activities, as sometimes reflected in the names by which they are known, such as the Orcadian 'Strip the Willow' line dance which conveys a loose figuring of willow being stripped while also enabling the turning-and-interlinking-with-one-another passage of the leading couple as they 'strip' along the lines from head to foot (or tip to butt) to the rhythm of musical accompaniment. In Scottish dancing a set of repeated movements is known as a figure, a word rooted in the Latin *figura*, meaning a form or shape, which was in turn a translation of the Greek *skhêma*, (σχῆμα, schema) and which referred not only to shape and form but also to dance. A 'figure' in dancing, conceived thus as a formation, or a shaping, creates a pattern of movements that are repeated. It's also worth noting that the familiar phrase 'figure of eight' not only indicates the shape of the number 8 or describes a knot but also describes a motif in Scottish dancing in which one or more dancers follows the path of a figure of eight, moving around either standing figures or one another, creating a figural braid-like reticulation through succession.

A comparison between the way in which dance movements and braid patterns are graphically 'figured' as notation or diagram further articulates the interstices between the two domains, while also mapping a territory between material and verbal aspects of cognition. The Bauhaus artist and choreographer Oscar Schlemmer drew many 'gesture dance' diagrams or '*gestentanz*', many of which suggest a spatial weaving or braiding of threads which have their origin in the kinesthesia and physiognomy of the body (Gropius and Moholy-Nagy 1925; Fig. 32.2).

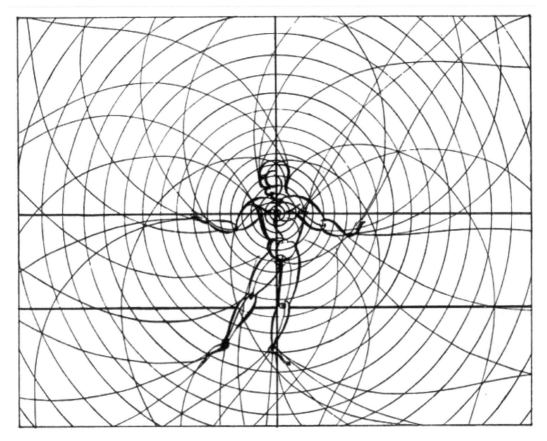

FIGURE 32.2 *Oscar Schlemmer,* Man as Dancer, *1921. Pen and ink. (Gropius, W., and Moholy-Nagy, L., (eds.) 1925).*

Contemporary practices in craft and performance can also shape the potential interface between braid and dance whereby the lived-in performative body becomes an effective and enabling instrument through which aesthetically rhythmic activities such as braiding and dancing can share crossing points. This is evident in recent work by Dutch designer Maria Blaisse in which the movements of dancer Kenzo Kusudo are combined with interwoven bias structures of bamboo, 'from body scale towards architecture', together illustrating what she describes as 'the emergence of form' (Blaisse 2013, 160). Each element is distinct but also acts intra-actively, as if in a pervasive process of inosculation. In some manifestations it is as if the pliable bamboo functions as a garment-like extension of the dancer's body, but Blaisse also envisages a braided dome on an architectural scale. Within this framework, dancer and bamboo engage in symbiotic shaping (Fig. 32.3), reflecting the braiding rhythms and patterns of each and both.

Braiding is one of the simplest, oldest and most significant means through which engagement with materials is integral to our formation of pattern. A fibrous structure of connectivity is brought into play in which not only the hands but the body as a whole is active in its engagement with

FIGURE 32.3 *Maria Blaisse,* Bamboo structure open sphere, *2014. Design photography: Maria Blaisse: Dancer Marcela Giesche.*

materials which are themselves formative of the decision-making and rhythmic patterning that ensues, both individually and socially. Within my amateur struggle to remain in control of the braiding process there are moments when an almost meditative sense rises to the fore, when the ongoing dialogue between *epistêmê* and *technê* gives way to a satisfying working rhythm and the various strands of braid and body are brought together, intertwined figuratively and literally, as if dancing.

Note

1   In conversation with Felicity Irons at Rush Matters, Bedfordshire, U.K., 27.11.2018.

Bibliography

Barad, K. 2007 *Meeting the Universe Halfway: Quantum Physics and the Entanglement of Matter and Meaning*. Durham, NC: Duke University Press.

Barthes, R. 1974 *S/Z* (translated Richard Miller). New York: Hill and Wang.

Baskerville C. R. 1929 *The Elizabethan Jig*. Chicago, IL: University of Chicago Press.

Bateson, G. 1972 *Steps to an Ecology of Mind*. Chicago, IL: University of Chicago Press.

Blaisse, M. 2013 *The Emergence of Form*. Rotterdam: nai010 publishers.

Boivin, N. 2010 *Material Cultures, Material Minds*. Cambridge: Cambridge University Press.

Buckland, T. J. 2013 'Dance and cultural memory: Interpreting Fin-de-Siècle performances of "Olde England"', *Dance Research* 31 (1): 29–66.

Gropius, W. and Moholy-Nagy, L. (eds) 1925 *Die Bühne im Bauhaus*, Bauhausbücher 4. Munich: Albert Langen Verlag

Haraway, D. 2016 *Staying with the Trouble: Making Kin in the Chthulucene*. Durham, NC: Duke University Press.

Judge, R. 1983 'Tradition and the plaited Maypole dance', *Traditional Dance* 2: 1–22, Alsager: Crewe and Alsager College of Higher Education.

Langer, S. 1953 *Feeling and Form: A Theory of Art*. London: Routledge & Kegan Paul.

Merleau-Ponty, M. 1969 *The Visible and the Invisible*. Evanston, IL: Northwestern University Press.

Mitchell, V., 2020 'Tangles and Tectonics: the expanding range of contemporary basketry'. In T. A. Heslop and H. Anderson (eds) *Basketry and Beyond: Constructing Culture*, Norwich: Sainsbury Research Unit, University of East Anglia.

Ruskin, J. 1904 [1865] *The Ethics of the Dust*. Orpington: George Allen.

Speiser, N. 2018 *A Manual of Braiding*. Bern: Haupt Verlag (reprint of 2nd edition of 1988).

Spencer, P. 1986 *Society and the Dance*. Cambridge: Cambridge University Press.

Spuybroeck, L. 2016 *The Sympathy of Things: Ruskin and the Ecology of Design* (2nd edition). London: Bloomsbury.

Trewavas, A. 2014 *Plant Behaviour and Intelligence*. Oxford: Oxford University Press.

Wendrich, W. 1999 *The World According to Basketry: An Ethnoarcheological Interpretation of Basketry Production in Egypt*. CNWS publications no. 83, University of Leiden: Research School of Asian, African and Amerindian Studies.

33

Weaving together:

Human-robot-relations of basketry and knitting

Cathrine Hasse and Pat Treusch

Making implies unmaking, remaking, making connections whether through deliberate entanglement or drafting code. Through manipulation of textile signs – cloth, related materials, processes, histories, and technologies – people produce knowledge.

JEFFERIES IN JEFFERIES ET AL, 2015:3

Today's robots, in the shape of 'helping hands', are moving from the production line to offices, homes and the care sector. In an age when the idea of the high-tech, flexible, mobile robot arm that will supposedly become useful in every aspect of human everyday lives takes centre stage, we question: How are humans and robots woven together at the emerging interface of collaboration? What do humans and robots respectively bring to the entanglements of human hands and arms and robotic 'hands' and 'arms'?

In asking this, we draw on weaving, firstly in its direct meaning as a collective, socio-material practice of linking and connecting while also disconnecting and relinking apparently separate entities and secondly, weaving as metaphor, in as much as it carries a rich metaphorical function for grappling with methods of knowledge production, reconciling the body/mind split for example. We are especially interested in the ways in which weaving, in both its direct and metaphoric senses, embodies processes of socio-material and collective learning. However, what we would like to emphasize is a new context in which handwork is realized, namely at the emerging interface between human and robot.

In order to do so we draw on two examples of experimental collaborative situations which weave humans and robots together. The first is a workshop bringing robot-makers and basket weavers together to explore the potential of each learning from the other. In the second example human and robot collaborate, engaging in a manipulation of textile patterns together, through the cultural technology of knitting.

However, let us begin by defining robots. Weaving by hand and robot-like machines have been entangled at least since the seventeenth century when, in 1675, the first Spitalfields weavers 'rioted against machines by which one man can do as much . . . as near twenty without them' (Hobsbawm 1964: 6). The looms were forerunners of a robot revolution, which has not only developed industrial robots, but has increasingly focused on robotic machines developed to work closely with human bodies. The machines share some features with the early industrial looms but are much more advanced. Although it is debatable whether such robots can weave and make baskets like those made by humans, machines appear to be becoming increasingly adept at replicating human limbs and their capabilities. This does not imply, however, that robots can be made to behave exactly like humans.

Even if people in general connect robots with human-like intelligence, the people who make robots connect them with technical features. As defined by the International Organization for Standardization (ISO-Standard 8373:2012), '[a] robot is an actuated mechanism programmable in two or more axes with a degree of autonomy, moving within its environment, to perform intended tasks. Autonomy in this context means the ability to perform intended tasks based on current state and sensing, without human intervention.'

Though robots thus are envisioned as autonomous beings (whether they have a full human-like 'body' or a robot arm), empirical studies show that robots always depend on social settings for their functionality (Alač et al. 2011, Hasse 2013, Blond and Schiølin 2018, for example). There is a lack of analytical concepts for indicating how robot technology consistently mediates surroundings (Verbeek 2005, Ihde 1993) and in practice robots become a challenge for humans who stretch themselves to learn from and adjust to them (Hasse, 2015). Basketry, knitting and weaving are embodied processes which often function without any conscious awareness by the human of all the bodily processes involved. When working with robots, humans have to learn to apply all the intuitive movements and at the same time become aware of their own embodied being by learning from robots. As we show with the examples, the relation between robot and human can be captured through a process of alignment. We highlight the way in which this relation evolves through a tension between the flexure and stiffness of the materiality of bodies and artefacts and – also through this – that the process of alignment is an embodied one. Our account of how robots and humans are woven together, through making together, thus centres on the materiality and embodiment of the human-machine relation.

Weaving robots and baskets

In May 2017 an event took place at the Department for Learning at Aarhus University in Denmark, where a group of skilled basket weavers from Denmark and the UK met with Danish engineers to explore the potential for learning from each other. The basket weavers came from a local organisation, The Willow Braiding Association, in which many skilled makers meet regularly and exchange ideas for basket-weaving, patterns and knowledge about materials. Furthermore, a neurobiologist, a therapist and a weaver working on archaeological projects visited the event.

From the engineering side a group of engineers from the IT University of Copenhagen participated. They were fascinated by the techniques presented by the weavers. Led by Professor Kasper Støy at the Robotics, Evolution and Art Lab in the department for Robotics and Artificial Intelligence, they had already begun to explore how machines could be made of textures other than the hard (as in metal). Wires necessarily have to be there (to conduct current) but for Støy and his team robots will in the future become soft, made for instance, of silicone or other bendable materials.

This has opened the possibility of looking at robots in an entirely new way. Instead of industrial robots, robots could perhaps themselves be woven with techniques that the roboticists could learn from skilled basket weavers. As Støy envisages such robots,

> We are in a situation where the technology makes many things possible, but that does not help us if the robots physically do not work in cooperation with humans. Some elements of the robots we build today are based on 18th century technology – like metal rods and cogwheels. We have to find a different way of building robots and ITU see potential in *soft robotics*, an emerging field where researchers experiment with building robots from soft materials like silicone. This requires entirely new production methods. (. . .) We would like to weave, knit or weave robots with a structure that humans will feel good being around, which are light, and which are made of materials that don't hurt you if you bump into them.
>
> STØY 2016: 1

What appears central in this plea for reconsidering the mechanical structure of a robot is the development of lighter, more flexible and thus also less frightening machines. The softness of the

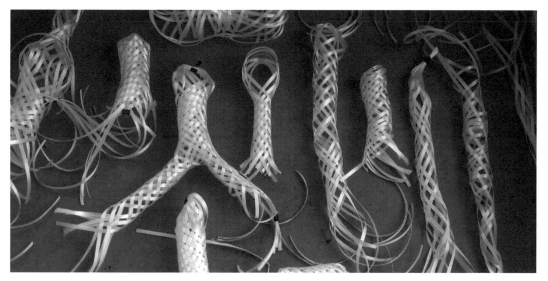

FIGURE 33.1 *Hand-manufactured braids. Flexibility of filament organization allows for diversity of attributes, such as branching and interlacing pattern. Courtesy Phil Ayres, Centre for Information Technology and Architecture, The Royal Danish Academy of Fine Arts Schools of Architecture, Design and Conservation.*

robot is regarded as a factor in relating a robot to humans. Furthermore, with a change of perspective in choosing which materials should be used, the 'style of engineering' also changes dramatically: from building with metal to weaving or knitting with soft materials (Fig. 33.1).

At the seminar, robot-makers and basket weavers explored each other's skills and debated how robots may affect human skills in the future. Robot-makers may learn to weave robots in innovative materials that make them soft and stretchable, so to a larger extent they can meet human demands and bodily engagements. However, the weavers also emphasized that they did not believe that robots themselves can become basket weavers mastering the old skill of human weaving (the word weaving coming from the old English *wefan,* which has an Indo-European root meaning 'entwine'). As Stephanie Bunn (2016) highlights:

> [T]he three-dimensional form of the basket as it develops in the making, acts as both the technology – the kind of loom or frame on which the basket is made – and at the same time it forms the structure of the basket itself. The basket is like its own loom, and this emergent, 3-D making process is primarily what makes it so difficult to transfer to machine. [. . .]This inability to mechanize and sub-divide tasks in basket-making is further compounded by basketry's use of materials, which, being plant matter, are thus organic, uneven, short and frequently needs adjustment and creative decision-making from stroke to stroke, inch to inch, and strand to strand.

BUNN, 2016: 27

At the seminar the weavers demonstrated their skills for learning to adjust to materials, thus in a continuous flow between bendable straws or willow branches, rhythmically weaving hands and fingers with the basketry materials in a process defined by the anthropologist Tim Ingold as a meshwork that weaves together atmosphere and the rhythms of life (Ingold 2011: 63).

Although the robot-makers can learn weaving techniques, the makers of soft robots will still depend on the capacities of algorithms to formulate discrete and digital approaches to embodiment and learning. However, if robot-makers can themselves learn the weaving techniques that inform their design of 'embodied' robots, how could soft robots enable an approach to embodiment and learning which is no longer purely discrete and digital? We suggest a deeper and more detailed understanding of collaboration between humans and their robots. What exactly does it mean to align one's self to a robot? Developing an account of human and robots as being woven together, that maps the opportunities as much as the challenges of learning from one other, we underline the embodied and material nature of learning at the human-robot interface. This could then become the point of departure for leaving behind a discrete and digital approach to embodiment and learning in robotics.

Becoming an affiliated human to PANDA: learning collaboratively to knit anew

In the project *Do robots dream of knitting? Recoding collaboration between human and robot* (DRDK), Pat Treusch is working with an interdisciplinary team at the Technical University, Berlin, towards realizing different scenarios of knitting together with a robot arm (Treusch 2020). The project thus not only brings humans and robots into collaborative relation through an unusual task – at least within the context of high-tech technology development – but also underscores the historical linkages between craft practices and computer science. One of our foci here is to reconstruct one aspect of DRDK, namely the teaching/learning between a human and the robot arm when realizing the knitting together task. In what follows, this realization is reconstructed through an auto ethnographic perspective of feminist studies of science and technology, which then also underscores the importance of experience for understanding learning processes.

In one major scenario that the project has been working on, a person begins to knit a small piece, such as ten stitches over three rows. The selection of needles and yarn has already been adapted to earlier experiments with the robot arm which means, for instance, using bamboo needles instead of needles of plastic or metal, as the wool will show different 'sliding qualities' depending on the material of the needle. After the person has knitted the three rows, she or he will put the empty right needle into the gripper of the robot – which is the PANDA model of the Bavarian company, FRANKAEMIKA. At the same time, the 'guide mode' of the robot will be enabled.

The next step then is to guide the gripper and robot arm as if it was the right arm of the person in order to 'teach' the movements of the right needle to the robot. Teaching in this regard means instructing how to press the 'enter' button at the pilot of the robot arm. When doing so, the robot arm will 'remember' the location of its gripper on the x-, y- and z-axes. Once this process is completed, we can decide how many times the 'learnt movement' should be repeated, for instance, as many times as there are stitches on the left needle that need to be knitted in order to complete the row. Then we can start to knit together.

What might appear like a quite easily realizable serial process of following steps along a path of implementation requires an engagement with the robot arm that can be reduced neither to a step-by-step-path nor to the handling of buttons and controlling a computer screen. This becomes palpable when describing the – as we argue – mostly neglected efforts and labours that are necessary to make interaction at the human-robot arm interface a success. In this, we are interested in reconstructing the experience of realizing collaboration through the cultural technology of knitting. In doing so, our focus is on exactly those 'ongoing – or truncated – labours of its [the robot's] affiliated humans' (Suchman 2011, 119). That these labours are truncated appears to be taken-for-granted in representations of the useful high-tech robot arm. In this regard, knitting together means to become an affiliated human.

We now map the details of this process. When PANDA's guide mode is enabled, the guiding button right above the gripper has to be pressed by taking the robot above the grippers between thumb and forefinger (Fig. 33.2). If pressed too hard some kind of panic mode of the robot will be triggered, which means it will freeze and stop. Then, the person guiding the robot arm has to let go of the button briefly and press again in order to be able to continue with the guiding. How gently the button has to be pressed in order not to trigger the panic mode and how hard it has to be pressed in order to enable the guiding necessitates a form of practical embodied knowledge learning which the person working with PANDA has to acquire.

Further, this practical knowledge can be regarded as a prerequisite for a person to become – with reference to Suchman – PANDA's affiliated human, that is, a person who adjusts her/himself to the robot by, for instance, investing her/himself in a host of prerequisite efforts and labours.

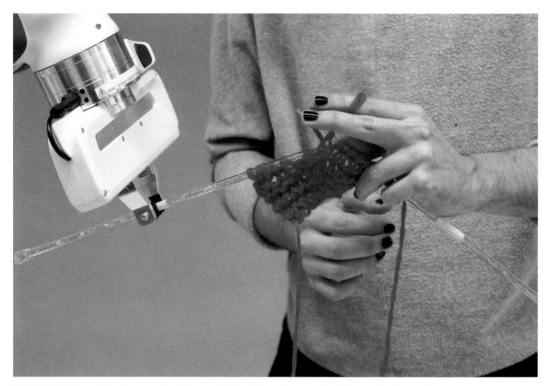

FIGURE 33.2 *Collaborative knitting with PANDA. Copyright: Katrin M. Kämpf.*

However, emphasizing the practical dimension of becoming familiar and therefore affiliated to the robot, we also underscore the embodied nature of this learning process. The person who is guiding PANDA has to find out where to stand in relation to the robot in order to be able not only to press the guiding button in the correct way but also to be able to move and therefore guide the arm. Becoming attentive to the *embodied* details of affiliating oneself with the robot means to 'attend[. . .] closely to material practices' (Suchman 2011: 134). Central to the material practices of affiliating oneself with PANDA is not only to experience how the robot arm moves but, and concomitant to that, to adjust one's own movements to the range and nature of the robot's movement.

The same applies to the execution of the task 'knitting together'. The 'first five warm up stitches' have become an established 'rule' when starting to engage in knitting with PANDA and delegating the right needle to the robot (Field Notes PT, November 2018). During these stitches several things might happen, for instance, the new stitch might slide from the right needle before it is pulled through. Based on that, it was also decided that the number of repetitions that the arm will execute after pressing start should be much higher than that of stitches on the row.

On collaboration as being woven together/apart

Using human engagement with robots in order to explore learning has several advantages. From a robot-maker point of view it can demonstrate where humans and robots delink from each other and how humans differ from machines in their worldly engagements when they engage in Human-Robot Interactions (HRI). From a learning perspective it can teach us that the rational and scientific approaches to learning, that for so long has dominated the learning sciences (Packer 2001), has its limits. Human learning is not an algorithmic cognitive development in the thinking brain where knowledge transfer is a goal. It is rather a sustainable ongoing process of weaving human bodies and materials together.

Our engagement with robots constantly teaches us that in spite of 'numerous attempts to constrain natural systems within fixed and measurable constructs (. . .) this world does not behave in scientifically predictable ways' (Cato 2014: 6). Robots can help us develop a holistic insight into processes where humans and machines adjust as uncertainty abounds.

With Alač (2009) and Treusch (2015), material practices of affiliation through movement can be described as mobilizing one's own body through practices such as that of association – a process of 'getting into the body' (Alač 2009: 496) of the robot. The suggested analytical scope allows us to contemplate collaboration through knitting, in terms which necessarily involve processes of making as a linking and unmaking as a delinking of natural and artificial intelligence, and through which separable entities with properties, including agency and specific materialities or embodiments, emerge. This implies not reducing the realization of the task of knitting together to an effort of the human, but also to take into account of the collective efforts involved in learning how to realize such a task with the robot arm.

At the 'Weaving Robot' seminar, the robot-makers learned from the basket weavers the complexity of the process that goes into human basketry. In Pat Treusch's work, the humans learn about themselves and how to adjust movements to a robotic arm which in turn adjusts to humans – just as Støy's soft robots will mould themselves following human touch. An account of being woven together/apart highlights the provisional character of id/entities and the constitutive nature of collaborative efforts of learning as experiencing how to realize a task together. Knitting together is to 'act in concert' (Treusch 2017). This acting in concert, however, is not based on pre-figured id/entities, but rather is characterized by a dance between the subject- and object-like qualities that are linked at the human-robot interface. We suggest grappling with this dance through the material practices of affiliation. As Suchman points out, 'Re-specifying the roboticist's labours, and her and others' intra-actions with her machines, might contribute to demystification and re-enchantments restorative to the life of subjects and objects alike' (Suchman 2011: 134).

The detailed re-specification thus not only serves the reconstruction of collaborative efforts which weave humans and robots together. Rather, it also delinks the threads of the narrative of automation as frictionless delegation, as easy as pressing a button. Mobilising one's own arm as the robot's arm shows how automation at this interface is a socio-material and fine-grained concerted process of learning that weaves the human and her or his robot together.

Weaving brings together previously distinctly separated communities of engineers and basket weavers, human knitters and robot arms and creates new socio-material practices that connect and disconnect humans and machines in novel ways, thus moving boundaries as to what humans are and what robots are. As a metaphor, weaving shows how knowledges emerge with new methods of merging and (re)connecting machine parts, software, basket materials, willows, needles and humans from different backgrounds and embodied rhythms into the formation of new embodied entities. However, as learned both at the seminar and by knitting with robots, there are also threads and materials that resist being woven together as their rhythms are fundamentally different.

Bibliography

Alač, M. 2009 'Moving Android: On Social Robots and Body-in-Interaction', *Social Studies of Science*, 39 (4): 491–528.

Alač, M., Movellan J., and Tanaka F. 2011 'When a robot is social: spatial arrangements and multimodal semiotic engagement in the practice of social robots', *Social Studies of Science* 41 (6): 893–926.

Blond, L. and Schiølin, K. 2018 'Lost in Translation? Getting to Grips with Multistable Technology in an Apparently Stable World'. In Cathrine Hasse and Jan Kyrre Friis (eds), *Postphenomenological Methodologies – New Ways in Mediating Techno-Human Relationships*. Lanham, MD: Lexington Books, pp. 151–167.

Bunn, S. 2016 'Who Designs Scottish Vernacular Baskets?' *Journal of Design History* 29 (1): 24–42. https://doi.org/10.1093/jdh/epv027

Cato, M. S. 2014 'What the Willow Teaches: sustainability learning as craft', *The International Journal of Higher Education in the Social Sciences*, special issue, *Teaching and Learning* 7 (2): 4–27.

Hasse, C. 2013 'Artefacts that talk: Mediating technologies as multistable signs and tools', *Subjectivity* 6 (1): 79–100.

Hasse, C. 2015 'Multistable robo-ethics'. In Jan Kyrre Berg Friis, Robert P. Crease (eds), *Technoscience and Postphenomenology: The Manhattan Papers (Postphenomenology and the Philosophy of Technology)*. Lanham, MD: Lexington Books, pp. 169–189.

Hobsbawm E. 1964 'The Machine Breakers'. In *Labouring Men. Studies in the History of Labour*. London: Weidenfeld and Nicolson, pp. 5–23.

Ihde, D. 1993 *Postphenomenology – Essays in the Postmodern Context*. Evanston, L: Northwestern University Press.

Ingold, T. 2011 *Being Alive: Essays on Movement, Knowledge and Description*. London: Routledge.

Jefferies, J. 2015 Editorial Introduction. In Janis Jefferies, Diana Wood Conroy, and Hazel Clark (eds), *The Handbook of Textile Culture*. London: Bloomsbury.

Mindell, D. A. 2015 *Our Robots, Ourselves: Robotics and the myths of autonomy*. New York: Viking.

Packer, M. 2001 'The Problem of Transfer, and the Sociocultural Critique of Schooling', *The Journal of the Learning Sciences* 10 (4): 493–514.

Støy, K. 2016 https://en.itu.dk/about-itu/press/news-from-itu/new-professor-wants-to-make-human-friendly-robots (retrieved 06.01.2019).

Suchman, L. 2011 'Subject objects', *Feminist Theory* 12 (2): 119–145.

Treusch, P. 2015 'Robotic Companionship: The Making of Anthropomatic Kitchen Robots in Queer Feminist Technoscience Perspective'. Linköping: LiU, http://urn.kb.se/resolve?urn=urn:nbn:se:liu:diva-118117.

Treusch, P. 2017 'Humanoide Roboter als zukünftige assistive Artefakte in der Küche? Einblicke in die Herstellungspraktiken eines aktuellen robot companions'. In Peter Biniok and Eric Lettkemann (eds), *Assistive Gesellschaft*. Wiesbaden: Springer.

Treusch, P. 2020 *Robotic Knitting. Re-Crafting Human-Robot Collaboration Through Careful Coboting.* Bielefeld: transcript.

Other resources

Project Blog of DRDK: https://blogs.tu-berlin.de/zifg_stricken-mit-robotern/

Afterword:

To basket the world

Tim Ingold

No one lives forever, nor does the longest stalk of grass, reed or straw extend indefinitely. Yet social life carries on, and a cord, twisted from grass fibres, can be continued without limit. With the multi-stranded cord as with the life of many lives, the reasons are the same. Lives, like fibres, are bundled together, which is to say that their alignment is longitudinal. In the bundle, strands overlap along their length: even as old strands begin to give out new strands are introduced. The old and the new, as they twist around one another, establish in the tension and the friction of their contact a grip that is even stronger than the combined tensile strength of the strands themselves. The analogy between the twisting of cordage and the entwining of generations is not loose but exact. It is why a history told over again is called a record; why – in the record – every life retains its own individuality however tightly it is bound with others; and why, in the passage of time, this binding is of the essence. It is no wonder that among peoples around the world, knotted cords were not only among the most frequent repositories of ancestral lore; they were also commonly employed as measures of time. As cords were paid out, time would elapse, and stories would be told.

This is no longer true today. It is not easy to put one's finger on what has happened, or to fathom the reasons that led to it. But even as the twisting and spinning of fibres, once a ubiquitous task of daily life, has largely become confined as a niche art for hobbyists and the purveyors of heritage, and as cord disappears from common use, so records have ceased to be stories to tell and to follow, and have instead become benchmarks of their own era, laid down as limits to be broken. Generations, then, don't twist around one another like corded strands, but are layered like sheets in a stack, such that the work of each is flattened in its own time. Far from coming together in forging the conditions of the present, the old and the young are wedged apart by them – the young not yet ready, the old already past it – and are denied the opportunity to contribute to their evolution. As a prisoner of the present, every generation can receive nothing from the past save that which can be represented, in some transmissible form, independently of its lifetime achievement. This is what psychologists know as 'social learning', as distinct from the 'individual learning' entailed in the application of acquired representations. Whatever is not socially learned drops out. While future generations may attempt to reconstruct practices from their extant benchmarks, much is forever lost.

Among arts on the endangered list is basketry. The weaving of baskets, like the twisting of cords from which they are very often (though not universally) constructed, closely models the processes of social life. People would bring the same tactile sensibility, the same sense of movement and pattern, into the choreography of their lives with one another as into that of their hands in working with materials. Every basket is like a little community, binding its constituent fibres, as the community binds lives, into a supple and durable form. And as communities produce baskets, so baskets reproduce communities. In the practice of the craft, basketry produces its makers as well as the things themselves, building a feel for the work into their muscle memory, sense of rhythm and perceptual attunement. But there is much more, once the field of basketry is enlarged beyond weaving itself, to embrace the entire life of its materials, and what happens to the things after they are made. It would then include the cultivation and harvesting of the grounds from which the materials are collected, ranging from grassland to willow beds, as well as the harvest of the sea or land they will eventually hold, not to mention all the relations, whether of grandparents and grandchildren, or of masters and apprentices, which ensure that skills are carried on.

Basketry, then, is more than mere technique. It is a life process. Its generativity lies in the unfolding of an entire field of vital relations from which not only things, but also people and their provisions, are as much grown as made. It is no surprise that in so many myths of origin, the world itself was conceived in a basket. There is a sense of containment as encompassment, as all-in-one, that makes no distinction between inside and outside. The in-and-out weave of the basket, from which its surfaces are formed, defies any such distinction. Yet again, it is the same with community, which in its classical sense of 'giving-together' (from the Latin, *com*, 'together', plus *munus*, 'gift') is not closed in on itself but open-ended: open to others, to the past and to the future. Nevertheless, along with cords, baskets – and the skills of making them – are close to dying out. Were there no more to basketry than technique, there would be nothing exceptional about this. With techniques in human history, as with species in evolution, extinction has been more the rule than the exception. Yet life carries on, regardless. But the loss of basketry is not just a case of technical extinction. What is unique about the contemporary moment is not the loss of techniques to life, but the draining of life from technique.

This trend is not easily reversed. No amount of curation, repair or documentation will, of their own accord, restore baskets to life. The much greater challenge is to rethink the passage of generations. To meet the challenge means imagining a society in which young and old can once again join together in the making of a common world. This has massive implications for the way we think about education, about the wisdom of the elderly and the curiosity of the young, and about the potential of their collaboration. Both seasoned wisdom and juvenile curiosity entail an openness to the world, and an attentiveness to what is going on there, that hold little esteem in a system that values objective knowledge, and the operations of abstract reason, above all else. Within such a value system, the humility of wisdom is assessed as a deficiency of mind, and the innocence of curiosity as a deficiency of knowledge: the former branded as dementia, the latter as ignorance. To those who guard the gates of our institutions of education and social care, the idea that the demented and the ignorant might together forge the future is manifestly absurd. To unite wisdom and curiosity, however, appears not only prudent but necessary for there to be a future worth living at all. This is not nostalgia, or a hankering for a lost past. It is rather a foundation for hope.

Nowhere do wisdom and curiosity come together more than in the practice of basketry. That's why the practice has been so shamefully denigrated by mainstream institutions, and why it is so important to bring it back. We have, to coin a verb, to 'basket' the world. By this, I mean to oppose the common view that the right place for what are pigeonholed as 'arts and crafts' is as optional supplements to the core curriculum of so-called academic subjects designed to instil authorised knowledge into the minds of the young and improve their powers of reason. One such subject is mathematics. At first glance, to compare mathematics to basketry is like placing a grand palace of classical proportions, inhabited by the finest minds, on a par with a ramshackle hovel whose naive or demented occupants lack the wit to improve their condition. How could the mathematics of the basket be anything other than a degenerate imitation of the real thing, simplified for ease of comprehension by vulgar minds? But in reality, it is the inhabitants of the palace who are deluded into thinking that mathematics can float above the realities of bodily experience with vital materials, oblivious to the grounding of their most basic concepts of number, line, surface, symmetry and pattern in crafty operations of folding, twisting and weaving with which the inhabitants of the hovel would have been entirely familiar. Who, then, are the real mathematicians?

Anyone who has worked with materials, for example, knows that intersecting fold-lines cannot be produced simultaneously but require successive operations. Hands and fingers must get to work on the material, folding it first in one way, and then in another. Baskets, likewise, take time to weave, and cords time to twist. To basket the world is to restore things to the temporal current of their ongoing creation. It is to recognise that there can be no pattern without rhythm. For every pattern records the movement of its formation, and to read it one must be able to enter into this movement and to join it with the arc of one's attention. Herein lies the work of memory. To remember is to pick up lives from the past and pull them through into the vivid present so as to bind them with one's own. Remembering another person is like having them there before us, after a long absence, and resuming our conversation; remembering a material is feeling it again in our hands, and responding with gestures that seem to well up from within. This is also what the weaver does in looping. In a basket-world, memory loops the threads of the past through the eyes of the present. And it is by bringing these past lives into our presence, listening to them and attending to their needs, that we care for them.

The contemporary production of heritage, however, breaks the loop. Instead of pulling the past into the present, we turn our backs on it, only to appropriate its products as heirlooms. With this, the basket no longer affords, in its weave, a way of remembering or a path of care, and becomes instead an *object* of memory, to be conserved and curated rather than followed. It tells of another world that is not ours, one that we have irrevocably left behind. And it is as such that it enters the museum, an institution tasked with preserving objects of the past for posterity. In the museum the basket, once a record in itself – or better, a bundle of records, each a story waiting to be told – is turned into an object *in* the record. This is the record as it appears in the official accounts of history and archaeology, in which every object is catalogued by its place and date of manufacture. Confined to its point of origin, the object stays put while time and history march on. Museums, of course, are doing all they can to resist this objectification, and to bring the things in their collections back to life. But they are in a double bind, torn between their public duty to archive the record of material culture and their desire to revive endangered skills. It is inevitable, in the museum context, that such revival appears freighted with nostalgia.

Indeed the very designation of basketry as a 'craft' seems virtually guaranteed to keep it on the margins, to push it underground from higher to lower levels of awareness, or even from mind to body. This feeds on a well-established discourse according to which the learning and practice of a craft provides an outlet for the development of knowledge and skills variously branded as tacit, non-verbal and embodied, to complement and counterbalance higher powers of reasoning that are taken to be explicit, literate (or numerate) and abstract. In educational circles this complementarity is sometimes expressed by converting the acronym STEM (science, technology, engineering and mathematics) to STEAM, by adding in an A for art. Turning STEM to STEAM is compared to reconnecting the left hemisphere of the brain to the right, or even the mind as a whole to its body. My aim, however, in advocating for basketing the curriculum rather than adding basketry to it, is quite different. It is to destabilise the entire edifice on which the complementarity rests. Basketing is about more than making baskets. It is about making a world. It is in this sense a way of breathing life into the world or – if you will – of reanimating it. We animate numbers and words, in arithmetic and literature, not by burying them, as in appeals to tacit knowledge and the embodiment of skills, but by restoring them to currents of life and feeling.

Numbers and words are neither concrete nor abstract, neither embodied nor disembodied. They are rather lived and felt. Consider numbers first. They come from counting things. Nowadays we call them data, and their manipulation data handling. The phrase calls to mind a scientist, technician or business analyst, seated before a screen and operating a keyboard. As he works, numbers come up on the screen, lots of them. These are his data. They have been extracted from somewhere, precipitated from the real-life processes for which they serve as indices. But his hands, though they tap the keys, have no material contact with the data. Literally, of course, a datum is a thing given, an offering. Receiving the gift, you take it in your hands. If anyone really ever handled data in this literal sense, it would have been the cord-keepers of old, reading accounts from the loops and knots of their material. The Inca people read numbers from their *khipus*, constructed on the same principle as the communal suspension bridge, likewise made from twisted fibre cords. But making a basket is also a practice of data handling in this sense. Picking up and threading through, the maker receives with her hands what the evolving work offers as it proceeds. She counts as she goes, over and under, over and under. But her numbers do not add up. They rather follow on, marking in their recurrence the rhythm of time passing.

Words, too, whether spoken or written, issue from a body that is not wrapped up in itself but open and alive to the world. They pour out: on the breath in speech, from the restless movement of hand and fingers in writing. To suggest, as we so often do, that the verbal arts on the one hand, and crafts such as basketry on the other, tap into different reservoirs of knowledge, respectively explicit and tacit, incorporeal and embodied, or higher and lower in an imaginary column of consciousness, is to make a false comparison. For it is to set what is incipient in the practice of a craft – a gesture on the brink of expression – alongside what is already flown in the articulation of words. But words, too, bubble up; they are momentarily felt on the tongue or in the fingers, prior to their release. And the gestures of a craft, in their enactment, give birth to forms that are no longer tethered to their makers. It is unfair to both craft and speech to see the one only prospectively, in its incipience, and the other only retrospectively, in its outcomes. The maker and the wordsmith are both poets of a kind, who live and feel on the cusp of their work, between the incipient and the articulate, or between the flying and the flown. Therein lies the source of their creativity. It is the work of time.

Nowadays we worry that time has lost its rhythm, that it has been ejected from its proper orbit into a rampant and uncontrolled acceleration. If only we could slow down! Perhaps, then, we could live a simpler life, more measured in its pace, with fewer demands. We could walk instead of taking the car, write by hand, grow our own food and wait for it to ripen before harvesting. And we could go back to making baskets. There is much to be said for these alternatives, at least for those with the leisure to afford them. They are good for health, and environmentally sustainable. Yet in practice, they are neither slow nor simple. The skills of basketry are of such complexity that in times past, it took apprentices years of laborious effort to master them. And under pressure, they had to work fast. A time traveller hoping to discover slowness and simplicity in the labour of bygone ages would be disappointed. He would likely find people working in conditions that, compared with today's comforts, appear hard and unrelenting. Yet he might also discover that his modern understanding of speed, and of complexity, would be out of place in a world where working fast meant seizing the moment rather than running against the clock, and where complexity lay in the depth and subtlety of attention and response rather than in the superabundance of information and the principles of its integration.

Our traveller comes from a world ruled not by the practice of the basket but by the logic of the algorithm. These are fundamentally incompatible. The algorithm is computational. It lays out a step-by-step programme for problem-solving. Experiments in robotics have shown that such programmes can be progressively improved through trial-and-error learning. Robots can get better and better in doing what we humans do as a matter of course. But so far, no robot has been designed that could make a basket. This is because the practice of the basket is not computational but ambulatory. It goes along. Recall the maker, counting as she proceeds on her way. She works *with* her materials, but does not work them *out*. The basket is not a problem that already contains its own solution. Rather, maker and materials, going along together, arrive at a solution that emerges only in and through their collaboration. Here, attention and response take precedence over computation and execution. Instead of mediating between inputs and outputs, basketry kinetically couples forces and materials. This, finally, is what it means to basket the world. It is not to slow down, or to simplify. But it is to restore life and feeling to a world in which both are vulnerable to algorithmic decomposition. As we rush to escape from this world into the bubble of artificial intelligence, leaving our very humanity behind, it is worth remembering that in the practice of the basket, another way is possible.

Glossary of terms

Aha Hawaii sacred cord in Hawaii; also binding cord of Tahitian to'o.

Apus (Peruvian Andes) mountain gods.

Bann (Scottish Gaelic) bind, tie, girth, belt, sash.

Bent (Scots) marram grass. In English, bent is the name for a grassland grass, (Latin name: Agrostis tenuis or Agrostis gigantic).

Bicornual baskets (Australia) Australian two-cornered baskets.

Bilum (Papua New Guinea) looped bag from Papua New Guinea.

Bødi (Shetland) Shetland creel-like basket used for fishing, made from black oat straw or docks, and woven with wild rush twine.

Caisie (Orkney) Orcadian creel-like back basket tapering towards the base, made from black oat straw, dockens, heather or rattan, and woven with wild rush twine. These are usually used for carrying things such as neaps, peats, dung, even shopping and could also be made to hold a certain weight or measure.

Chaîne opératoire (French) technological term indicating understanding an object as a result of its making process, highlighting key points of decision-making at each stage of the process.

Ciosan (Scottish Gaelic) grain meal basket made from marram.

Ciosan-arain bread basket

Ciosan-bafair bread basket made from marram or sea-bent.

Ciseán (Irish Gaelic) basket.

Cliabh, clèibhe (Scottish Gaelic, Irish Gaelic) Highland pannier or creel used for carrying burdens, (from the Gaelic for chest or breast – hence how you carry it).

Corra-shìomain or cor-shìomain (Scottish Gaelic) Highland term for rope-twister, twist handle, thraw cock or thraw crook, for making straw ropes.

Corra-shùgan (Skye) Skye term for rope-twister for making rope from straw.

Creel Scots term for back basket. There can be many forms of creel – fishing creel, peat creel etc.

Cubbie (Orcadian) a tightly woven straw basket used for many indoor domestic purposes, including storage of salt or holding spoons. They are also made for horse muzzles, carrying bait for sowing seed, and even for hens to lay eggs in.

Cuimhne (Scottish Gaelic) memory

Curach (Scottish Gaelic, Irish Gaelic) craft constructed of willow, equivalent of 'coracle'.

Dockens (Shetland) Shetland, Orcadian and Skye term for dock.

Dokki (Shetland) child's doll in Shetland, twisted from and bound with black oat straw.

Dulan, dulagan (Scottish Gaelic) loop.

Flaki, flackie (Shetland, Orkney) respectively, Shetland or Orcadian term for mat woven from straw with rush twine, used for winnowing.

Flechten (German) to braid, bind, weave.

Flos, floss (Shetland, Orkney) respectively, Shetland and Orcadian term for wild rush.

Gloy (Shetland, Orkney) Scots term for oat straw cleaned of grass and weeds for use in basketry and thatching.

Haku (Hawaii) ruler, also term meaning to bind, weave, put in order, compose a chant.

Hovi/høvi (Shetland) an openwork fish creel carried on the back, or fish trap set in a stream.

Hylomorphism ((from Greek *hule*=matter *plus* morph=form) anthropological term referring to a conceptual model of making, where form is imposed on to substance.

Imbolo pattern name for an interlocking design

Jawun (Australian Girramay) Australian bicornual basket.

Kaisie (Orkney) Orcadian creel-like back basket made from black oat straw, dockens, heather or rattan, and woven with wild rush twine.

Keshwa chaca (Peru) Peruvina Andes grass bridge.

Kessi (Shetland) Shetland back basket of black oat straw or docks, woven with rush twine, and used for land work; phonetically 'kishie'.

Khipu, quipu (Peruvian Andes) Andean knotted or twisted cords used by Inca to store information used.

Koddi (Shetland) Shetland small woven bag made for storing salt or holding bait.

Lipe alternative term for coil work.

Machair (Scottish Gaelic) low-lying fertile plain on the west coast parts of the Hebrides, such as the Uists.

Malanggan (New Ireland) Pacific Islands either carved figures from wood, woven from cord, or moulded from clay with the appearance of a wrapped form. Invested with the powers of the gods.

Manguri (Australia) hair rings.

Mùdag (Scottish Gaelic) oval egg-shaped basket used for holding fleece when spinning. In Dwelly, the Gaelic dictionary, it is described as being 3 ft in height made of straw – we have now come to know the 'rugby ball' type.

Muran, (Scottish Gaelic) **sometimes spelt 'murran', see also bent above** marram grass.

Murlin hemispherical frame basket used for weighing out fish in Eastern Scotland.

Ngufe (Futuna-Aniwa, Vanuatu) ni-Vanuatu term for several ribbons woven following the same twill sequence.

Nyim ruler of the kingdom of the Kuba.

Pa'iatua (Pacific) gathering and undressing of the gods.

Pandanus (Pacific) the pandanus tree produces leaves that are used in basket- and mat-work throughout Vanuatu, the Pacific and South-East Asia and nearby regions.

Pardog (Irish Gaelic) D-shaped Irish creel.

Pituri bag (Australian) aboriginal Australian bag to hold tobacco.

Plataichean-feamainn (Scottish Gaelic) Hebridean seaweed mat.

Plataichean-muillinn; plaid a' mhurain (Scottish Gaelic) Hebridean mill bag or grain sack made from rush or *muran*.

Rattan climbing tropical plant used in many baskets imported from the Far East, often called 'cane'.

Rotoa (Futuna-Aniwa, Vanuatu) incremental increase or decrease of twill in ni-Vanuatu basket-weaving.

Sabbat tilifun (Egyptian Arabic?) a tray with a handle for carrying a telephone from room to room.

Scalloms (English basketmaking term) thin lengths shaved at the thick end of a rod used to tie it on to a frame.

Sciathog (Irish Gaelic) Irish basket for straining potatoes.

Sciob (Irish Gaelic)**, anglicized as skib** Irish basket for straining potatoes.

Scull (Scots) flat frame basket of varying dimensions used for gathering 'tatties' or laying out fishing lines.

Seanair (Scottish Gaelic) grandfather.

Seic (Scottish Gaelic) bag made of rush rope for holding grain.

Simmen (Shetland) rope made from rushes, straw, marram, or heather. Similarly termed in Orkney.

Sìoman (Scottish Gaelic) straw rope.

Sìoman luachair (Scottish Gaelic) rope made of rushes.

Skekler (Shetland) Shetland masquerader, part of a winter custom where youngsters disguised in straw costumes.

Slath (English basketmaking term) the tying together and opening out of the base or lid sticks on a round or oval base.

Slype (English basketmaking term) obliquely angled long cut.

Sugan (Scottish Gaelic, Irish Gaelic)**, sughan** (Orcadian and Shetland) single strand rope, twisted rope of hay or straw.

Tapa (Tonga) bark-cloth.

Thraw crook, thraw-hook UK-wide term for rope-twister.

Tir a' Mhurain (Scottish Gaelic) land of marram grass, name for Uist.

Tjanpi (Australia) special kind of Australian grass used for making baskets.

Tjanpi Toyata (Australia) famous sculpture of a Toyota 4-wheel drive made from Tjanpi grass.

To'o (Tahiti) figural 'God image' made from tightly bound cord in Tahiti.

Tripitaka Buddhist term for three baskets of wisdom.

Verflechtung (German) intertwining.

Wanaku (Peru) wrapped.

Woody willow bridle used among travellers.

Please note, Northern Isles words are bedevilled by spell-as-you-please, but thanks to advice from Ian Tait, we have used the standards (Jakobsen *Norn Language in Shetland*, Marwick *Orkney Norn*, and for dialect Johnson *Shetland Words*). Some chapters may feature variants. For Gaelic terms, thanks to advice from Hugh Cheape and Caroline Dear, we have used Dwelly as our standard.

Index

The letter *f* following an entry indicates a page that includes a figure.
The letter *t* following an entry indicates a page that includes a table.